Developing In-House Digital Tools in Library Spaces

Laura Costello
Stony Brook University, USA

Meredith Powers
Brooklyn Public Library, USA

A volume in the Advances in Library and Information Science (ALIS) Book Series

Published in the United States of America by
IGI Global
Information Science Reference (an imprint of IGI Global)
701 E. Chocolate Avenue
Hershey PA, USA 17033
Tel: 717-533-8845
Fax: 717-533-8661
E-mail: cust@igi-global.com
Web site: http://www.igi-global.com

Library of Congress Cataloging-in-Publication Data

Names: Costello, Laura, 1985- editor. | Powers, Meredith, 1984- editor.
Title: Developing in-house digital tools in library spaces / Laura Costello and Meredith Powers, editors.
Description: Hershey, PA : Information Science Reference, [2018] | Includes bibliographical references.
Identifiers: LCCN 2017008839| ISBN 9781522526766 (hardcover) | ISBN 9781522526773 (ebook)
Subjects: LCSH: Libraries--Automation--Management. | Libraries--Information technology--Management. | Libraries--Information technology--Case studies. | Academic libraries--Information technology--Case studies. | Application software--Development--Case studies.
Classification: LCC Z678.9 .D456 2018 | DDC 025.00285--dc23 LC record available at https://lccn.loc.gov/2017008839

This book is published in the IGI Global book series Advances in Library and Information Science (ALIS) (ISSN: 2326-4136; eISSN: 2326-4144)

British Cataloguing in Publication Data
A Cataloguing in Publication record for this book is available from the British Library.

Advances in Library and Information Science (ALIS) Book Series

ISSN:2326-4136
EISSN:2326-4144

Editor-in-Chief: Alfonso Ippplito, Sapienza University-Rome, Italy &
Carlo Inglese, Sapienza University-Rome, Italy

MISSION

The **Advances in Library and Information Science (ALIS) Book Series** is comprised of high quality, research-oriented publications on the continuing developments and trends affecting the public, school, and academic fields, as well as specialized libraries and librarians globally. These discussions on professional and organizational considerations in library and information resource development and management assist in showcasing the latest methodologies and tools in the field.

The **ALIS Book Series** aims to expand the body of library science literature by covering a wide range of topics affecting the profession and field at large. The series also seeks to provide readers with an essential resource for uncovering the latest research in library and information science management, development, and technologies.

COVERAGE

- Subject Specialists in Libraries
- Censorship
- Ethics of Information
- University Libraries in Developing Countries
- Visual Literacy
- Ethical Practices in Libraries
- Social networking technologies
- Cases on Library Management
- International Library Statistics
- Future of Computing in Libraries

IGI Global is currently accepting manuscripts for publication within this series. To submit a proposal for a volume in this series, please contact our Acquisition Editors at Acquisitions@igi-global.com or visit: http://www.igi-global.com/publish/.

The Advances in Library and Information Science (ALIS) Book Series (ISSN 2326-4136) is published by IGI Global, 701 E. Chocolate Avenue, Hershey, PA 17033-1240, USA, www.igi-global.com. This series is composed of titles available for purchase individually; each title is edited to be contextually exclusive from any other title within the series. For pricing and ordering information please visit http://www.igi-global.com/book-series/advances-library-information-science/73002. Postmaster: Send all address changes to above address.

Titles in this Series

For a list of additional titles in this series, please visit:
https://www.igi-global.com/book-series/advances-library-information-science/73002

The Developing Role of Public Libraries in Emergency Management Emerging Research ...
Michael Mabe (Chesterfield County Public Library, USA) and Emily A. Ashley (Chesterfield County, USA)
Information Science Reference • ©2017 • 119pp • H/C (ISBN: 9781522521969) • US $120.00

Library and Information Services for Bioinformatics Education and Research
Shri Ram (Thapar University, India)
Information Science Reference • ©2017 • 291pp • H/C (ISBN: 9781522518716) • US $190.00

Managing Knowledge and Scholarly Assets in Academic Libraries
Bhojaraju Gunjal (National Institute of Technology Rourkela, India)
Information Science Reference • ©2017 • 381pp • H/C (ISBN: 9781522517412) • US $180.00

Interdisciplinary Digital Preservation Tools and Technologies
Tariq Ashraf (University of Delhi, India) and Naresh Kumar (American Center Library, India)
Information Science Reference • ©2017 • 281pp • H/C (ISBN: 9781522516538) • US $190.00

Library Technology Funding, Planning, and Deployment
Edward Iglesias (Stephen F. Austin State University, USA)
Information Science Reference • ©2017 • 257pp • H/C (ISBN: 9781522517351) • US $155.00

Academic Library Development and Administration in China
Lian Ruan (Illinois Fire Service Institute at the University of Illinois at Urbana-Champaign, USA) Qiang Zhu (Peking University, China) and Ying Ye (Nanjing University, China)
Information Science Reference • ©2017 • 391pp • H/C (ISBN: 9781522505501) • US $195.00

Handbook of Research on Emerging Technologies for Digital Preservation and Information...
Alfonso Ippolito (Sapienza University of Rome, Italy) and Michela Cigola (University of Cassino and South Latium, Italy)
Information Science Reference • ©2017 • 649pp • H/C (ISBN: 9781522506805) • US $275.00

For an enitre list of titles in this series, please visit:
https://www.igi-global.com/book-series/advances-library-information-science/73002

IGI Global
DISSEMINATOR OF KNOWLEDGE

701 East Chocolate Avenue, Hershey, PA 17033, USA
Tel: 717-533-8845 x100 • Fax: 717-533-8661
E-Mail: cust@igi-global.com • www.igi-global.com

Table of Contents

Section 2
Services and Workflow Processes

Section 3
Collections

Detailed Table of Contents

The authors discuss user-centered design and agile project management using the development of the Omeka Curator Dashboard as a case study. The University of California, Santa Cruz University Library developed a suite of 15 plugins for the Omeka open source content management system. This chapter describes the library's use of agile principles and methods for the management of this project, detailing the creation of user stories and acceptance criteria. This chapter also outlines the usability testing conducted by the library in the form of online surveys and moderated field tests. The authors conclude that user-focused, inclusive, and iterative development are key components to the success of the software development process.

Framing a technology question as a simple choice between developing an in- house application system and off-the- shelf proprietary system, or simply put, as a choice between build and buy, runs the risk of ignoring myriad options available in between the two extremes. In this era of cloud computing and run anything-as- a-service model, the very notion of developing an in-house application would raise a few eyebrows among C- level executives. How then can academic libraries, under mounting pressure to demonstrate their value (Oakleaf, 2010), justify investments in software development in particular? What follows in these sections is a brief discussion on the importance of investing in software development in libraries, three mini-case studies demonstrating the wide possibilities of integrating software development in library operations and a non- prescriptive model to assess which projects may be worth pursuing from the software development standpoint.

This chapter will detail the use of mobile applications in libraries. It will begin by briefly exploring the history of mobile application development, its inception, and progress to its relevance and use within libraries as a means of improving access and resource delivery for patrons. The prevalence of mobile devices, both inside and outside of the library, has affected the way individuals locate and use information. Libraries play an essential role in delivering resources to enhance the way users retrieve information, and therefore it is important to facilitate learning and scholarship through meaningful experiences in a variety of areas and mediums. A mobile application, not just a mobile-friendly website, can appeal to an increasingly digital population of library users in an environment that is both familiar and modern.

Section 2
Services and Workflow Processes

New technologies have changed the way people interact with information and space—as well as expectations of the library as a service provider. This section details how new technologies are harnessed, adapted, and developed to create efficient workflows for library staff as well as provide new means of accessing library services for users.

The chapter is based on experience of authors who work at different positions at University Library "Svetozar Markovic" in Belgrade, Serbia. This library has been aiming at creation of efficient, creative work environment in the last decade and one of the main pay-offs has been the development of a unique set of digital tools for handling METS/ALTO files. The chapter will present both managerial background and ICT related details that encompass this complex process. It will also aim at providing examples of good practice in implementation of Enterprise 2.0 and fostering of intrapreneurship that may be employed in other library environments with notes on specifics of the University Library Belgrade and its relations to more general managerial issues and challenges that may be useful for other librarians.

The author describes his experiences working in the Leon E. Bloch Law Library designing and prototyping in-house digital tools to improve communication among internal and external stakeholders. The projects discussed include a custom study room schedule application syncing university calendar to affordable tablets to increase staff productivity, an online data visualization dashboard to help digest large and complex sets of data for better understanding and decision making, and a mobile application to offer students and community an easy access to library resources and services.

Like many academic libraries throughout the United States, the James C. Kirkpatrick Library at the University of Central Missouri has increasingly documented its impact on the university and its students. A library statistics dashboard tool was developed internally to assist with increased assessment activities. The Information Technology Librarian and the Library Assessment Team collaborated to create the dashboard tool. This case study discusses the impetus for developing the tool and provides a detailed explanation of the creation and testing of the dashboard. The chapter also describes the outcomes of using the dashboard tool in the library's assessment activities, along with recommendations for how other libraries may develop similar tools and skills within their organizations.

Digital platforms offer new ways to showcase and disseminate library collections, as well as provide a means for preserving ephemeral works. The chapters in this section offer detailed accounts of building new apps and customizing existing platforms in order to create interactive digital experiences and communities of online users.

The University of Nevada, Reno Libraries is building a project and assessment-based organization that utilizes applications to increase the discovery of digital collections, enhances the online user experience, supports a growing Digital Humanities measure on campus, and encourages faculty and students to create projects using digital curation and various existing tools. A GeoHumanities Digital Project Specialist and Digital Humanities Historian were added to the library organization to create interactive exhibits. ESRI software was employed to create place-based storytelling using digital content held by CONTENTdm, CatDV, and other library platforms. By reimagining how we use such tools at our disposal, we can create new ways of interacting with information to create innovative ways for our patrons to re-engage with our materials.

This paper explores the possibilities of using digital technologies in an archival setting. The hypothesis examined and investigated was: street art can be preserved and archived through archival websites and mobile applications. In order to explore this problem a community driven digital archive, Drips Gallery, was created. Drips Gallery is a new archive consisting of graffiti photograph collections and is available through a website and mobile app. The database, website, and mobile app was created, coded, and programmed specifically for the archival and community needs of Drips Gallery. Drips Gallery allows the community to drive the archive and changes the role of the archivist from record keeper to facilitator. By creating an archival mobile app and website, new and immediate ways of capturing and preserving culture as it is being created and consumed is now possible.

Preface

Library service is dependent on the technology tools we use to host, distribute, and control content, our data collection strategies, and user-focused tools that promote discovery and recommendation. Libraries have historically relied on contracted vendors to develop and support these tools, but many libraries are now creating, testing, and supporting their own tools to better suit their particular communities. In response to this trend, many vendors have started offering more responsive platforms outfitted with developer tools to help libraries build these systems out in new ways. This is particularly observable in library management systems like Innovative Interfaces' Sierra and Ex Libris' Alma and discovery tools like Proquest's Summon and the Ebsco Discovery System, and is of course a large part of the appeal for open source software systems such as Koha, Opals, and Evergreen.

As libraries continue to expand their digital collections, online services, and technological offerings, librarians increasingly must rely on new technologies to deliver their content and services. Even as vendors open up APIs and try to adapt their products to suit libraries' evolving needs, existing library technologies and software vendors are not always able to sufficiently or cost-effectively meet these new challenges, and some libraries are turning inward to tackle the development process themselves. This volume seeks to empower librarians to create and develop their own software solutions and technologies, rather than merely implementing existing technology, and is aimed at institutions hoping to put together technology teams or enable existing staff to accomplish in-house technology projects. Some of the case studies and examples are in the very earliest stages of development and may inspire librarians to dip their toes into the world of software development for the first time; other chapters will prove more useful for institutions with existing functional technology teams looking for new projects and collaborations.

For a library to assemble a new functional team or build new tools is not a decision to make lightly; however, as more processes are automated, it may make sense to revisit the day-to-day functioning of the library as well as the roles of library staff. As this volume's chapters from a diverse range of libraries demonstrate, limitations based on cost, flexibility, and nimbleness are often merely organizational factors that can be overcome with some practical guidance and creative redistribution of resources. Additionally, developing library software in-house or scaffolding from existing open source resources reinforce the core missions and values of many libraries. Not only is it often preferable to customize software to suit library users, rather than shoehorn library services into an existing software product, but libraries are in many ways already the antithesis of proprietary; open source or homegrown technologies are a natural progression for libraries today.

With its detailed case studies of the development process and organizational structures of libraries who have successfully created their own in-house technology solutions, this volume fills a gap in the library technology book market and provides ideas and opportunities for libraries of any kind—public, academic, or highly specialized—looking to expand their existing tools and services. Some of the chapters offer practical guidance to fostering the kinds of environments and organizational structures that allow teams and individuals to accomplish technology projects; by including sections on assessment and the iterative process of development, many chapters could also serve as a benchmark for setting goals and evaluating the effectiveness of library software.

The following chapters represent use cases of libraries that have taken the development process into their own hands, through an internal or outsourced development team creating their own tools from scratch or on top of existing library software. Authors go into detail about the products and their development, including the organizational structure that enabled development and any user feedback or testing; chapters also discuss organizational issues (such as internal and external collaboration and overcoming institutional barriers), examples of library automation, case studies of developing library products, and assessing the impact and usefulness of in-house technologies.

Houda El Mimouni of Drexel University, Jennifer Anderson of Hook & Loop, Nadaleen F Tempelman-Kluit of New York University, and Alexandra Dolan-Mescal of University of California Riverside provide a clear overview and rationale of applying UX (user experience) methods to library services in "UX Work in Libraries: How (and Why) to Do It." Their chapter provides some theoretical background on the traditional goal of library user satisfaction and introduces UX as an approach that benefits libraries and their users. It gives an overview of popular UX methodologies and describes real-life UX in libraries through the stories from three librarians in their respective institutions: the New York Public Library, New York University, and University of California, Riverside. Most critically, this chapter provides practical guidance for librarians, whether they are specifically in charge of UX work at their library or aspire to integrate UX into their work on other library services and products.

Susan Chesley Perry and Jessica Waggoner, both from University of California Santa Cruz, also discuss user-centered design in their chapter, "Processes for User-Centered Design and Development: The Omeka Curator Dashboard Project." Perry and Waggoner provide background and guidance on using an agile project management framework for software development, and offer the development of the Omeka Curator Dashboard as a case study. The University of California, Santa Cruz University Library developed a suite of 15 plugins for the Omeka open source content management system, and this chapter describes the library's use of agile principles and methods, including the creation of user stories and acceptance criteria, for the management of this project. This chapter also outlines the usability testing conducted by the library in the form of online surveys and moderated field tests, and conclude that user-focused, inclusive, and iterative development are key components to the success of the software development process.

University of Utah's Harish Maringanti eschews the false dichotomy of "build or buy" when it comes to software products, and instead goes into depth on the myriad options available when implementing new technologies and library systems in the chapter "Software Development in Libraries." Maringanti focuses on academic libraries in the discussion on the importance of investing in software development in libraries. This chapter also highlights three mini-case studies that demonstrate the wide range of possibilities of integrating software development in library operations, and offers a non-prescriptive model to assess which projects may be worth pursuing from the software development standpoint.

Dana Haugh of Stony Brook University details the use of mobile app development in libraries in "Mobile Applications for Libraries." Haugh begins by briefly exploring the history of mobile application development, from its inception and progress to its relevance and use within libraries as a means of improving access and resource delivery for patrons. The prevalence of mobile devices, both inside and outside of the library, has affected the way individuals locate and use information; Haugh argues that because libraries play an essential role in delivering resources to enhance the way users retrieve information, it is therefore important to facilitate learning and scholarship through meaningful experiences across a variety of formats and mediums. Haugh suggests that mobile applications—not just mobile-friendly websites—can appeal to an increasingly digital population of library users in an environment that is both familiar and modern.

Nikola Smolenski, Milena Kostic, and Adam Milorad Sofronijevic from the University of Belgrade describe their digital tool development at the University Library ''Svetozar Markovic'' in Belgrade, Serbia in "Intrapreneurship and Enterprise 2.0 as grounds for developing in-house digital tools for handling METS/ALTO files at the University Library Belgrade." The authors work in different roles at the library, which has been aiming at building an efficient, creative work environment over the last decade, and one of the main outcomes of their efforts has been the development of a unique set of digital tools for handling METS/ALTO files. The chapter presents both managerial background and ICT related details that encompass this complex process, and provides examples of best practices in the implementation of Enterprise 2.0. In particular, the library's successful fostering of intrapreneurship is of great relevance for other libraries. The chapter provides notes on both the specifics of the University Library Belgrade and its organizational relationships, as well as an overview of more general managerial issues and challenges that may be useful for other librarians.

In "Developing In-House Digital Tools: Case Studies from the UMKC School of Law Library," Ayyoub Ajmi describes his experiences working in the Leon E. Bloch Law Library at the University of Missouri Kansas City School of Law, where he designs and prototypes in-house digital tools to improve communication among internal and external stakeholders. The projects discussed include a custom study room schedule application syncing university calendar to affordable tablets to increase staff productivity, an online data visualization dashboard to help digest large and complex sets of data for better understanding and decision making, and a mobile application to offer students and community an easy access to library resources and services. In addition, the author calls for the need to engage in innovative and experimental practices in libraries by encouraging collaboration with external partners to help develop new services and improve existing ones.

Colleen Bradley-Sanders and Alex Rudshteyn of Brooklyn College explores some of their library's work in technology development in their chapter "MyLibrary at Brooklyn College: Developing a Suite of Digital Tools." The Office of Academic Information Technologies (AIT) at Brooklyn College is based in the college library and the authors describe a history of successful innovation in developing in-house digital tools for the use of students, faculty, and the library staff. This chapter is of particular interest to any library operating under tight budgetary restrictions, as the authors argue that developing software solutions in-house has not only been cheaper than purchasing commercial software products, but has also improved services and tailored them to the library's needs. There is also some discussion of earning income by selling custom tools to other libraries; however, commercialization is not a prime motivator for the creation of the software at Brooklyn College's AIT department. This chapter explores the development of a set of digital tools called MyLibrary Suite—just one aspect of the work done by AIT—and offers a glimpse into a library with a long and successful history working on technology projects.

Room reservation systems are important in an increasingly collaborative library environment, but can also be technically challenging for all types of libraries to implement, whether they are using off the shelf vendor products or creating tools from scratch. Stony Brook University's Laura Costello and Shafeek Fazal explore two case studies of libraries experimenting with room-bound, electronic reservation kiosks in "Developing Unique Study Room Reservation Systems: Examples from Teachers College and Stony Brook University." Teachers College, Columbia University built a native app to run on room-coded iPads, while Stony Brook University developed custom code to run Steelcase's RoomWizard system in a university environment. The authors discuss the particularities and challenges of both systems, as well as review a range of potential applications and solutions that have emerged in recent years from other libraries.

Laura Horne-Popp, Elisabeth Bliese Tessone, and Joshua Welker of the University of Central Missouri describe their library's data-driven decision making process in "If You Build It, They Will Come: Creating a Library Statistics Dashboard for Decision-Making." Like many academic libraries throughout the United States, the James C. Kirkpatrick Library at the University of Central Missouri has increasingly documented its impact on the university and its students. The Information Technology Librarian and the Library Assessment Team collaborated to create a library statistics dashboard tool to assist with increased assessment activities. This case study discusses the impetus for developing the tool and provides a detailed explanation of the creation and testing of the dashboard. The chapter also describes the outcomes of using the dashboard tool in the library's assessment activities, along with recommendations for how other libraries may develop similar tools and skills within their organizations.

In "Pulling Content Out the Back Door: Creating an Interactive Digital Collections Experience," Amy J Hunsaker, Natasha Majewski, and Laura E Rocke discuss how the University of Nevada Reno is developing a project and assessment-based organization that utilizes applications to increase the discovery of digital collections, enhances the online user experience, supports a growing Digital Humanities measure on campus, and encourages faculty and students to create projects using digital curation and various existing tools. Part of the chapter describes organizational structuring, such as the hiring of a GeoHumanities Digital Project Specialist and Digital Humanities Historian to create interactive exhibits. The authors describe how ESRI software was employed to create place-based storytelling using digital content held by CONTENTdm, CatDV, and other library platforms. By reimagining how libraries use such tools, this chapter explores new ways of interacting with information to create innovative ways for patrons to re-engage with library collections.

Lastly, Alexandra Lederman and Farah Jindani investigate the possibilities of using digital technologies in an archival setting and describe the development of a community-centered, graffiti-documenting mobile app in "Drips Gallery: A Community-driven Graffiti Library & Archive." The chapter examines how street art can be preserved and archived through archival websites and mobile applications, and details the development of Drips Gallery, a new archive consisting of graffiti photograph collections that is available through a website and mobile app. The database, website, and mobile app were created, coded, and designed specifically to allow the graffiti art community to drive the archive. By creating an archival mobile app and website, new and immediate ways of capturing and preserving culture as it is being created and consumed is now possible, and the authors explore how new technologies can shift the role of the archivist away from record keeper towards facilitator.

Libraries are collaborative organizations by nature, whether through traditional resource-sharing initiatives like interlibrary loan or forming consortia to gain leverage and offset operational costs. Developing new or open tools need not be an entirely in-house process; if libraries can identify shared goals and needs, library technology initiatives can grow beyond the individual use case. Neither the trend towards collaboration nor the trend towards homegrown software solutions are likely to abate any time soon, so the next steps in library technology may well represent a convergence of these two ideas. The goal of this volume is not only to foster the formation of new library technology teams, but also to provide a resource so that new teams may not have to start from scratch with every project. As we move towards open sourcing and using open standards, our tools may be increasingly reusable and interoperable. By offering a comprehensive examination of the structures, environments, and skills that are conducive for successful technology projects—and by featuring case studies from a diverse range of libraries and librarians—this volume proffers to expand the toolkit of the modern librarian and provide a deep dive for libraries interested in developing software or other technology projects.

Acknowledgment

The editors would like to acknowledge the help of all the people involved in this project, and especially, to all of the insightful authors and reviewers who dedicated their time and expertise to create this resource. Most of the authors also served as referees in the review process, and we greatly appreciate their double task. Without their support, this book would not have become a reality.

Thank you also to our colleagues, and to all the librarians whose work and research are constantly pushing towards the uncertain future.

Laura Costello
Stony Brook University, USA

Meredith Powers
Brooklyn Public Library, USA

Section 1
Starting With Users

Software development is about more than the final product—it is a process that starts and ends with users. This section describes how and why libraries are natural hosts for user-centered development projects, as well as goes into detail on fostering user-centered design and development processes.

Chapter 1
UX Work in Libraries:
How (and Why) to Do It

Houda El Mimouni
Drexel University, USA

Jennifer Anderson
Hook & Loop, USA

Nadaleen F Tempelman-Kluit
New York University, USA

Alexandra Dolan-Mescal
University of California – Riverside, USA

ABSTRACT

The application of UX expertise is beneficial in all the areas and aspects of library services and products. All what a librarian needs is an understanding of those principles and some tools with which to practice them. The goal of this chapter, therefore, is to provide a guide for librarians, whether they are specifically in charge of UX work at their library or aspire to integrate UX into their work on other library services and products. This chapter provides some theoretical background on the traditional goal of library user satisfaction and introduces UX as an approach that benefits libraries and their users. It gives an overview of popular UX methodologies and describes real-life UX in libraries through the stories from three librarians in their respective institutions: the New York Public Library, New York University, and University of California, Riverside.

DOI: 10.4018/978-1-5225-2676-6.ch001

INTRODUCTION

It is often assumed that libraries, like museums, are guarded strongholds of knowledge and history, kept alive (albeit cloistered) by specialized staff whose primary aim is to protect, preserve, and only occasionally reveal the valuable artifacts. It is true that many research libraries and specialized collections must protect fragile materials by requiring visiting scholars to wear gloves or employing low lighting—and only after proving their need to expose the artifact with a letter of introduction. But the modern library—and indeed any library—remains relevant when the knowledge it preserves is absorbed and disseminated by new readers. For the library, access to knowledge is its reason to exist.

So how to provide sufficient access to a modern readership that rapidly grows in number, alters in composition and variety of needs, and increasingly expects instant admittance? It's a boon to the mission of libraries that the web and other forms of digital information access have been successfully introduced. Digitization of finding aids and materials means faster access and more widespread availability. But digitization also means a certain level of technical sophistication on the part of both patrons and librarians. So the question becomes: how can librarians, who are not necessarily trained in computer science or software programming, make sure that digital tools are not a further impediment to access?

The answer, perhaps ironically, comes from a concept most often associated with software interface design: user experience (or UX). The emergence of publications such as Weave Journal of Library User Experience, conferences such as Designing for Digital and User Experience in Libraries, and the establishment of graduate degrees in Information Experience Design at library schools such as Pratt Institute all support the notion that UX is a serious element of modern librarianship. The more that access to information is digitized, the more important it is that the modern library provide the best tools for browsing and searching. Having a good user interface for digital library tools is like having a friendly, knowledgable, trained reference librarian—both are crucial to serving patron needs.

The application of UX expertise is beneficial in all the areas and aspects of library services and products, not just electronic interfaces; UX principles can also be applied to the design of physical space. All you need is an understanding of those principles and some tools with which to practice them. The goal of this chapter, therefore, is to provide a guide for librarians, whether they are specifically in charge of UX work at their library or aspire to integrate UX into their work on other library services and products.

The first part of this chapter provides some theoretical background on the traditional goal of library user satisfaction. It will then introduce UX as an approach that benefits libraries and their users, and give an overview of popular UX methodologies. In the second part, three librarians will describe real-life examples of UX work at their respective institutions: the New York Public Library, New York University, and University of California, Riverside. These stories will demonstrate not only different ways UX is being used today to make a difference in library patron experience, but also how aspiring UX librarians can make a difference at their own libraries.

PART 1: THEORETICAL BACKGROUND

Library User Satisfaction

The concept of library user satisfaction cannot be traced to a point in time. Around 1928, Ranganathan, the great Indian library theorist, enunciated The Five Laws of Library Science[1]. These laws have been taught to library students worldwide. Reflecting on Ranganathan library laws, Leiter (2003, 413) argues that they "provide a paradigm of how libraries function, how they grow and serve, how they live, and so provide for us a framework through which to examine our professional lives and our libraries." While this paradigm is meant to advise the management of the library, two of the rules are directly related to the patron's satisfaction, mainly that, 1: every reader his or her book and 2: save the time of the reader. These two laws underscore the importance of providing the patron with the materials they need as a basic right, and facilitating access to them. However, to achieve this goal, the librarian needs to know the users well enough to be able to know what they read, what time the library resources should be available, how to arrange the collection, and how to design the website for the user to be able to access it easily. Nevertheless, knowing what the users read depends on the users approaching the librarian with requests for acquisition, which leaves a huge gap when the needs are latent and not expressed.

Research on how to evaluate the products and services in traditional librarianship usually imitates Shannon's Mathematical Theory of Communication (Shannon, 2001), where library services adjust based on the feedback received after the communication process culminated. In other words, the librarian designs products and services for the patrons, then evaluates after service/product delivery to adjust based on the satisfaction of the patron.

Satisfaction surveys and evaluation instruments were adapted from marketing research and practices not only to gauge library users' satisfaction but also to justify their contributions to the achievement of their parent organizations' goals. Thus, services evaluations are carried out to quantify the benefits of the library products and services to users and justify continued funding (Cullen & Calvert, 1993).

Service quality according to Grönroos (1984) is of three dimensions: the technical quality of the outcome, the functional quality of the service, and the company's

Figure 1. Adapted from Shannon's Mathematical Theory of Communication Model

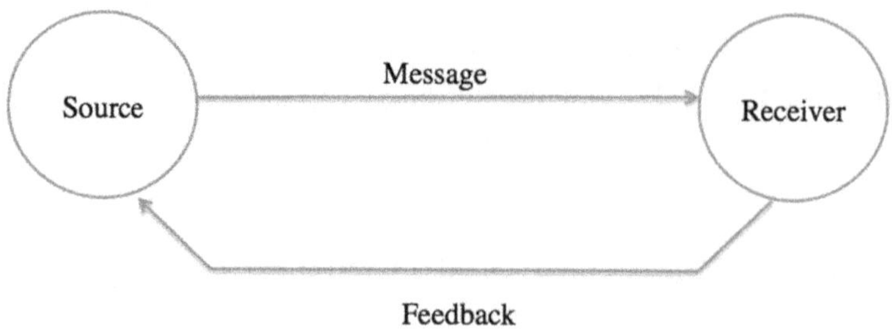

corporate image. Grönroos (1984) differentiated between the quality associated with the process of service delivery and the quality associated with the outcome of service, judged by the consumer after the service is performed.

One of the early models of quality evaluation is ServQUAL, developed by Parasuraman, Zeithaml, and Berry (1985). SERVQUAL has been considered one of the important tools of service quality evaluation in marketing research and practice, and has been used by many researchers across various fields of services, including information systems (Pitt, Watson, and Kavan, 1995). Based on ServQUAL, LibQUAL was developed by the Association of Research Libraries (ARL) (Cook, 2001; Thompson, Cook, and Kyrillidou, 2006; Heath, 2011). Similar surveys since developed include the SCONUL Satisfaction Survey (Payne and Conyers, 2005; Bainton, 2001) and Counting Opinions LibSat survey (Nie, 2009; McCulley, 2010). However, these tools have been criticized for the lack of a clear link between satisfaction and perceived service quality (Duffy and Ketchand, 1998). In addition, the substantial administrative costs exceed the budget of many libraries, especially those attached to small colleges (Angell, 2013). This has pushed many libraries to either develop their own evaluation tools (Hossain, 2016) or use free software developed by the open source movement (Angell, 2013).

The relationship between the library and the user has evolved over time. In the early years of the 20th century, a great library that aimed at satisfying its user took pride in the size and quality of its collection, including rare and newly printed books, as well as the quantity and quality of its scholar librarians. Buckland (1975) argues that intellectual access to information is a major preoccupation of librarians, and that physical access needs to accompany intellectual access. Lancaster (1978) also sees library evaluation as an evaluation of user satisfaction, which can be checked at three possible levels: 1: effectiveness evaluation; 2: cost-effectiveness evaluation; and 3: cost-benefit evaluation. Traditional methods of inquiry such as surveys, interviews and focus groups were also used for library evaluation but never to know the users and design for the process of providing access to the resources.

The relationship between the user and the library has developed over time. Librarians strove to make the patron happy, while nowadays UX librarians want the user to be happy. Forrest (2009) describes such relationship. At the early stage, the relationship was a transaction between patrons and the library-as-books-warehouse, where the librarian's role was to control transactions. As the library started providing services, the patron became a client and the librarian an assistant. More recently, the user has become considered a guest, while the library is a collaborator delivering an experience. The library's success is measured by impacts such as fostering student learning success, supporting faculty productivity, enhancing institutional reputations, and so on. Therefore, the known concept of patron satisfaction is user satisfaction in UX practices, where experience is what matters most.

UX in Libraries

User experience emerged from the Human Computer-Interaction domain. UX has recently inspired many librarianship practices in terms of best practices and user satisfaction, mainly through the practice of empathy, which can make library services and products usable, useful, and desirable. Here we present an overview of user experience benefits and methods.

UX Overview

The concept of UX can be traced to Don Norman and his seminal book, *The Design of Everyday Things* (Norman, 1988). In the book, the phrase "user-centered design" introduced the very important idea of designing with the user in mind and taking his or her perspective into account. While there is no consensus about the nature and scope of UX (Law et al., 2009), an agreement has been made about what determines UX; namely, the user's internal state (i.e., emotion), the user's past experiences, the user's goals and needs, and the user's external context (Lallemand, Gronier & Koenig, 2015).

Hassenzahl (2008, 12) defines UX as "a momentary, primarily evaluative feeling (good-bad) while interacting with a product or service." Kuniavsky (2010) provided a more detailed definition. For him UX is "the totality of end users' perceptions as they interact with a product or service. These perceptions include effectiveness (how good is the result?), efficiency (how fast or cheap is it?), emotional satisfaction (how good does it feel?), and the quality of the relationship with the entity that created the product or service (what expectations does it create for subsequent interactions?)."

Thus, UX relies on understanding user needs, behaviors and attitudes through empathic methods.

The term empathy is central to any UX work. Bell (2014, 370) argues: "In the absence of empathic design, there is a disconnect between what the designer intended and how the user experiences the system." In the psychological literature, empathy is beyond perspective-taking. Perspective-taking and empathy may overlap (Galinsky et al., 2008). However, there is a fine line that differentiates between the two concepts. Perspective-taking is defined as the process of taking an alternate point of view and thus is associated with a cognitive skill. It does not necessarily lead to feelings of empathy, which are associated with an emotional capacity, which may be made after the perspective-taking process has concluded (Davis, 1983).

The UX designer, by being empathetic, needs to recognize not only users' thoughts, but also their emotions. Being empathetic leads to a better understanding of users' needs, pain points, and attitudes.

Benefits of Using UX in Libraries

The traditional satisfaction model sought feedback after service delivery and mostly took pride of the collection and staff members. UX, however, aims at transforming the essence of the library from book warehouses to places where people want to come and hang out, and librarians from bookkeepers to life transformers. Users nowadays can have access to materials in bookstores and can download them from the Internet from the comfort of home. In short, accessing books and information resources in the library no longer satisfy the users. Users need the library to have access to equipment and staff expertise. They want that which is not available elsewhere. UX helps you know about what the users know and need without having to guess.

UX work benefits the library services and products, the institution, and the patrons in the following ways:

- **Product and Services Benefits:** UX work advises on what products and services are solicited, and when and how they will be used. UX research helps decide what choices can be taken in terms of acquiring products and services.
- **Institution Benefits:** UX work helps increase the value of the library in the eyes of the patrons. When the importance of the library becomes clear to the community, justifying why a library should exist and be funded is no longer needed.
- **Patrons' Benefits:** when patrons' expectations are met, they are satisfied and happy. Performing UX research helps reveal the real needs and wants of the users that can direct the deployment of library resources.

Recent researchers revealed that a good user experience makes the users not only satisfied, but also happy (Kuniavsky, 2003; Desmet and Hassenzahl, 2012; Hassenzahl et al., 2013). Bell (2015) posits that libraries can provide a happy experience as they contribute to community members' positive feelings. The library delivers a wide range of services, such as lending materials, providing equipment, providing space for meetings, in-person research consultations, or lectures.

Librarians who care about the experience of their users need to be completely engaged. They need to design library interfaces as well as physical spaces, and intentionally design them as happy environments. They need to involve the users and place them in the center of their design process. Designers who do not think of the users are biased, since patrons do not necessarily think the way designers do.

Areas Where UX Can Be Applied

UX can be applied not only to electric interfaces such as Electronic Resources Management Systems (ERMS) (Fagan et al., 2012), library homepages (Stephan, Cheng & Young, 2006), virtual reference services (Nilsen & Ross, 2006), and mobile library websites (Pendell and Bowman, 2012), but also space arrangement such as the location of the help desk and shelves, signage and wayfinding, and so on:

- **Services:** Engaging with a library's service should not be a complicated, time consuming process. Users need to be able to check out and return materials without having to worry about the wait time. When a service is provided quickly and easily by approachable staff members, and the less confused and more satisfied is the user.
- **Signage and Wayfinding:** The library can be intimidating if there is a lack of appropriate tools to map its features. Indoor library mapping tools such as StackMap and Capira, or in-house developed tools and signage, can help users navigate the physical space and reduce directional questions. These tools can help users know the number of floors in the library, the stacks, workstations and printing facilities and bathrooms' locations. Signage also needs to convey the identity of the library and establish a visual consistency.
- **Library Space Ergonomics:** The arrangement of the library features is highly important. Such arrangement needs to be designed with the objective of making the space comfortable. Avoiding clutter in all the library spaces and placing the services desk at the entrance will make the users feel welcome.

Whether they hold positions dedicated to UX or are involved in the management and the development of libraries, librarians need to equip themselves with UX expertise. Every librarian can apply UX design thinking by considering how their decisions impact the experience of the users. Applying UX practices does not necessarily require a special degree, and librarians can start with simple yet effective fixes. In the following section we will detail some UX methods that will help you start employing UX work in your library.

A Guide to UX Work in Libraries: Approaches, Methods, and Tools

Before describing some approaches and methods used in UX research, it is beneficial to review the five steps of UX research developed by Erin Sanders and illustrated below in the Research Learning Spiral (Sherwin, 2013).

These steps are reflected in the following questions related to library UX research:

- **Objectives:** What are the knowledge gaps about our library users we need to fill?
- **Hypotheses:** What do we think we understand about our library users?
- **Methods:** What methods should we select based on our library resources?
- **Conduct:** Collect data through the selected methods.
- **Synthesize:** Analyze the results and fill in the gaps, verify the hypotheses, deduce implication and future research ideas.

Figure 2. Research learning spiral

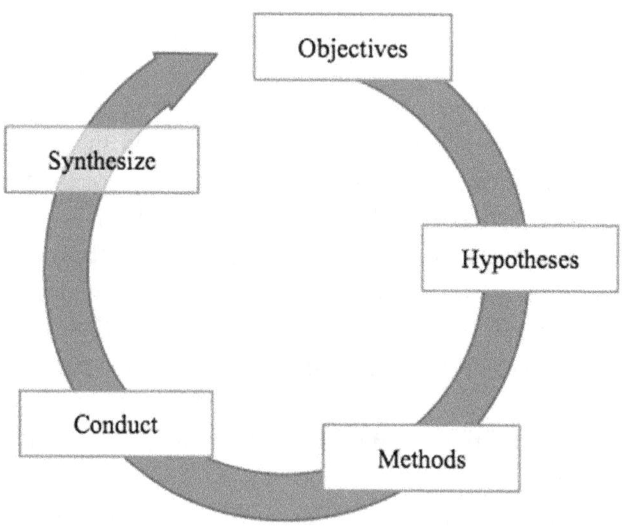

In the same regard, conducting research and developing products and services can take two process approaches: Waterfall and Agile.

Waterfall is a linear approach to product development wherein the stages of development are successive, and each finishes before the following begins. These stages are: Analyze, plan, design, build, test, deliver. Agile, on the other hand, is an iterative approach wherein teams collaborate for the rapid delivery of the end product. The following table represents the advantages and disadvantages of both.

The UX librarian needs to choose an approach based on the resources available, as well as the kind of product or service being developed. In some cases a hybrid approach can work better if the research is well planned.

Figure 3. Waterfall vs. Agile approaches

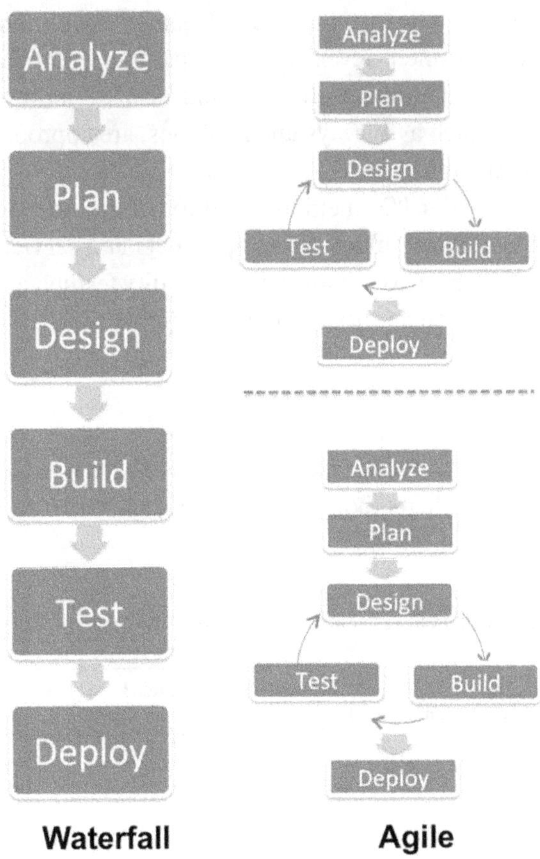

Table 1. Agile and waterfall advantages and disadvantages

	Advantages	Disadvantages
Waterfall	• Stakeholders and developers agree on the final product or service • Progress is easily measurable • Team members can be involved or work independently	• Difficulty in gathering all the necessary data before the beginning of the following step • Stakeholders may not be satisfied by the end product
Agile	• Stakeholders are involved as they get the chance to view the end result earlier and make changes • Possibility to iterate based on an early version of the product • More focused on the user	• Might be time consuming for the stakeholders • Needs more dedication by all team members • Frequent adjustment of the prototype might delay the delivery of the final product

UX Approaches

Both qualitative and quantitative approaches benefit user experience research in libraries. However, choosing an approach depends on the kind of information you are seeking, and your overall research goals. A qualitative research method would involve usability testing, interviews, user groups, and ethnography. Qualitative methods can help elicit answers as to why and how to address a certain issue. Quantitative methods, such as surveys and analytics, are appropriate for discretely measuring certain elements.

Here we present popular UX methods used to better understand the users and improve the usability and usefulness of the products and services. Some of these methods are qualitative (such as ethnography, usability testing, and interviews) and others are quantitative (such as surveys and analytics)

Methods

Prior to selecting a method, clear goals and objectives need to be set. Such goals will define the specific approach, method and procedure, and will help you stay relevant.

Table 2. Example of quantitative research question vs. qualitative research question

Quantitative research question: How often do users use advanced search? Qualitative question: How do users navigate the advanced research interface?

Surveys

Surveys are another traditional method that can be used for learning about the users' preferences, attitudes, and views of a specific element of library products and services. Surveys are useful for collecting quantitative data. As a method, it is less time consuming and can reach a larger number of patrons. Most online survey platforms can provide some analysis of the gathered data (i.e., Google forms, Survey Monkey, Qualtrics etc.).

The length of the survey can determine the response and completion rates, as many people avoid long surveys. Hence, it is advisable to keep the survey brief, simple, and to vary the type of questions (i.e., multiple choice, semi-open, and open ended questions) to keep participants interested until the end of the survey.

Interviews

Interviewing is a traditional method used across disciplines to learn about a participant's attitudes and perspective. In UX research, it is typically used in the early stages of the product development cycle to become familiar with the needs of the users. Interviews can also supplement surveys. They can be used prior to surveys to refine the questions or used after surveys to help explain the results of the survey. While in-person interviews allow you to capture verbal and nonverbal cues (such as facial expressions, emotions, and body language) interviews can be conducted in-person, online, or over the phone.

Prior to conducting an interview it is necessary to plan well for it. A written script with the questions can help manage the relevance and time of the interview. Informed consent paperwork needs to be prepared to document that participants agreed to be interviewed and get participants' permission to record the session. At least one trial run of the interview can be conducted to test the questions and the flow of the interview session.

The interview is ideally conducted by an interviewer and a note-taker. While the interviewer is asking questions and guiding the interviewer, the note-taker can record notes of the answers as well as the interviewee's facial expressions and intonation. If a note taker is not available, recording audio and/or video might be a good idea if the interviewee consents.

At the beginning of the interview, the interviewer needs to explain the purpose and objectives of the interview, and how the data will be used without leading the participants and biasing the results. Ideally an hour is enough. It's a good idea to schedule a break between interviews in order to make notes while everything is still fresh in your mind.

There are some caveats to be aware of:

- The interviewee cannot always remember details about previous experiences, so they may not be able to remember what made their experience positive or negative.
- The interviewer might prime the interviewee and risk prescribing the direction of their answers.
- The way users say they do things might be very different from the way they actually do things (Nielsen, 2001).

In short, participants should not be asked about what they think about a design and how do they use it, but rather about their impressions and attitudes such as issues that they have encountered while using the system.

If the interview method is conducted correctly and triangulated with other methods, it can be very beneficial, especially for exploratory purposes.

Ethnographic Studies

Ethnography is a traditional method of understanding the norms and goals of particular social settings (Fisher, 2007; Latour & Woolgar, 1979). It is one of the most commonly used methods used in qualitative research. Ethnography often relies on implanting an observer or participant-observer in the context of the study (Fleischmann & Wallace, 2005). The ethnographer delves deeply into behaviors and strives to identify not only patterns but also the variability of the patterns and outliers. The fact that ethnography is immersive and more interpretative can make it time-consuming, but very informative.

While there are no guidelines of how to use ethnography in libraries, the general practice of ethnography is applicable. The ethnographer is not supposed to enter the field with an empty mind but rather with an open mind (Fetterman, 2010). Thus the librarian practicing ethnography should be reflexive as he or she considers users' behaviors; in other words, the librarian should not put aside his or her background and his or her cultivated ideas about the users, but rather consider those ideas while trying to understand the users' and being empathetic towards them.

Table 3. Examples of interview questions

1- how difficult or easy you find using the advanced search interface? 2- where do you usually find resources for you classwork? 3- what do you usually do in the library?

A good tool to consider while doing ethnography in your library is the AEIOU Framework. This framework is a heuristic that helps collecting and coding data.

AEIOU stands for five components (Hanington and Martin, 2012): Activity, Environment, Interaction, Object, and User.

- **Activities (Goal-Directed Sets of Actions):** What do patrons often research?
- **Environments (The Arena in Which Activities Take Place):** How is the space used in the library?
- **Interactions (Between a Person and Someone or Something Else):** What are the interactions that usually happen between the librarians and the patrons?
- **Objects (Building Blocks of the Environment):** What are workstations in the reading room used for?
- **Users (The People Whose Behaviors, Preferences, and Needs are Being Observed):** Who are the users and what are their objectives?

An example of a way to solicit ethnographic data is to have patrons write a love letter or a break up letter (Hanington and Martin, 2012), or tell stories (Quesenbery & Brooks, 2010) about their use of the library can help you get valuable insights about the users' satisfaction, needs, and pain points.

Personas

A user persona is a fictional representation of an archetypical user. Personas are meant to be as realistic and representative as possible to the key segments of the actual users. Three to four personas are considered to be a fair number. The goal is not represent individual needs, but rather a segment of the audience that has common needs, goals and behaviors.

Personas inform the design of the system in a systematic way throughout the design process; designers can consider different needs, goals, and capabilities at every stage of the design cycle and layer (ideation, information architecture, design, flow, and content).

The personas need to be based on user research to be reliable and truly reflect the needs, goals and behavior patterns of the audience. The user study needs to answer the question of: who are the users? Why they are using our system? What are their behaviors? At this step, employing surveys and/or interviews of actual users can help to get users' demographic information, needs, and preferences. The results are then condensed and classified into themes, patterns, and groups, which are then refined into three to five segments with identified characteristics. Finally, developing a description (background, motivations, and expectations) to the personas is makes the persona a realistic representation.

Evaluating and reiterating the personas can help improve the representation of the users' segments.

Usability Testing

Usability testing is defined on Usability.gov as "evaluating a product or service by testing it with representative users." It enables the designers to uncover issues pertaining to a specific aspect of the design. Conducting usability testing is not a complicated task. It requires only good preparation, a few participants, and an efficient iteration. The power of usability testing compared to other forms of inquiry is that it allows the designer to know how the patrons actually use the system. This offers more accurate and detailed information on users' use rather than when patrons say or think how they use the system (Nielsen, 2001).

The librarian or team in charge of the usability testing needs to have clear objectives. Specify what aspects of the design need to be tested and the focus of the test, for instance: the advanced search in a library's website. A script of the test that includes tasks in the form of scenarios needs to be developed as well as the flow of the multiple tasks if any (see Table 4).

Krug (2009) argues for including initial questions dedicated to set the tone and put users at ease, as well as reminding the users that you are testing the site and not them.

Usability testing is meant to collect detailed data about the use of a system. Thus, a handful of users that represent the population of patrons is enough to run the test. While Krug recommends three (Krug, 2009), Nielson recommends five (Nielsen, 2012). Nielsen (2001) argues that testing with more users yields marginally fewer insights and thus time can be saved by conducting more tests, rather than finding more testers (Nielsen, 2012). Recruiting participants could be easier when incentives are offered. These may include but are not limited to cash, gift cards, book bags, etc. The testing location and equipment are also important to prepare. While a lab may not be within the reach of many librarians, a quiet space with a table, chairs and a networked computer are the minimum.

Table 4. Example of a usability test script

1. Using the simple search interface: Find the first book in the Harry Potter series. (After task completion, take the user to the advanced search interface) 2. Using the advanced search interface: You've learned about a newer edition of this book. How would you find it? 3. Do you have any observations? Which of these tasks did you find quick and easy and which was difficult?

During the test, participants are guided through the script and are asked to perform the tasks while the librarian is observing. While there is free software that can record the flow of the task performance, if recoding is not possible, taking notes is also a prudent idea. Interesting behaviors such as points of confusion need to be documented (Krug, 2009).

Debriefing right after the test is highly encouraged. The testers should make an inventory of the issues uncovered by testing and list them according to their importance. Krug (2009) suggests prioritizing in terms of what they will address or fix first. Changes are introduced as suggested by the test, and then iterative improvements are made. It is important to evaluate the success of the introduced changes by keeping a record of the tasks completed successfully while iterating (Nielsen, 2001).

Participatory Design

Participatory design (or more recently, "Co-Design") (Szebeko & Tan, 2010) involves untrained end-users or stakeholders working jointly with researchers and designers to create artifacts (i.e., sketches, wireframes, and prototypes) that lead directly to the end product. Users can be involved in all the stages of design, starting from ideation, to prototyping, testing, and re-iterating.

The benefits of involving the stakeholders in the design process are diverse. First, stakeholders can provide an ongoing evaluation of the design. Second, the final product is not prescribed to the users but rather is a result of a collaborative work. Finally, the continuous feedback from a diverse group of stakeholders strengthens the design of the product.

The participatory design team can be very powerful if stakeholders are carefully selected and reflect the segments of the library audience.

Analytics

Content analysis, either as a manual or computer-assisted method, can be a very useful in learning about the users (Cheng et al., 2010; Fleischmann et al., 2009) and overcoming some data collection limitations. Koepfler and Fleischmann (2012) described this method as non-invasive, since it allows reaching users who may not be interested in usability testing or surveys. It also mitigates issues of social desirability that often emerge in interview and survey techniques, as some users may be afraid of critiquing and showing disagreement.

Through data analytics, the frequency of some services and products' use can be calculated and faults with some library features can be uncovered. For instance, a space that is rarely used may reveal an issue with signage or a page that is never visited may indicate a broken link.

PART 2: EXAMPLES OF LIBRARIES PRACTICING UX AND DEVELOPING IN-HOUSE TOOLS

UX at New York Public Library (NYPL)

In 2007, I was the first UX Designer hired into the NYPL web team, who are responsible for the content, design, and coding of the Library's main web presences (especially NYPL.org). At the time, the department was transitioning from a "webmaster" model (where the few team members were generalists who did everything from editing HTML pages to restarting the server) to a more distributed model of both specific and general expertise. "User experience" and "UX" were new terms, and neither well defined nor well understood. But the introduction of a UX role meant a way to prioritize patron needs at the level of resource creation. If we had a UX Designer, then we were committing to designing experiences that were directly connected to the behaviors of our users.

The existing members of the web team transitioned naturally into project manager roles, since they had institutional and architectural knowledge. New roles added to the team included developers and content producers. As the UX Designer, I was connected to the structural design, the information architecture, the interaction design, and the graphic treatment of the site. I worked with members of my own department and also with the Communications department, which housed content creators and graphic designers.

My responsibilities included wireframing, some graphic design (translating the NYPL brand into the web context), and presentation-layer coding. Having those skills on the team allowed for us to better distinguish between content and UI work; I focused on layout and interaction, and my colleagues focused on managing the rapidly expanding amount of information available via the main site.

As the web team grew, so did the UX team it contained. At one time, the UX team was four roles: a product manager, a user analyst, a front-end/Drupal developer, and myself. The four of us both specialized in and also shared parts of the design process. The introduction of an analyst role established a tangible connection between the practice of UX design and our patron response to its results: site analytics. The UX Analyst was responsible for reporting on key performance indicators of site health as well as running user tests. Everything we designed was informed by research, and every new design was measured with user surveys and usage statistics.

This UX team was active throughout the launch of an entirely Drupal-based, CMS-driven site in 2009. After the launch, the UX analysis work was incorporated into a higher-level role (the UX Analyst was promoted to a managerial role on the site), but those skills came into play again when the team hired an Information Architect in 2013. Our IA's responsibilities included planning site structures, developing content strategy, and running user tests, while I worked on UX design and code. Together we created prototypes to be tested, incorporated test results into my designs, and otherwise iterated on each other's work.

Ultimately, NYPL's web team consisted of the following roles:

- Content producers
- UX Designer
- Information Architect
- Front-end developers
- Drupal and other back-end developers

The strength of this structure was our connection to each other, and to groups of content producers in the Library. The skills that we each contributed to the team included:

- Project management
- Content strategy
- Writing/editing
- User research
- User flow/interaction design
- Graphic design
- Wireframing
- Rapid prototyping
- Web development
- CMS/asset management

Within the team we had all the skills necessary to maintain and grow a content-driven website. Our department could easily have become a small web design agency. It was crucial to have the right team in place not only to do modern UX work, but to convince the administration of the value of this work. Without making this major organizational transition, UX as a practice for NYPL may not have become so significant, so well-disseminated within the organization, or so successful.

It is significant to note that many of the team members, developers included, have library science degrees. The establishment of UX in the NYPL web team coincided with the expansion of information science in graduate programs. It makes sense, since information design informs any profession concerned with the discovery and absorption of knowledge. But it is worth pointing out that this education path had not been solidly codified at the time of the creation of NYPL's UX practice; perhaps the two paths found each other serendipitously.

APPROACHES, METHODS, AND TOOLS

The formation of the contemporary NYPL web team was an evolution, which necessarily involved the step-by-step addition of parts of the UX process.

Wireframing

When I first began collaborating with the Communications team on the design of the website, the design methodology was far more analogous to waterfall than Agile. That means that finished, high-fidelity, non-interactive designs were developed and presented to stakeholders for review. Problems arose when stakeholders focused on the graphic treatment of the content rather than on the content itself. It was therefore difficult to get agreement on the content strategy, which should inform the design.

I noticed that wireframes were not part of the design process, not even as an internal tool for the designers. So I decided to use a small project (an exhibition site) as a test. Along with the project manager, I scheduled regular meetings for everyone on the project: the stakeholders, the designer, the developer, and the content producer were all there. During the kickoff meeting, everyone heard from the stakeholders about their content needs at the same time. Based on this conversation, I developed a first draft of the site in low-fidelity wireframes. At every subsequent meeting, I would show the wireframes on the big screen of the meeting room, and guide everyone through the gradual design (which increased in fidelity at each iteration). After every meeting, everyone received a PDF of that wireframe version.

As a result, the design process was no longer a guessing game but a conversation—and because it was a conversation, everyone was able to learn from each other. The entire group developed the content and the design together, aided in seeing how content related to the user's experience of it by the wireframes. Wireframing allowed interactivity and user flow to be developed without the constraint of final graphic design. Because wireframes illustrate what content will look like in context, everyone was able to comment from their particular perspective (for example, developers cautioned against a design that was challenging to build in the CMS). Finally, those various perspectives learned to have empathy for each other. The stakeholders in particular were welcomed for the first time into a process that demystified design and web development.

Online User Testing

At the time (around 2009), sophisticated web apps for running specific user tests (such as Optimal Workshop or Usability Hub) didn't exist. So we created our own.

Our UX Analyst had some knowledge of Ruby on Rails, and was inspired by another project (Usability Hub, n.d.) (based on Jared Spool's "Five Second Test" idea) to build an in-house tool for serving quick, single-question user tests. Because he had "rolled it himself," he called it Infomaki.

We hypothesized that visitors to the site might be more inclined to take a test if they knew it would only take a minute of their time. So we designed the tests to be very simple preference or click tests. For example, we wanted to test the labeling of the topmost items in the site's global navigation: did users understand where to go to find what they needed? We mocked up a few variations of the global navigation, exported flat images of the mockups, loaded the images into Informaki's test manager admin, and published the test. Visitors to the home page were invited to "answer a single question" via a text link at the top of the page. The test asked where they would click in the mockup to find a specific piece of information, and recorded their click. The final screen of the test thanked the user and invited them to take another test (if any other tests were running at the time).

Infomaki allowed us to test variations quickly, and also hone our understanding of patrons' behavior patterns and expectations. We often got a couple hundred responses within 48 hours of a test being published. Also, patrons tended to take all the tests that were available at any given time. Many patrons reported that taking all the tests was fun!

Infomaki was most effective at collecting a large number of responses to very specific questions in a short timeframe. As long as the test was small in scope, we could use Infomaki to gauge patron response and then iterate our design based on the results. But this tool also helped illustrate the importance of UX practices to the Library's leadership. Low-fidelity wireframes and the ability to test them quickly proved that UX wasn't difficult to incorporate into design workflow.

(Infomaki's developer, Michael Lascarides, has written about the project in the Code4Lib Journal) (Lascarides, 2009)

A/B Testing

In 2010, we added another UX tool to our arsenal: multivariate testing. This was the next logical step after testing small pieces of UI design on their own; now, how would they perform in the context of the rest of the site?

We used Optimizely to run our A/B tests, largely because it's easy for non-coders to use. Neither I nor the Information Architect at the time wrote JavaScript, so Optimizely's interface made it easy for us to set up the variations without a developer's assistance. Like Infomaki, Optimizely allowed us to launch tests and get results quickly. We found it especially useful whenever there was a difference of opinion regarding how patrons might engage with a design. High-level stakeholders tended to respond positively to a case made for a design change if we could show data proving "real" users engaging during a "real" visit to the site.

Prototyping and Live User Testing

During my years as the Library's UX Designer, I learned that if someone can see and/or touch an idea, then it becomes real. I learned that prototypes were crucial not only for user testing, but also for gaining project approval.

I also found that the creation of prototypes was helpful during periods of time when we weren't able to launch new designs (for example, during a major CMS migration). I couldn't kick off new projects for development, but I could explore and test new designs.

I started by building simple HTML/CSS/Jquery prototypes and hosting them on my internal "sandbox." Many early iterations of global navigation patterns and page layouts were created this way, and tested among the team. It had a similar effect as did my first wireframes: both team members and interested parties had the opportunity to affect the developing design, and the project benefitted from early, widespread approval.

This practice of prototyping in code led to creation of NYPL's first rapid prototyping system. The website suffered from design inconsistency, and I had long wanted to find a way to correct that. I wanted whatever style guide or pattern library I created to be code-based, and therefore something that could change and grow easily, as well as be shared with outside developers. As a small team, we didn't have a lot of internal resources, so re-use and multi-use of a single tool is important. So I took the code I'd been using for my prototypes and rewrote it using Harry Roberts' InuitCSS (GitHub, n.d.) as the framework. I worked with our Communications department to make sure the styling matched our branding, and with our front-end developers to incorporate our existing Jquery plugins. The first iteration took about three months altogether to build. I called it "NYPL Base" because it would be the basis for all our web designs.

We put NYPL Base to the test during the redesign of our Locations section. First we built designs for user testing (which we did in-person in the branches, guerilla-style), and then we incorporated the code into our release. While this resource made prototyping much easier, we did find that the amount of styling variation necessary for a good prototyping system was unnecessary for production code. Future plans for NYPL Base included using a build automation tool (such as gulp or grunt) to produce two "flavors" for prototyping and for production.

The Locations redesign was the culmination of all the UX tools we'd amassed: wireframes, user tests, analytics, and prototypes. We completely redesigned one of the most frequently used sections of the site based on analytics and qualitative data, to overwhelmingly positive effect. This project also led us to expand our skills, include more user persona research, and consider content strategy techniques (such as content creation research and content auditing). Today's web team is the result of effective research and development; by trying new techniques in real projects and slowly adding to our toolset, we built a UX practice that strengthened the team's capabilities and changed the institution's design culture

UX AT NEW YORK UNIVERSITY LIBRARIES

Our UX department was founded in 2013, and, like others I've spoken to who lead a library UX department, there is no blueprint for building teams, creating strategies, and getting buy-in for the work we do.

Because of this, we can develop our strategies without having to deviate from any norms, or feel pressure to conform to those norms. At the same time, knowing how successful departments have modeled themselves can be helpful in creating a roadmap. Fortunately, most UX teams are not only innovative and agile by nature, but are also able to adapt as needed, and develop new strategies if existing ones aren't proving successful. Since the NYU Libraries UX department was created, our approach has changed, as has our focus.

Background and History

The User Experience (UX) department at NYU Libraries (n.d.) was created in 2013 when it became clear that our users' needs (both in the physical environment of our libraries and across digital interfaces) required a dedicated group focused on exploring those needs.

For a number of reasons, the department was conceived as the first "virtual department." This translated to a department of one (me), with a small dedicated percentage of time (10%) by relevant staff (a Digital Library Technology Services (DLTS) designer, and graphic designer). The department was created, and remains within, Public Services, which also includes the following departments:

- Access, Delivery, & Resource Sharing Services
- Avery Fisher Center for Music & Media
- Business & Government Information Services
- Dibner Library Public Services
- Instructional, Undergraduate & Global Services
- Reference Services

Our responsibilities were as follows:

- Provide leadership and vision for addressing user needs across the libraries.
- Apply best practices of user-centered design to develop interfaces that address user needs and behaviors, promote our brand, and reflect our philosophy of outreach and service.
- Ensure interfaces are functional, efficient, and intuitive.
- Provide systematic mechanisms to gather feedback and suggestions from staff and users in order to improve the user experience (training sessions, online surveys, workshops).
- Identify and promote the use of new and innovative technologies.
- Routinely evaluate UX procedures and methods to ensure the most effective and efficient processes are being utilized to improve interfaces.
- Develop and promote a content strategy to create consistency amongst local and global library interfaces.
- Manage projects, and work towards standard integration of UX processes in projects with interfaces in domains of responsibility.

This is a tall order for a department of any size, let alone a department of one! Luckily, soon after the department was formed, I was able to recruit six UX-focused library school interns. With their help, I was able to test methods and models and processes, which was helpful in shaping the department and learning what worked and did not within our larger organization.

This work was valuable, not only because we were able to test, shape and solidify UX methods, but also because it helped refine the scope and frame the shaping of the department within the larger organization. Because the UX department reports to a different group than our Web Development team, our partnership is situational rather than structural. Therefore, unless organization development time was dedicated to a project, no development progress would be allotted to user-centered changes.

While shifting our focus to organizational priorities with development time allotted made the most sense in terms of being able to improve experiences for our users, it took some time to integrate UX methods and strategies into existing workflows. Fortunately, once we were able to build UX methods and research into the scope of a few projects, adding our department as project members and stakeholders on other projects and working groups became standard.

Methods and Approaches

Our UX department explores many different models and methods, and is constantly testing new strategies to improve and extend our work, create better workflows, garner stakeholder buy-in, and work efficiently and effectively.

Some of the overarching research we've done which has proven useful is our work on personas. By culling Ask a Librarian chat transcripts, a colleague and I were able to gather and synthesize user feedback, creating personas from the data clusters (Tempelman-Kluit & Pearce, 2014). Because we have a number of different audiences, using personas to map out our users' journeys and think through their particular needs, has been highly effective. User stories and scenarios based on the needs and behaviors of our personas helped inform much of our recent website redesign work. We've also used the Ask a Librarian chat transcripts to identify common pain points for users, which in turn helps us prioritize work. In knowing the main areas of frustration, we are able to make data-informed arguments about how work should be weighted.

Our approach to usability testing includes a strategy that allows us to collect qualitative feedback while also gaining stakeholder buy-in. We set up the tester and testee in the department's UX lab, and stream the test live to stakeholders in a conference room. Everyone watching integrates their observations using Stickies.io, a post-it note app that allows teams to create and cluster post-it notes on a shared virtual board. We've also experimented with Tomer Sharon's rainbow spreadsheet (Sharon, 2013), a collaborative observer spreadsheet. By having stakeholders observe and take part in adding observer notes, the impact has been greater and has tended to lead to design changes which may not be made without the way we promoted the methods of methods include usability testing. For example, when we performed formal usability testing on our rooms application, an in-house tool built for users to sign up for group study rooms, we invited the developers to observe. Very quickly, they were able to understand the frustration users were having with areas of the system. We were then able to work together as a team to come up with shared solutions.

We also regularly employ guerilla usability testing, which is quicker and requires less overhead. Through trial and error, we've solidified a process that works well within our environment. We set up a table in the atrium of Bobst Library, and create forms that collect data based on user interaction (via hotspots), which we deploy on an iPad. As our users visit the library, we ask if they'll answer a few quick questions in exchange for an energy bar. Because we are the main branch NYU Library (with over 11,000 visitors a day), within an hour we're usually able to get feedback from over 60 of our users.

Another regular UX method we employ is the heuristic evaluation. These evaluations have largely been done for stand-alone collections, though as we've solidified our department, we've received increasingly more requests to evaluate stand-alone interfaces based on grants, or professors creating sites for classes. Because of our workload and small team size, we only take on a few of these projects a year. In order to select the appropriate projects, we've created a form for potential partners, asking them if their teams are able to enact changes we recommend. Because our goal is to help users, our aim is to work on projects in which the work we do can result in actionable interface changes.

We also partner with colleagues in the NYU UX community. As our department developed, we received more and more enquiries about our work from the larger NYU community. Though there are no other formal UX teams at NYU, there are many others interested in pursuing this work, and learning more about it. We've cultivated a community of those of our colleagues who are interested in UX, and regularly host webinars, talks, and lunch and learns.

Our department places a high value on professional development. As a team, we regularly schedule and watch webinars, and have hosted speakers to discuss various UX methods and ideas. We also try to regularly post link roundups, which encourage us to read and post about a particular UX topic.

Our department remains small. Besides me (Head of UX), we have a UX Researcher & Strategist, a part-time quantitative UX analyst, and a part-time content strategist. Despite the size of our team and the newness of our department, we've managed to synthesize into a tight collaborative group with complementary skills. By iterating our department as we do our UX work, we've defined ourselves in the organization as a group whose expertise and input is critical to projects with a user focus.

UX AT THE UNIVERSITY OF CALIFORNIA RIVERSIDE LIBRARY

The University of California, Riverside (UCR) Library created their User Experience (UX) Design Unit in 2014 as part of a cluster of positions hired to make the Library's cyber infrastructure the most robust, forward-thinking, and secure on campus. The unit currently consists of solely myself as both User Experience Designer and Web Developer for the library's internal and external websites and applications. A long-term plan for expansion was written into the 2020 Library Strategic Plan and as of 2017, a Digital Initiatives Project Manager is in recruitment.

The UX unit reports directly to the Associate University Librarian for the Digital Library, who also oversees the Cyberinfrastructure, Metadata Services, and Preservation departments. I work closely with both the Cyberinfrastructure Department and the Web Development Management Committee.

The Cyberinfrastructure Department is responsible for maintaining and upgrading the library's networks, public and staff computers, data security, hardware, software. All web development is done in consultation with Cyberinfrastructure. The department was restructured in 2014 and has entirely new staff consisting of the following positions:

- Manager of Cyberinfrastructure
- Infrastructure Systems Engineer
- Client Systems Engineer
- Client Support Engineer
- Lead Software Developer

The Web Development Management Committee has been in existence for more than a decade, and has representatives from across the library who have a vested interest in the websites and web applications the library manages. The committee meets monthly to review active projects, consider proposals, review analytics and assessments, and plan enhancements. Though the membership changes, the following positions are typically present:

- Web Developer/UX Designer (Chair)
- Archivist
- Reference Librarian (2)
- Director of Teaching and Learning
- Head of Access Services
- Manager of Cyberinfrastructure
- Software Developer

This departmental and committee level collaborative model is integral to making my job possible in lieu of other positions in my unit. The input and coordination from colleagues allows me to focus on getting the work at hand done. As the User Experience Designer, my job so far has been threefold: to move the library website from a 15+ year old home-grown content management system (CMS) to Drupal 7, a sustainable open source CMS; to re-imagine how we engage with our users and market our services online and in-person; and to develop the unit and embed UX principles into all aspects of the library's work.

Relaunching the Library Website

In 2014, the new University Librarian, Steven Mandeville-Gamble, hired Chapter Three (a design consultant firm) to help move the library website to a new CMS. At that time, the site was powered by a homegrown CMS and application framework called Centaur. Centaur had been built over time and influenced by the webmaster model in which anything requested was built without a strategy for security, sustainability, purpose, or impact. 57 (of around 100) employees had editing access to the website, and by 2014 the site had ballooned to over 2,000 pages which suffered from stale design, inconsistent writing style, out-of-date content, and broken functionality. The original developers of Centaur moved on from UCR, and the new Cyberinfrastructure team had no documentation on how the site was built or how to use it. A complete overhaul was in order. As I had just been hired and was learning the lay of the land at UCR Library, the consultants were particularly useful in auditing old content, gaining stakeholder support for the changes to come, and convincing my colleagues of the need to give up their editing rights in pursuit of a unified, clean, and accurate branding of our library and services. As project manager for the content and design of the site, I worked with a committee of 18 colleagues (representing almost every department in the library and the campus Computing & Communications department) to agree upon a site map, wireframes, content editing guidelines, interaction design, and enhancement strategy. Though we wanted to avoid the pitfalls of "design by committee,"we felt that it was important to get stakeholder buy-in at all points in the process. Having all voices at the table gave us a shared understanding of our entire organization and its unifying goals (though it did greatly extend the project's timeline). While the project's concrete deliverable was a new website, the larger goal was to change our institution to be more adaptable, responsive, professional, and user-centric.

Approaches, Methods, and Tools

By 2014, many practices in user experience design were tried, assessed, and well-documented. After reviewing relevant contemporary literature, and with the guidance of our design consultants, we took the following path, iterating along the way:

- Surveys
- Content Review & Card Sorting
- Persona Development
- Site Mapping
- Wireframing & Design
- Content Editing
- Development & Internal QA Testing
- Beta Launch
- Usability Studies
- Assessment

- Enhancement Planning

We used a variety of products (both free and paid, open and closed-source) to do this work, but the products used are less important than the UX methods we pursued. Where private enterprise products were used, I try to note free and open alternatives.

Research and Content Auditing

At the beginning of the website redesign, we conducted a 10-question user satisfaction survey on SurveyMonkey (any survey tool will work). We posted it on social media and the website itself, and had volunteers with iPads out in front of each library location soliciting responses. We also raffled gift cards for coffee shops to increase response rate, with a total of 1,500 users surveyed (90% students and 10% faculty). I used DataWrapper, an open source data visualization tool, to easily present results to the team. The survey helped uncover the major pain points for our users. We then conducted a series of meetings with the committee and design consultants to review the content of the then-current site and usage statistics. With over 2,000 pages and 18 committee members, this process was arduous and took the form of a series of card sorting exercises. We took the names and URLs of all pages on the site and wrote them on cards. We then tried to sort the content into a new sitemap, re-writing on different color cards to show hierarchy. As we discussed each card, we reviewed the webpage content. Through this we found many issues: duplicate pages updated erratically, content that should be separated into multiple pages, content that did not match the page headers or URLs, and content that was assumed deleted but actually just un-linked, so that it still surfaced in search results.

A tentative sitemap, largely repurposing current content, was developed in Omnigraffle (purchased software for Mac) from the card sorting exercise. While we used Omnigraffle, site mapping can be done in many tools, including using post-it notes on a wall and photgraphing it!To develop tone for editing and new content, we defined personas of the users we wanted to engage. As a quickly-growing research institution, we were, and are, interested in developing relationships with new faculty and graduate students in addition to providing general research services to undergraduates. Looking at circulation statistics by patron type, we were also able to see the activity of the community and outside researchers.

Our personas helped refine the sitemap, set tone for content, and determine what new content should be created to highlight our services to desired users. A handy visualization of the personas was made with DataWrapper and added into our project document. We continue to use these personas to prioritize enhancements and determine news items on the website.

Figure 4. Breakdown of personas

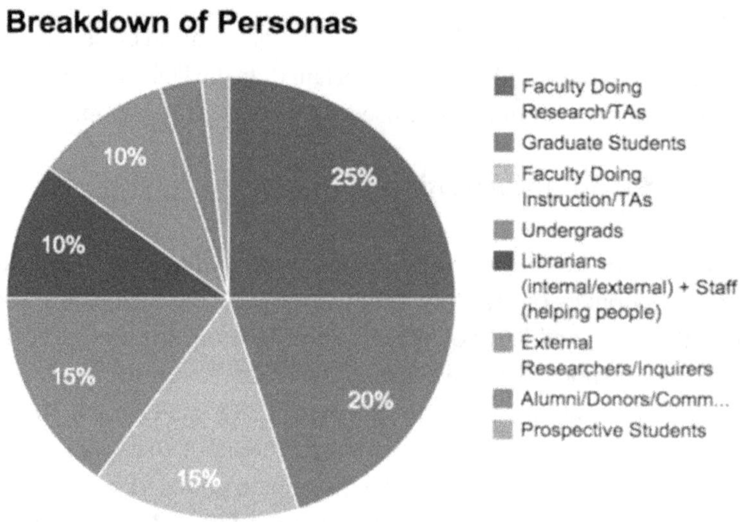

Design and Development

With an agreed upon site map, we moved into the wireframing phase. We ended up developing almost 50 wireframes of different content types and landing pages. We loaded the images into our Content Management Tracker, a content commenting system developed in house with PHP and Laravel, taking design comments from the team and redesigning over four rounds. With each round, we added in additional graphic design and branding elements to get a more complete picture of how the site would eventually look. Chapter Three then began software development while I set to the task of working with content owners to move our content into the new model. This was the longest part of our process, and involved cutting 57 editors down to 12 through shifting content responsibilities, negotiating content removal through data- and persona-driven research, and developing the UCR Library voice and style through a series of "Writing for the Web" workshops. The Content Management Tracker was then used by content owners to load in their page content alongside the design files, so that I could easily load content when the site was ready.

Beta Launch

In December of 2015, we launched the beta site to all library staff, requesting that everyone test interactions and forms, review content for typos and style errors, and provide general feedback. We also held all-staff meetings to explain the impetus behind the redesign and our new user-centric approach. Following this we had a beta launch period of four months, in which users could test the new website and provide feedback. We received more than 150 comments and questions, which I personally answered. During this time, our temporary developer added and redesigned features as need arose. This waterfall methodology, while not ideal, was a stop-gap solution while our Lead Software Developer position was being recruited. The site went into production on June 15, 2016.

Continuing Enhancements

Since launch, we have done a few small-scale or "guerrilla" usability tests. As a one-woman shop, I necessarily have to keep the tests lightweight and reproducible by colleagues. I have worked with librarians to do usability tests at graduate student coffee socials where the librarians ask students to complete three to five tasks and record videos with their phones of the students' attempts. The videos are then sent back to me for analysis, which I then visualize in Datawrapper. I also observe instruction sessions whenever possible. These analyses, along with the public comments and in conjunction with Google Analytics, are then reviewed by the Web Development Management Team and slated for enhancement releases by our Lead Software Developer, who is moving us toward an Agile methodology. We plan to increase our responsiveness and expand our UX toolkit with the addition of the Digital Initiatives Project Manager soon. A Communications Specialist is now on staff, which allows the content ownership to live in another department so that I may focus more on layout and interaction design in future iterations. The Communications Unit has also developed a comprehensive style guide which is referenced every time content is published, helping solidify our brand.

In reviewing and reporting on the Website Redesign Project, I would have liked to engage with user groups more through A/B testing, more deeply focused usability tests, and a more active feedback and enhancement loop. Given the minimal resources at hand, however, we have been successful in creating a user-centered website and framework for other projects. As our team expands and roles are defined and developed, UCR Library will be better poised to provide continually enhancing services to our users.

Engaging With Our Users Online and In-Person

A major goal of the Library is to service our various users more directly, and two immediate needs came out of the website redesign: our faculty needed a system to easily put materials on course reserves quarter after quarter, and students needed to easily access our study spaces.

Working with faculty, Research & Instruction, and Access Services staff, we created an in-house application with PHP and Laravel for putting materials up for course reserves. This system authenticates via CAS, allows faculty to transfer materials into new quarters, and provides digital asset management. To build this, we gathered functional requirements, wireframed layouts, solicited feedback, conducted a beta launch, and set schedules for enhancements. Faculty engagement has been key to this endeavor, building upon the foundational relationships developed by our subject specialists. Release 1.2 was just launched, and we plan on enhancing quarterly, as needed.

For students, we purchased DIBS room reservation software, eliminating the need to check keys in and out at circulation desks and allowing students to book rooms up to two weeks in advance online. The software allows us to see how often rooms are booked, how many people are in each room at a time, and who the "power users" are. This then informs the Facilities team for repair and furniture ordering schedules, and decreases lines at circulation desks.

The ability to purchase enterprise software has been a major supplement to our limited staffing and we have developed a system for reviewing and comparing products to find the best fit. We have used trial packages to test with users which system they prefer before purchasing. While we always consider users in our software decisions, sometimes campus priorities trump our users' needs. For example, our campus printing service is both cumbersome (unclear and complicated instructions for use) and exclusionary (change is not allowed, patrons must have a campus ID card to use them, etc.) but we are required to use this system as per campus license.

In addition to taking advantage of faculty relationships and interactions at circulation desks, reference desks, and study spaces, I have an open-door policy to my office, which is situated at the corner of a high traffic corridor. Curious students provide ample feedback, suggest new projects, and have even offered to create a user testing group on campus!

Developing UX Practices and Embedding Them Library-Wide

User experience design principles can (and should!) be applied to all library services. The last two years have been a series of experiments in what established UX practices work well in the UCR Library environment. Many of the techniques, such as wireframing, user personas, and conducting post-launch usability studies, have become integral to my daily work. Others have been less successful. For example, a survey to test user discovery of our Water Resources Collections and Archives received a grand total of zero responses over three months. What is crucial at this phase in developing our unit is to be able to quickly move across methods and be willing to try new things while we build expertise in our expanding team.

All library staff have been encouraged to build a culture of user-centric assessment and enhancement through professional development opportunities, including cross-training, seminars, and conferences. Ongoing projects include applying UX principles to our physical spaces by assessing our wayfinding and marketing signage, placement of our service desks and equipment, and digital signage marketing. I consider myself a service point for all other library departments, and strive to be available for any projects with potential user interaction. The Research & Instruction Division has formed partnerships with the Instructional Technology group on campus and will soon conduct a comprehensive analysis and reform of library instruction sessions, with my help as needed. Our team is small but scrappy, so engaging with our library and campus colleagues amplifies our reach and helps cement UX principles library-wide.

CONCLUSION

The practice of UX research and user-centered design is a natural fit for libraries. It supports the goal of librarianship to help patrons find the right material quickly, efficiently, and enjoyably. Satisfied users will return to the designs that please them; so too will satisfied patrons return to use their library.

Because UX work prescribes continuous evaluation and improvement, librarians who use UX methods can demonstrate to their returning patrons that their satisfaction is a priority. The data that results from user testing and collecting analytics is also crucial to a librarian's responsibility to prove the worth of the services and materials that their library provides. During a time in the evolution of libraries when physical space is a premium, and digital space is expanding and transforming quickly, librarians can employ UX to make sure both kinds of library spaces are as valuable and valued as possible.

Fortunately for the often-underfunded librarian, UX tools are easy to acquire, and many of them inexpensive or free. UX practitioners tend to share their ideas and methods freely, and online publications such as UX Movement[2] and UX Magazine[3] provide good starting places. No single methodology or suite of tools is required, which is part of the benefit of UX to libraries; the methods and tools available can be combined in whichever way will best suit each particular library's needs. The most important thing a practitioner can do is to try something, adjust as needed, and build upon successes.

It's a daunting task that Ranganathan sets for librarians with his five laws of library science. Essentially, librarians need to please all of the people all of the time. But while Ranganathan's laws give librarians our mission, the five steps of UX research tell us what we need to know in order to fulfill that mission. If we seek to know the reader, we can point the way to his or her useful book for use, save that reader some time, and make sure the growing library keeps the happy reader coming back.

ACKNOWLEDGMENT

Thanks to Kristen Droesch for her thorough edits of our work.

REFERENCES

Angell, K. (2013). Open source assessment of academic library patron satisfaction. *RSR. Reference Services Review*, *41*(4), 593–604. doi:10.1108/RSR-05-2013-0026

Bainton, T. (2001). *Information Literacy and Academic Libraries: The SCONUL Approach (UK/Ireland).*

Bell, S. (2015). Life, Library, and the Pursuit of Happiness. *Library Journal.*

Bell, S. J. (2014). Staying true to the core: Designing the future academic library experience. *portal. Libraries and the Academy*, *14*(3), 369–382. doi:10.1353/pla.2014.0021

Buckland, M.K. (1975). *Book availability and the library user.*

Cheng, A. S., Fleischmann, K. R., Wang, P., Ishita, E., & Oard, D. W. (2010). Values of stakeholders in the Net neutrality debate: Applying content analysis to telecommunications policy. In *Proceedings of the 2010 43rd Hawaii International Conference on System Sciences (HICSS).*

Cook, C.C. (2001). *A Mixed-methods Approach to the Identification and Measurement of Academic Library Service Quality Constructs: LibQUAL.*

Davis, M. H. (1983). Measuring individual differences in empathy: Evidence for a multidimensional approach. *Journal of Personality and Social Psychology*, *44*(1), 113–126. doi:10.1037/0022-3514.44.1.113

Desmet, P., & Hassenzahl, M. (2012). Towards happiness: Possibility-driven design. In Human-computer interaction: The agency perspective (pp. 3-27). Springer. doi:10.1007/978-3-642-25691-2_1

Donald, N. (1988). *The design of everyday things*. Doubled Currency.

Duffy, J. A. M., & Ketchand, A. A. (1998). Examining the role of service quality in overall service satisfaction. *Journal of Managerial Issues*, *10*(2), 240-255.

Fagan, J. C., Mandernach, M. A., Nelson, C. S., Paulo, J. R., & Saunders, G. (2012). Usability test results for a discovery tool in an academic library.

Fetterman, D. M. (2010). *Ethnography: Step-by-step* (Vol. 17). Sage.

Fisher, E. (2007). Ethnographic invention: Probing the capacity of laboratory decisions. *NanoEthics*, *1*(2), 155–165. doi:10.1007/s11569-007-0016-5

Fleischmann, K. R., & Wallace, W. A. (2005). A covenant with transparency: Opening the black box of models. *Communications of the ACM*, *48*(5), 93–97. doi:10.1145/1060710.1060715

Fleischmann, K. R., Oard, D. W., Cheng, A. S., Wang, P., & Ishita, E. (2009). Automatic classification of human values: Applying computational thinking to information ethics. *Proceedings of the American Society for Information Science and Technology* 46 (1):1-4. doi:10.1002/meet.2009.1450460345

Forrest, C. (2009). Academic libraries as learning spaces: Library effectiveness and the user experience. *Georgia Library Quarterly*, *46*(3), 4.

Cullen, R. J., & Calvert, P. J. (1993). Further dimensions of public library effectivenes: Report on a parallel New Zealand study. *Library & Information Science Research*, *15*(2), 143–164.

Galinsky, A. D., Maddux, W. W., Gilin, D., & White, J. B. (2008). Why it pays to get inside the head of your opponent the differential effects of perspective taking and empathy in negotiations. *Psychological Science*, *19*(4), 378–384. doi:10.1111/j.1467-9280.2008.02096.x PMID:18399891

GitHub. (n. d.). Retrieved from https://github.com/inuitcss

Grönroos, C. (1984). A service quality model and its marketing implications. *European Journal of Marketing*, *18*(4), 36–44. doi:10.1108/EUM0000000004784

Hanington, B., & Martin, B. (2012). *Universal methods of design: 100 ways to research complex problems, develop innovative ideas, and design effective solutions*. Rockport Publishers.

Hassenzahl, M. (2008). User experience (UX): towards an experiential perspective on product quality. *Proceedings of the 20th Conference on l'Interaction Homme-Machine*. doi:10.1145/1512714.1512717

Hassenzahl, M., Eckoldt, K., Diefenbach, S., Laschke, M., Len, E., & Kim, J. (2013). Designing moments of meaning and pleasure. Experience design and happiness. *International Journal of Design*, *7*(3).

Heath, F. (2011). Library assessment: The way we have grown. *The Library*, *81*(1).

Hossain, M. J. (2016). Determining the Key Dimensions for Evaluating Service Quality and Satisfaction in Academic Libraries. *The International Information & Library Review, 48(3), 176-189.*

U. Hub. (n. d.). Five second test. Retrieved from http://fivesecondtest.com/

Koepfler, J. A., & Fleischmann, K. R. (2012). Studying the values of hard-to-reach populations: content analysis of tweets by the 21st century homeless. In *Proceedings of the 2012 iConference*, Toronto, Ontario, Canada. doi:10.1145/2132176.2132183

Krug, S. (2009). *Don 't make me think: A common sense approach to Web usability: How we really use the Web.*

Kuniavsky, M. (2003). *Observing the user experience: a practitioner's guide to user research.* Morgan kaufmann.

Kuniavsky, M. (2010). *Smart things: ubiquitous computing user experience design.* Elsevier.

Lallemand, C., Gronier, G., & Koenig, V. (2015). User experience: A concept without consensus? Exploring practitioners perspectives through an international survey. *Computers in Human Behavior, 43*, 35–48. doi:10.1016/j.chb.2014.10.048

Lancaster, F. W. (1978). Guidelines for the evaluation of information systems and services. In *Guidelines for the evaluation of information systems and services*. Unesco.

Lascarides, M. (2009). Infomaki: An open source, lightweight usability testing tool. *Code4lib 8.*

Latour, B., & Woolgar, S. (1979). *Laboratory life: The social construction of scientific facts*. Beverly Hills: Sage.

Law, E. L. C., Roto, V., Hassenzahl, M., Vermeeren, A. P., & Kort, J. (2009). Understanding, scoping and defining user experience: a survey approach. In *Proceedings of the SIGCHI Conference on Human Factors in Computing Systems.*

Leiter, R. A. (2003). Reflections on Ranganathan's five laws of library science. *Law Library Journal, 95*, 411.

N.Y.U. Libraries. (n. d.). User Experience (UX). Retrieved from https://library.nyu.edu/departments/user-experience/

McCulley, L. (2010). Sustaining Feedback: Assessment in the Liberal Arts College Library. In *Proceedings of the 2010 library assessment conference*.

Nie, G. P. (2009). Customer Satisfaction Management with Counting Opinion Surveys. *Public Library Quarterly*, *28*(3), 204–211. doi:10.1080/01616840903106980

Nielsen, J. (2001). First rule of usability? Don't listen to users. *The Alertbox: Current Issues in Web Usability*. Retrieved from http://www.useit.com/alertbox/20010805.html

Nielsen, J. (2012). How many test users in a usability study. *Nielsen Norman Group*.

Nilsen, K., & Ross, C. S. (2006). Evaluating virtual reference from the users perspective. *The Reference Librarian*, *46*(95-96), 53–79. doi:10.1300/J120v46n95_05

Parasuraman, A., Zeithaml, V. A., & Berry, L. L. (1985). A conceptual model of service quality and its implications for future research. *Journal of Marketing*, *49*(4), 41-50.

Payne, P., & Conyers, A. (2005). Measuring the impact of higher education libraries: the LIRG/SCONUL impact implementation initiative. *Library and information research,* 29(91).

Pendell, K. D., & Bowman, M. S. (2012). Usability study of a librarys mobile website: An example from Portland State University. *Information Technology and Libraries (Online)*, *31*(2), 45. doi:10.6017/ital.v31i2.1913

Pitt, L. F., Watson, R. T., & Kavan, C. B. (1995). Service quality: A measure of information systems effectiveness. *Management Information Systems Quarterly*, *19*(2), 173–187. doi:10.2307/249687

Quesenbery, W., & Brooks, K. (2010). *Storytelling for user experience: Crafting stories for better design*. Rosenfeld Media.

Shannon, C. E. (2001). A mathematical theory of communication. *Mobile Computing and Communications Review*, *5*(1), 3–55. doi:10.1145/584091.584093

Sharon, T. (2013). A Collaborative Lean UX Research Tool. *Smashing Magazine*. Retrieved 10/14/2016 from https://http://www.smashingmagazine.com/2013/04/rainbow-spreadsheet-collaborative-ux-research-tool/

Sherwin, D. (2013). A 5-step process for conducting user research. *Smashing Magazine*. Retrieved from: http://uxdesign.smashingmagazine.com/2013/09/23/5-step-process-conducting-user-research/

Stephan, E., Cheng, D. T., & Young, L. M. (2006). A usability survey at the University of Mississippi Libraries for the improvement of the library home page. *Journal of Academic Librarianship*, *32*(1), 35–51. doi:10.1016/j.acalib.2005.10.011

Szebeko, D., & Tan, L. (2010). Co-designing for Society. *Australasian Medical Journal*, *3*(9), 580–590. doi:10.4066/AMJ.2010.378

Tempelman-Kluit, N., & Pearce, A. (2014). Invoking the User from Data to Design. *College & Research Libraries*, *75*(5), 616–640. doi:10.5860/crl.75.5.616

Thompson, B., Cook, C., & Kyrillidou, M. (2006). Stability of library service quality benchmarking norms across time and cohorts.

ENDNOTES

[1] 1. Books are for use; 2. Every reader his or her book; 3. Every book its reader; 4. Save the time of the reader; 5. The library is a growing organism

[2] http://uxmovement.com/

[3] http://uxmag.com/

Chapter 2
Processes for User-Centered Design and Development:
The Omeka Curator Dashboard Project

Susan Chesley Perry
University of California – Santa Cruz, USA

Jessica Waggoner
University of California – Santa Cruz, USA

ABSTRACT

The authors discuss user-centered design and agile project management using the development of the Omeka Curator Dashboard as a case study. The University of California, Santa Cruz University Library developed a suite of 15 plugins for the Omeka open source content management system. This chapter describes the library's use of agile principles and methods for the management of this project, detailing the creation of user stories and acceptance criteria. This chapter also outlines the usability testing conducted by the library in the form of online surveys and moderated field tests. The authors conclude that user-focused, inclusive, and iterative development are key components to the success of the software development process.

INTRODUCTION

This chapter discusses user-centered software development projects and their management using the development of the Omeka Curator Dashboard by the University Library at the University of California, Santa Cruz as a case study. This chapter introduces the reader to Omeka, an open source content management system

DOI: 10.4018/978-1-5225-2676-6.ch002

designed by the Roy Rosenzweig Center for History and New Media at George Mason University for digital asset management and digital exhibit creation. Omeka is used by a variety of libraries, museums, and academic researchers.

The University of California, Santa Cruz University Library developed a suite of 15 plugins to expand the functionality of Omeka in the areas of collection building, description, management, and preservation. The library managed the development project using an agile project management approach. This chapter describes the benefits of using agile for this type of development work and details the library's utilization of user stories to support a user-centered approach to plugin design. The library also conducted usability testing to reveal problematic aspects of plugins and discover potential future enhancements. This chapter describes the library's use of both online surveys and moderated field testing.

BACKGROUND

Libraries and archives are increasingly focusing their staff expertise on curating and disseminating the digitized primary source materials in their archival collections. As part of this effort, archivists and curators see an increased need to engage and connect researchers directly to those materials (Theimer, 2010). Crowdsourcing transcriptions and other descriptive information is one way to engage users, but as Trevor Owens (2012) of the Institute of Museum and Library Services (IMLS) stated in his blog post, crowdsourcing transcription or tagging should not be considered the ultimate end goal. Instead the goal of participatory archives projects should be to improve user engagement and understanding of the institution and its collections. The *2015 NMC Horizon Report: Museum Edition* states that two short-term trends for museums and archives include the expansion of the concept of patrons to include both in-person and virtual visitors and the increasing focus on participatory experiences on-site and online (p. 16). The report further explains one of the significant challenges facing museums is the need to improve digital literacy of museum professionals (p. 24). The authors of this chapter assert that libraries and archives face that same challenge. The director of the Scholars' Lab at the University of Virginia Library, Bethany Nowviskie calls on libraries with research and development teams to engage in "creative, iterative, unfettered, informal, (even gonzo?) development of digital scholarly interfaces and content" (p. 55). Digital humanist Cris Alen Sula describes a model where libraries can truly engage digital humanities scholars and support their projects by promoting skills and leveraging the user-centered service paradigm accepted by most libraries (p. 24). Faced with the challenge of developing systems to support digital humanists and to engage users with digital content while keeping that development creative and iterative, the UC Santa Cruz University Library chose the agile development approach to managing software projects. Agile methodologies assert that the user is always the final authority on product quality, and quick iterations of developed functions allow for frequent and prompt feedback from those users (Beyer, Holtzblatt, & Baker, 2004, p. 56). Following is an explanation of the functions the UC Santa Cruz team developed in order to facilitate engaged user participation with the digital archive and a step-by-step approach to developing those functions for the Omeka open source content management system.

CASE STUDY: THE OMEKA CURATOR DASHBOARD DEVELOPMENT PROJECT

What Is Omeka and What Can It Do for Me?

Omeka is a free, flexible, open source Web publishing tool used largely by libraries, museums, and scholars. Omeka has a unique hybrid disposition as both a fully featured digital exhibit platform and a capable digital asset management system. In this chapter, the authors will outline the development process for creating plugins, or additional modules that extend the core functionality of the software. The downloadable Omeka software requires a LAMP-configured server (including the Linux operating system, Apache, MySQL, and PHP), along with ImageMagick for image manipulation. Omeka is a project of the Roy Rosenzweig Center for History and New Media at George Mason University, and the creators provide several options for institutions without system administration resources. They list suggestions and options for running Omeka as a virtual machine on Mac and Windows servers or in the cloud on a variety of fee-based hosting platforms ("Preparing to Install," 2016). A hosted version of the full downloadable version of Omeka is best for institutions with limited server and system administration resources. Omeka.net is a third option with a fully hosted and supported instance. Omeka.net has a free basic plan that includes 500 MB of storage, one site, 15 plugins, and five theme choices (Corporation for Digital Scholarship, 2015). Other fee-based tiers allow additional sites, files, and features. Omeka.net is the best for institutions looking to test-drive the software before fully committing the resources, or those with very limited IT resources.

The Omeka system itself is a structured database of files with metadata assigned to those objects in element sets. It handles most file types, including media. Each item can have multiple files attached to it, such as alternative views for images. Items are described using the Dublin Core metadata standard with additional metadata element sets for several different item types. These additional element sets can be modified by the institution. Items can be organized into collections and exhibits. Plugins are optional features that extend the functionality of Omeka, and they are developed by the Roy Rosenzweig Center for History and New Media as well as the open source community of developers using Omeka. Examples include the Geolocation plugin, which allows users to pin items to a Google Map and capture the geographic coordinates for that item in the metadata, or the YouTube plugin, which embeds video from the YouTube site and imports metadata such as creator and titles into the Omeka collection. Omeka themes control the look and feel of the site, including the colors and fonts. The Exhibit Builder plugin is a major feature of the system, which allows users to create Web pages that combine items from Omeka collections, including narrative text providing connections and context for items. Creators can incorporate visualizations such as maps and timelines to further illustrate their points.

The UC Santa Cruz University Library began using Omeka as a digital asset management system for the Grateful Dead Archive Online (GDAO). This large collection includes over 35,000 items, including images, documents, audio, and video. The site makes extensive use of the Solr Search plugin to index and create facets for the many categories of content. The online archive also accepts online contributions of materials from fans and scholars using the Contribution plugin. Library administrators chose the Omeka platform based on evaluations from other institutions such as the Metropolitan New York Library Council's experience with Omeka for their digitalMETRO project (Kucsma, Reiss, & Sidman, 2010). The Grateful Dead Archive Online is a blended collection of curated materials donated by the band along with artwork, images, and text uploaded by the community. In this sense, it works as an exhibit platform, a system for collecting user contributions, and a digital asset management system for both types of content. The Omeka core code's flexible approach to metadata representation was also particularly appealing. The Grateful Dead Archive is a significant 20th-century popular culture collection, and the project team needed the flexibility to create and incorporate local vocabularies specific to the collection. The Grateful Dead community members are truly the content experts, and the archive wanted to leverage their knowledge of names, places, and events. Omeka allowed the team to maintain a standards-based system employing Dublin Core metadata and controlled vocabularies along with crowdsourced tags and other content.

Archivists, librarians, and instructors at UC Santa Cruz also use Omeka to highlight materials from a range of collections held by the library's Special Collections and Archives departments in digital exhibits. The purposes of these sites have varied from digital components of physical exhibits, to classroom projects curated by students, to online-only sites with interactive elements and community contributions. Much of the Omeka development done by the UC Santa Cruz Library team supports these functions and will make up the case study in this chapter.

Several content management systems are available to libraries and museums, and the team of librarians and developers has experimented with several different packages and sites in addition to Omeka, including WordPress and Scalar. The basic functionality of these systems is similar, and they all meet the basic needs to display digital items along with contextual content. Omeka's strengths are the contribution functionality allowing users to upload files to the collections, its structured exhibit templates, and its wide range of plugins to manage content in different formats. Currently the community has created over 60 plugins to enhance functionality. At the UC Santa Cruz University Library, librarians, archivists, and students all use Omeka and have found it easy to use. Evaluations from other institutions praise its "low barrier to entry" (Marsh, 2013, p. 2). WordPress has a very large community of developers and is a common blogging platform, which makes it familiar to many users. However, it lacks the predefined Dublin Core metadata schema for items in the collections and the templated exhibits. Scalar is a similar digital exhibit platform and performs many of the same functions. The strength of Scalar is its ability to draw connections between objects and embed objects from external sites. Librarians and archivists often start with a collection and provide context, background, and visualizations based on those items. Researchers may start with a text or a thesis and then add objects and visualizations to illustrate that point. Scalar natively supports that workflow. In his evaluation of Scalar at the University of Illinois at Urbana-Champaign, Daniel Tracy (2016) highlights Scalar's ability to create multiple paths through a set of research objects (p. 164). As the Digital Scholarship and Digital Initiatives departments at the UC Santa Cruz library have evolved, they've begun to focus on the needs and research questions of faculty and curators in order to make a recommendation for the best digital exhibit platform. The user-focused agile development models used by the project team can be implemented for design and development of functionality in any platform.

Developing for Omeka

Although Omeka can be used as a turnkey solution for Web publishing and still allow the user a great deal of flexibility in the appearance and structure of the site through the use of themes and plugins, one of the benefits of Omeka is its open source nature and robust development community. After the library's work on the Grateful Dead Archive Online, archivists and librarians began conceptualizing use of Omeka as a general exhibit platform for all of the digital collections. However, Omeka lacked workflow and curatorial management tools that would have optimized this more expansive use of the exhibit platform. As use of GDAO progressed, the exhibit creators also began to recognize a need for additional tools that would enhance their ability to build, maintain, and preserve the collection.

The library administrators decided to take advantage of Omeka's open source code and began the initial planning of an Omeka development project in which a team of programmers, designers, archivists, and librarians would design, develop, and evaluate these tools in-house. At this point in time, the library did not have an applications developer or a dedicated project manager on staff; the dedicated developer and project manager positions for the Grateful Dead Archive Online project were temporary and had been funded through an IMLS grant. Therefore, pursuing a major development project would require the library to seek additional funding. However, library managers were confident that the Omeka tools they envisioned would be desirable and useful to the entire Omeka community, making this development work suitable for grant funding. In 2012 the UC Santa Cruz University Library was awarded a second IMLS national leadership grant to assist the team in creating new Omeka tools, which were dubbed the Omeka Curator Dashboard (OCD). The OCD would be a suite of 15 Omeka plugins delivering functionalities in the areas of collection building, description, management, and preservation.

The development team relied on a large number of library staff serving in diverse roles across the organization in order to support the development project. The IMLS grant provided funding that allowed the team to hire a project manager, who was funded to dedicate 50% time to the management of the OCD project, and a full-time applications developer. However, a development project of this scale would not have been possible with a project team composed of only these two staff members. The library recruited staff from the Digital Initiatives department to engage in usability testing and serve as subject matter experts for digital library workflows, from the Special Collections and Archives departments to advise on the needs of exhibit curators, from the Metadata Services department to instruct on the needs and workflows surrounding digital object metadata, and from the Information Technology Services department to design and build an Omeka prototype Web site for digital exhibits and for the system administration infrastructure necessary to support the prototype. As work progressed and the scope of the project expanded to include instructional use of Omeka exhibit building, the team also tapped the library's CLIR (Council on Library and Information Resources) Digital Humanities Post-Doctoral Fellow to shepherd the inclusion of pedagogical Omeka exhibit sites. The core team consisted of the project manager, developer, and the Digital Initiatives department manager who communicated about project and budget status regularly with the library administration. Other staff were pulled in as their expertise was required for determining their needs and testing the software.

Assembling a project team composed of staff from departments across the library can be a formidable task. Obviously, the departments from which staff members are pulled incur the opportunity costs, prolonging the timelines on some of their own departmental projects, or possibly forgoing them altogether. This makes advance buy-in a crucial element to this type of library development project. Library administrators and the project manager were able to cultivate buy-in among department heads and staff by framing the project as an opportunity for their staff to develop or enhance skill sets. Project team members would also have the opportunity to shape the tools that they would be utilizing in the future. The library dedicated funding for conference attendance for staff involved in the development project as a portion of the institutional cost-share for the grant. This funding served two roles. First, it allowed staff to be project ambassadors at national conferences. They met with other Omeka users, who shared details about their institution's Omeka implementation, and they informed these users about the OCD development project, possibly even soliciting the Omeka users as future beta testers of the OCD tools. Second, this conference funding allowed staff to attend sessions that developed or enhanced their skill sets, facilitating their work on the OCD development project and other future library projects.

The library used the experience gained during the Grateful Dead Archive Online project to estimate the development staffing needs for the OCD project. The library administration had hoped to hire the same programmer they had hired to develop for GDAO, but that person had moved on to a permanent position at another institution just as the grant funding ended for that project. Losing skilled staff is a definite risk when one-time funds are used for development projects. Hiring another experienced programmer into a temporary position for the OCD made for a challenging and long recruitment, which delayed the project by several months. Though it was a difficult lesson learned, it was helpful in making the case to library administration for a permanent programmer position. By the conclusion of the second IMLS grant, the project team was able to justify transferring the developer position from temporary to permanent, not only to pursue new development efforts, but also to sustain the existing projects.

Project Timeline

See Figure 1.

Assessing Development Needs

The UC Santa Cruz University Library took several steps to assess the library's development needs for the next phase of digital collection management and exhibits

Figure 1. Timeline for the OCD project

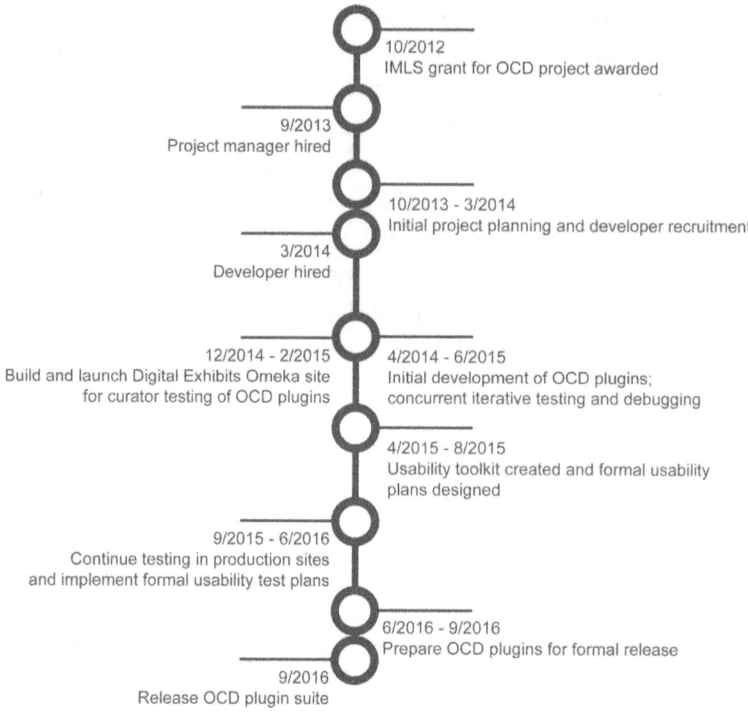

in Omeka. The first step included a retrospective evaluation of the construction and deployment of the Grateful Dead Archive Online. The postmortem of the project launch revealed a significant challenge to importing large batches of materials into Omeka. The project team also conducted interviews with GDAO stakeholders and administrative users. Now that the archivists and metadata specialists were using the system on a daily basis, they had specific recommendations on how to improve the site. The interviews revealed a host of unmet needs and ideas for increasing efficiency in object management and curation. For example, the metadata specialists discovered that they needed a way to edit metadata in bulk across the Grateful Dead Archive collection. This bulk editing included the need to delete, find and replace, append, and add new metadata to existing fields. Archivists also desired a history log for each object that would expose any curatorial updates made and the username of the staff member who made the change. Collection managers needed a mechanism for effectively pulling digital objects, both files and metadata, from our larger digital collection housed in CONTENTdm. Asking our exhibit curators to manually enter CONTENTdm metadata into Omeka and then find and upload the corresponding file was inefficient and tedious. The team wanted to provide curators with tools that would allow them to incorporate digital objects from collections outside the library systems, specifically image and video hosting sites such as YouTube, Flickr, and Vimeo. Facilitating the addition of these externally sourced materials would allow curators to add a great deal of richness to their digital exhibits. Another challenge the collections managers faced was the archival preservation of the digital files and metadata in the Omeka collections. Although the library used CONTENTdm to manage materials digitized in-house, Omeka was managing an increasing number of unique user-contributed files. Archivists needed a tool that would allow them to transform these Omeka items into METS (Metadata Encoding and Transmission Standard) and push them into an archival repository, such as the California Digital Library's Merritt digital preservation repository.

Once the project team had a draft list of functional needs, they consulted the main developer of Omeka, The Roy Rosenzweig Center for History and New Media at George Mason University, to compare these needs with the core manager's development roadmap. The Center for History and New Media staff were also very knowledgeable about projects in development at other institutions across the Omeka community. The UC Santa Cruz team wanted to be sure their plans complemented rather than duplicated the plans for core development. Because they were supported by federal grant funding, they also wanted to be sure their development would meet the needs of the larger Omeka and digital library communities.

The project team also consulted with the University of California Curation Center (UC3) at the California Digital Library to determine the feasibility of depositing objects from Omeka collections into their hosted repository as well as other standards-based repositories.

The team engaged in conversations with experienced Omeka developers around the country and their own administrative and IT departments to determine the resource requirements for such a development project. The assessment culminated with an environmental scan of other Omeka projects to determine how the development landscape had shifted between the deployment of GDAO and the awarding of the second IMLS grant. Through this assessment work, they identified broad requirements for project deliverables.

Managing Development

The UC Santa Cruz library had previously used a traditional "waterfall" project management approach for development projects. Although this method provided project teams with high levels of predictability and a more formalized structure, they found that it concentrated the development phase of the project timeline in a manner that did not accommodate any late changes in functional requirements.

When employing a user-centered approach to software development, it is essential to adapt functional requirements to changing user needs. This is particularly true when working with open source software. As new versions of Omeka were released and other developers in the Omeka community published new plugins, the team found that some of the functions in the original grant proposal were already in development at other institutions. The team found it necessary to consistently track the work of the Omeka development community and collaborate on similar plugins in development by other groups. Using a traditional project management method would have hindered the team's ability to quickly adapt to these changes in the development environment. As H. Frank Cervone (2011) opines when describing the disadvantages of traditional project management methods, ". . . requirements definitions are often so labor intensive and protracted that the requirements for the project have changed before development even begins" (p. 18). For these reasons, the team chose to use an agile project management framework for this development project.

Agile project management grew out of the Agile Software Development movement spearheaded by Beck et al. Agile software development articulated four key values for software development work: 1) individuals and interactions over processes and tools; 2) working software over comprehensive documentation; 3) customer collaboration over contract negotiation; and 4) responding to change over following a plan (Beck et al., 2001a). In addition to the four key values, Beck et al. laid out 12 principles to support the values declared in their Agile Manifesto. Agile project management methods reflect the four values and supporting principles. Although there are a variety of more prescribed agile methods (Scrum, extreme programming/ XP, etc.), the UC Santa Cruz library chose a less formal approach for their small team. They embraced the two core components of the agile approach, namely its iterative development cycle and regular direct communication and collaboration between stakeholders and developers. Cervone (2011) describes the importance of these elements, "The reasons these two concepts are emphasized is simple: both help a project team adapt quickly to the unpredictable and rapidly changing requirements most development projects are carried out in" (p. 19). The team also aligned their project with the principles behind the Agile Manifesto, particularly 1) early and continuous delivery of valuable software; 2) welcoming changing requirements, even late in development; 3) delivering working software frequently; and 4) working software as the primary measure of progress (Beck et al., 2001b).

The timeline for the development component of the Omeka Curator Dashboard project was one year. For the suite of 15 plugins, that allotted two to four weeks per plugin iteration to achieve the one-year timeline. Jim Highsmith, one of the creators of the Agile Manifesto, refers to these feature development timeframes as "timeboxes" and suggests that two to four weeks is an ideal length (2009, Kindle Location 2731). To decide whether a feature would require a two-, three-, or four-week timebox, the project manager and the developer reviewed the functional requirements to determine an estimated level of effort (LOE) for each complete plugin. Each plugin was assigned a low, medium, or high LOE corresponding to a two-, three-, or four-week timebox. The work performed inside the timebox was building/development time. Design and testing phases were also iterative in nature, but were not bound within the development timebox.

The project manager served as both the main stakeholder and the project facilitator. The project manager was responsible for working with subject matter experts (analogous to customers in an enterprise setting) to assess user needs for functional requirements expressed as user stories, communicating with the developer about features and user stories, developing acceptance criteria, conducting acceptance testing, and liaising with in-house users for feedback after the deployment of beta iterations. The developer was responsible for communicating with the project manager for information and clarification on requirements and acceptance criteria, giving feedback on LOE estimates for user stories and features, writing technical specifications based on functional requirements, developing the plugin iterations, fixing bugs and other issues found during bench testing, and providing LOE estimates for subsequent iterations.

The development cycle for each plugin had four distinct phases: 1) design, 2) develop/build, 3) implement/bench test, and 4) deploy/formal evaluation. During the design phase, the project manager created functional requirements, expressed as user stories, based on the needs of subject matter experts. Once these user stories and accompanying acceptance criteria were complete, the project manager and designer met to assign a level of effort to each plugin. As described earlier, this LOE estimate determined the size of the development timebox. The developer would then kick off the development phase by writing technical specifications. As agile emphasizes "working software over comprehensive documentation" (Beck et al., 2001), these technical specifications were often minimal. Rather than create extensive technical documentation, the developer ensured that the code itself was well commented. While the developer was building the plugin, the project manager created acceptance testing scripts based on the previously documented acceptance criteria. This simultaneous work allowed for a faster development cycle. Once the developer had a working iteration of the complete plugin, or for larger plugins a single function, the project manager bench-tested the iteration using the acceptance testing scripts. The developer would then fix any bugs or significant issues found during bench testing. The deployment phase involved use of the plugin within a production Omeka environment used by curators within the library. Curators gave feedback about the plugin to the project manager, who either shelved the feedback as a future enhancement or forwarded the issue onto the developer to address in a new iteration. This final phase also included a more robust evaluation of the plugin's usability. The phases of the project are indicated in Table 1.

Table 1. Tasks by project phase

Phase	Project Manager Tasks	Developer Tasks
Design	Write features and user stories Write acceptance criteria Determine LOE Set timebox size	Review features, user stories, and acceptance criteria Determine LOE
Develop	Write acceptance testing scripts	Write technical specifications Write code iterations
Implement	Bench-test iterations Report problems	Revise code to fix problems found during testing
Evaluate	Communicate with end users Document potential enhancements Report problems requiring immediate fixes Conduct formal usability testing	Revise code to fix problems found by end users

The team used the "freemium" (meaning free as well as paid tiers are available) project management web application Asana to assign and manage development tasks. Because the phases were identical for each plugin, the project manager created a template in Asana that was used for each plugin. The tasks for each plugin were assigned to a member of the project team (generally the project manager or developer) and given due dates. Asana was chosen over other more robust project management software options for several reasons. First, its deployment as a Web application meant that it could be accessed on any computer without the need to download software. Second, it was deployable in minutes, requiring very minimal setup by the project manager. Third, it had a clean intuitive interface requiring no training prior to use by the project manager or other members of the project team. Asana is a lightweight task-based solution and does not allow for the creation of Gantt charts. Therefore, Google Sheets was used for overall project scheduling, whereas Asana was used for task tracking and more detailed development due dates.

Designing the OCD Plugins

The development team began the design process armed with the broad deliverables outlined in the initial assessment. To create functional requirements for the Omeka Curator Dashboard plugins, the project team members interviewed potential users, examined their current and desired workflows, and discussed their specific objectives for using the broadly described OCD plugins. The project manager identified subject matter experts in departments throughout the library, ranging from exhibit builders in Special Collections to metadata experts in Metadata Services.

For example, one OCD project deliverable was a plugin that would import content from a video hosting site such as YouTube. The project manager met with exhibit builders from the Special Collections and Archives departments to examine the curatorial needs of such a plugin and the workflows surrounding the incorporation of externally hosted videos into a digital exhibit. The curators explained that although Omeka natively allowed them to embed videos within an exhibit, they sometimes preferred to have a video be its own distinct Omeka item. As an item, curators would have the flexibility to add the video to a collection, connect the video to other items throughout the Omeka site through indexed fields such as subject headings or tags, and expose the video's metadata. They wanted a plugin that would quickly and easily import a video as an Omeka item and include the video's metadata from its source. The import of metadata from the video hosting sites YouTube and Vimeo required a crosswalk between the external site's metadata schema and Omeka's basic Dublin Core fields. The project manager consulted with experts in the library's Metadata Services department to design this crosswalk.

Based on the information gathered in interviews with subject matter experts, the project team developed user stories detailing the desired capabilities of each plugin. Mike Cohn (2004), co-founder of the Agile Alliance, defines user stories as "short descriptions of functionality—told from the perspective of a user—that are valuable to either a user of the software or the customer of the software" (para. 1). Rather than describe user interface elements or detail system behavior, user stories briefly explain what the user should be able to do when interacting with the software. User stories should also be very specific and descriptive; ideally, two people independently reading a user story would share an understanding of what the user should be able to do even if they have different thoughts on how that functionality might be achieved. Cohn (2004) points to imprecision in language and the risk of differing interpretations between customers and developers as a key advantage in utilizing user stories (para. 5).

Due to the detailed nature of our user stories, the project team found it necessary to wrap them in a broader hierarchical context. In his book on agile project management, Jim Highsmith (2009) refers to these hierarchical elements as "stories" and "features," wherein features may be complete functions, whereas stories may be smaller components of a given feature, delivering useful but not complete functionality (Kindle Location 2817–2819). An example of this feature and story division can be seen in the Item Review plugin depicted in Table 2. The feature for this plugin stated, "As a curator/admin, I want to be able to view items created by Contributors and Researchers and approve them for publication." Alone, this feature would not be adequately specific for initiating development work so the project manager divided it into three distinct user stories: "As a Super User, I can determine which roles require approval for publication," "As a curator/admin, I can see a list of all objects pending approval," and "As a curator/admin, I can approve items for publication." Expressing the functional requirements as user stories allowed the team to pursue a more user-centered approach to the design by employing the user's perspective when envisioning and describing desired functionality. The user story approach also facilitated an iterative development process by concentrating development efforts on one user story at a time, then testing the completed user story while simultaneously beginning development work on a next user story.

The project manager derived acceptance criteria for each plugin based on the articulated user stories. Acceptance criteria are the minimum requirements for a given feature; once the developer feels that these criteria are met, the feature exits the initial development phase and enters the testing and refinement phase. Agile coach Sandy Mamoli argues that good acceptance criteria should not be overly detailed, should "state an intent not a solution," and should not be implementation specific (Mamoli, n. d.). Based on these guidelines, the acceptance criteria did not contain any technical specifications constraining the developer in his implementation of the user story, nor did they include any detailed instructions on the user interface design. Refinements to these aspects of the user experience would be made after acceptance testing, in line with the iterative approach to development.

To return to the example of the Item Review plugin, one acceptance criterion was "Users in designated Reviewer roles can approve items that are pending." This criterion did not specify details such as the wording, color, or placement of the approval button. Avoiding this level of detail facilitated the iterative development

Table 2. User story for the Item Review plugin

ID	Title	Feature	Priority	User Story ID	User Story	LOE Est.
17	Item Review	As a curator/admin, I want to be able to view items created by Contributors and Researchers and approve them for publication	2	17.1	As a Super User, I can determine which roles require approval for publication	Med
				17.2	As a curator/admin, I can see a list of all objects pending approval	
				17.3	As a curator/admin, I can approve items for publication	

process by allowing the developer to focus on delivering functionality. The project manager then identified refinements to these elements during acceptance testing.

Acceptance testing ensured that all acceptance criteria were met. The team developed detailed testing scripts enumerating the steps taken to test each criterion. Returning to the example for the Item Review plugin, the test for determining whether reviewers could approve pending items (approval of items being just one of the articulated acceptance criteria) was as follows:

1. Log in as a Reviewer-level account
2. Find items for review
3. Approve item(s)

The team referred to this acceptance testing as the "bench testing" phase for each plugin. During this phase, the project manager produced a bench testing report, reporting bugs, identifying necessary changes to user experience elements, and recommending possible future enhancements to the plugin. The developer then fixed any bugs and incorporated changes identified by the project manager during bench testing. Enhancements were either made at this point or shelved for future versions of the plugin, depending on available slack in the project timeline and the level of effort required for the enhancement.

After this second round of development work, the plugins were considered to be in "beta." Beta versions of the plugin were deployed in the library's own Omeka sites for use by exhibit curators. Curators subsequently suggested additional improvements to experience elements, such as buttons and wording. The project manager gathered these suggestions for potential incorporation into future versions of the plugin. May Chang (2010) describes this agile process for incorporating user feedback as follows: "Requirements elicitation is an ongoing activity, because needs are constantly changing, and user feedback is collected at the end of the development cycle. The development team is often willing to go back to the design phase to redesign the system around user feedback" (p. 673). This iterative cycle of development and refinement allowed the team to quickly deploy beta plugins for use in production Omeka sites and incorporate improvements into subsequent iterations on user feedback.

Because the library was already using GitHub as a repository for the OCD plugin code, the development team found it most efficient to use GitHub Issues for reporting bench testing outcomes. The project manager opened separate issues for bugs, user interface changes, and potential enhancements. Communication between the project manager and the developer about each issue occurred outside of the GitHub platform in greater detail. However, the team found GitHub Issues to be the most efficient way of tracking and monitoring the status of changes made after bench testing. Because the code was openly available in GitHub, other Omeka users at other institutions could also download and use the beta plugins. These users also opened GitHub Issues if they found bugs. Placing the official bench testing findings in GitHub gave the developer a single platform for storing and tracking all refinements.

Evaluation and Usability Testing

The Omeka Curator Dashboard project included more formal usability testing conducted outside of the development timebox after development work had been completed and plugins were ready to be used by the larger Omeka community. Usability is a subjective concept, with many definitions offered by a variety of authors. Most definitions center around the concepts of effectiveness (Can users do what they need to do?), efficiency (How easily can users do what they need to do?), and satisfaction (How do the users feel about using the tool?). Steve Krug (2014) offers a concise definition of what makes something usable: "A person of average (or even below average) ability and experience can figure out how to use the thing to accomplish something without it being more trouble than it's worth" (p. 9). Usability testing seeks to assess how usable something is and uncover changes that would make that thing more usable.

The project grant funding gave the team the opportunity to hire a usability professional. The consultant created a usability toolkit for use in testing the Omeka Curator Dashboard project plugins and future technology projects. Formal usability tests can take a variety of forms, ranging from asynchronous lightweight testing through surveys to more labor-intensive moderated field testing where testers observe and document users attempting to accomplish a task on a Web site. The toolkit focuses on four methods: focus groups, A/B testing, online surveys, and moderated field tests. Guidance is provided for determining which test(s) to use based on the type of development project, research questions to be addressed, and point in the development cycle. Playbooks that provide detailed instructions and templates for conducting the test are included for all four methods. This toolkit will be made publicly available for use by other libraries seeking guidance and templates for conducting their own usability testing.

For the Omeka Curator Dashboard usability testing, the project team determined that online surveys and moderated field tests would best meet their testing needs. In their *Handbook of Usability Testing*, Rubin, Chisnell, and Spool (2008) suggest that although surveys can be used at any point in the development cycle, developing language that elicits a common understanding among all survey takers can be challenging, and surveys cannot provide the quality of empirical data generated through moderated field testing (p. 18). Surveys allow testers to potentially gather data from a large number of participants. Whereas the resources required for moderated field testing may restrict testing to three to five participants, surveys can reach tens or even hundreds of users. Surveys are time intensive on the front end: the survey designer should ensure that questions are understandable by testing the survey itself prior to release. This testing phase might result in multiple revisions of survey questions. Once finalized, testers will need to publicize the survey in order to generate sufficient responses. Moderated field testing, referred to simply as "usability testing" by Rubin et al. (2008) involves developing a series of research questions or test objectives, recruiting test participants who represent the end user, observing participants conduct a series of tasks, and collecting quantitative (e.g., time to complete a task, number of clicks) and qualitative (e.g., post-test interview questions measuring satisfaction) data (p. 25). These field tests generate a wealth of usability data, but are very time and resource intensive to conduct.

The project manager developed separate online surveys for all 15 of the Omeka Curator Dashboard plugins. Surveys were designed to address 1) the effectiveness of the plugin: was the user successful in making the plugin do what it was designed to do; 2) the efficiency of the plugin: how easy the user found the plugin to use; and 3) the overall satisfaction of the user: how well did the plugin meet the user's expectations. The team attempted to minimize the number of questions in each survey, avoiding any unnecessary "nice to know" questions. The surveys employed Likert scales, where 1 meant "Strongly Disagree" and 5 meant "Strongly Agree" in the required questions and optional open questions where users could enter context for their scaled answers in a text box. They publicized the surveys in several ways. First, they included links to the surveys on the Web pages where users download the plugins: on the official Omeka.org list of plugins and/or the plugin's page in GitHub. Second, they included links to the surveys on the Omeka Curator Dashboard project Web site. Third, they sent links to the surveys out to the Omeka developer group and to a variety of library technology listservs.

Due to the resources required to conduct moderated field tests, the team limited field testing to a selected group of plugins rather than all 15. They selected plugins to test based on their levels of popularity and complexity. YouTube is the most popular plugin and was the first plugin for which the team conducted moderated field tests. They recruited three participants to test the YouTube plugin. The participants included two professional online exhibit curators and one undergraduate student with experience creating online exhibits in Omeka. Testing was conducted in an empty office at the University Library, and two members of the project team were involved in each test, one serving as the test moderator and the other as the observer. The field tests were divided into two parts: leading the participant through a series of tasks and a debriefing with the participant once the tasks were completed. For the first part of the test session, the moderator led the participant through a series of tasks using the Omeka plugin. The moderator followed a test script and encouraged the participant to think out loud and ask questions while engaging in the tasks. The observer silently watched the participant's screen and took extensive notes on how quickly the participant completed the tasks, points of confusion, questions or statements made by the participant, and "errors" made by the participant (e.g., selecting an incorrect option from a drop-down window, neglecting a necessary form field, etc.). For the second part of the session, the participant was presented with a list of words (both positive and negative) and asked to select the words that they felt represented their experience with the plugin. These selections served as a starting point for the debriefing conversation. The moderator asked the participant to explain their choices and attempted to probe the participants for more expansive descriptions of their thoughts and feelings while completing the tasks. During this debrief, the observer continued to take notes on the participant's responses. Once all three test sessions were completed, the project manager examined the notes taken by the observer. Based on these findings, the project manager created usability reports outlining changes needed in each plugin to enhance usability. These changes were divided into immediate needs and potential future enhancements. The project manager then created GitHub issues for each immediate need to be addressed by the developer.

FUTURE DIRECTIONS

The general principles of regular communication with users and attention to their input and feedback have been beneficial beyond the project detailed in this case study. Before the Omeka Curator Dashboard project concluded, the Digital Initiatives department was able to successfully make the case to UC Santa Cruz University Library and campus administration to permanently fund the library applications developer position. The short development cycles and iterations repeatedly demonstrated the progress and value of the project. This position has opened the possibility for continued development of Omeka and other open source software applications. The authors believe the user-focused agile project development method was a key component of the success of the project, and it will be used for all future development projects. The library continues to support Omeka for digital exhibits of archival materials, and the team has been working with researchers across the campus to create Omeka sites for courses. They've also developed additional Omeka plugins to support large research projects created and managed by faculty. This expanded the service, which includes graduate students, and has given the team insight into the different workflows and creative processes for different types of content creators. The team plans to include better support for helping researchers articulate their project goals during the needs assessment phase before the design and development stages begin.

Because usability principles are a major component of user-centered design, there is a growing movement to better incorporate usability features into the development cycle. Moreno and Yagüe (2012) argue that usability principles should be built into functional requirements for agile projects (p. 169), either as tasks within an existing user story or as separate user stories focused on usability (termed "usability stories") (p. 170–171). In future development projects, the UC Santa Cruz team will attempt to improve our functional requirements by incorporating usability principles. This might include the description of a button, the wording of a menu option, or the placement of explanatory help text.

CONCLUSION

The core project team at the UC Santa Cruz University Library found that involving a large team of staff stakeholders in the development of requirements and testing benefited the project in many ways. It increased the staff buy-in and professional investment in the project. Because the quick and iterative development cycle in agile project management focuses on delivering working software, staff were often able to see the results of their feedback within weeks of the initial needs assessment. The institution used the software as it was developed, and iterative development cycles supported that use. Users' stories were also extremely useful communication mechanisms, which helped the developers understand the needs of staff users of the software and helped the nontechnical users articulate their needs. Project team members can be so immersed in the details and iterations of a software function that they sometimes no longer see obvious flaws in the design. Usability testing helped the project team see their products through the eyes of a novice user. The project team also found that GitHub worked well for storing code and tracking issues from a variety of staff and sources. The GitHub Issues function gave the developer a clear list of tasks that could be prioritized by the rest of the project team. The team also found that the documentation from the deliverables, features, user stories, and acceptance criteria served as an extremely useful communication mechanism for all members of the project, including the project sponsors and library administration.

REFERENCES

Beck, K., Beedle, M., van Bennekum, A., Cockburn, A., Cunningham, W., Fowler, M., . . . Thomas, D. (2001a). *Manifesto for agile software development*. Retrieved October 25, 2016 from http://agilemanifesto.org

Beck, K., Beedle, M., van Bennekum, A., Cockburn, A., Cunningham, W., Fowler, M., . . . Thomas, D. (2001b). *Principles behind the agile manifesto.* Retrieved October 25, 2016 from http://agilemanifesto.org/principles.html

Beyer, H., Holtzblatt, K., & Baker, L. (2004). An agile customer-centered method: Rapid contextual design. In C. Zannier, H. Erdogmus, & L. Lindstrom (Eds.), Extreme Programming and Agile Methods – XP/Agile Universe 2004, LNCS (Vol. 3134, pp. 50–59). Berlin, Heidelberg: Springer; doi:10.1007/978-3-540-27777-4_6

Cervone, H. F. (2011). Managing digital libraries: The view from 30,000 feet: Understanding agile project management methods using Scrum. *OCLC Systems & Services: International Digital Library Perspectives*, *27*(1), 18–22. doi:10.1108/10650751111106528

Chang, M. (2010). An agile approach to library IT innovations. *Library Hi Tech*, *28*(4), 672–689. doi:10.1108/07378831011096303

Cohn, M. (2004, October 8). *Advantages of user stories for requirements* [Web log post]. Retrieved October 25, 2016, from https://www.mountaingoatsoftware.com/articles/advantages-of-user-stories-for-requirements

Corporation for Digital Scholarship. (2015). *Plans*. Retrieved November 3, 2016, from https://www.omeka.net/signup

Highsmith, J. (2009). Agile project management: Creating innovative products (2nd ed., Kindle version). Amazon.

Krug, S. (2014). *Don't make me think, revisited: A common sense approach to Web usability. (n.p.)*. New Riders.

Kucsma, J., Reiss, K., & Sidman, A. (2010). Using Omeka to build digital collections: The METRO case study. *D-Lib Magazine*, *16*(3/4). doi:10.1045/march2010-kucsma

Mamoli, S. (n.d.). On acceptance criteria for user stories [blog post]. Retrieved November 3, 2016, from http://nomad8.com/acceptance_criteria/

Marsh, A. C. (2013). Omeka in the classroom: The challenges of teaching material culture in a digital world. *Literary and Linguistic Computing*, *28*(2), 279–282. doi:10.1093/llc/fqs068

Moreno, A. M., & Yagüe, A. (2012). Agile user stories enriched with usability. *Lecture Notes in Business Information Processing*, *111*, 168–176. doi:10.1007/978-3-642-30350-0_12

New Media Consortium & Balboa Park Online Collaborative. (2015). *NMC horizon report*. Retrieved from http://cdn.nmc.org/media/2015-nmc-horizon-report-museum-EN.pdf

Nowviskie, B. (2013). Skunks in the Library: A path to production for scholarly R&D. *Journal of Library Administration*, *53*(1), 53–66. doi:10.1080/01930826.2013.756698

Owens, T. (2012.) Crowdsourcing cultural heritage: The objectives are upside down [blog post]. *User Centered Digital History*. Retrieved November 1, 2016, from http://www.trevorowens.org/2012/03/crowdsourcing-cultural-heritage-the-objectives-are-upside-down/

Roy Rosenzweig Center for History and New Media, George Mason University. (2016). *Preparing to install*. Retrieved October 27, 2016, from http://omeka.org/codex/Preparing_to_Install

Rubin, J., Chisnell, D., & Spool, J. M. (2008). *Handbook of usability testing: How to plan, design, and conduct effective tests*. Indianapolis, IN: Wiley.

Sula, C. A. (2013). Digital humanities and libraries: A conceptual model. *Journal of Library Administration*, *53*(1), 10–26. doi:10.1080/01930826.2013.756680

Theimer, K. (2010). *Web 2.0 tools and strategies for archives and local history collections*. New York, NY: Neal-Schuman Publishers.

Tracy, D. G. (2016). Assessing digital humanities tools: Use of Scalar at a research university. *Portal: Libraries and the Academy*, *16*(1), 163–189. doi:10.1353/pla.2016.0004

KEY TERMS AND DEFINITIONS

Agile Project Management: An iterative and adaptive method for managing projects that aligns with principles advocated by the Agile Manifesto.

Omeka: An open source content management system used for digital collections and exhibits. Omeka is a project of the Roy Rosenzweig Center for History and New Media at George Mason University.

Omeka Curator Dashboard (OCD): A suite of Omeka plugins that expand Omeka's functionality in the areas of collection building, description, management, and preservation. The OCD was developed by the University Library at the University of California, Santa Cruz.

Plugin: An add-on to the core Omeka code that expands the system's functionality.

Traditional/Waterfall Project Management: A sequential method for managing projects.

Usability Testing: Testing designed to evaluate the effectiveness and efficiency of a tool and the satisfaction of users when using the tool.

User-Centered Design: A design process in which the needs and wants of the user are considered prominently.

Chapter 3
A Decision Making Paradigm for Software Development in Libraries

Harish Maringanti
University of Utah, USA

ABSTRACT

Framing a technology question as a simple choice between developing an in- house application system and off-the- shelf proprietary system, or simply put, as a choice between build and buy, runs the risk of ignoring myriad options available in between the two extremes. In this era of cloud computing and run anything-as- a-service model, the very notion of developing an in-house application would raise a few eyebrows among C- level executives. How then can academic libraries, under mounting pressure to demonstrate their value (Oakleaf, 2010), justify investments in software development in particular? What follows in these sections is a brief discussion on the importance of investing in software development in libraries, three mini-case studies demonstrating the wide possibilities of integrating software development in library operations and a non- prescriptive model to assess which projects may be worth pursuing from the software development standpoint.

INTRODUCTION

Framing a technology question as a simple choice between developing an in-house application system and off-the-shelf proprietary system, or simply put, as a choice between build and buy, runs the risk of ignoring myriad options available in between the two extremes. As Langer puts it – "Choices of whether to make or buy do not

DOI: 10.4018/978-1-5225-2676-6.ch003

necessarily need to be binary, that is, one or the other, but rather could end up as a hybrid decision. For example, an organization can develop its own application using open source within its application development strategy or it can license a third-party product that also contains open source." (Langer, 2016). In this era of cloud computing and run anything-as-a-service model, the very notion of developing an in-house application would raise a few eyebrows among C-level executives. How then can academic libraries, under mounting pressure to demonstrate their value (Oakleaf, 2010), justify investments in software development in particular? What follows in these sections is a brief discussion on the importance of investing in software development in libraries, three mini-case studies demonstrating the wide possibilities of integrating software development in library operations and a non-prescriptive decision making paradigm to assess which projects may be worth pursuing from the software development standpoint.

Why Invest in Software Development?

Traditionally, businesses looked at IT systems as "black boxes" where it really did not matter what the interior looked like as long as those systems were able to deliver the value to the customer. Libraries were no different - one look at the literature points to a rich history behind library automation where proprietary systems played a major role (Breeding, 2006; Andrews, 2007). In the initial years, the focus was on automation where libraries cared about automating as many internal operations as possible. And as the years progressed, the expectations from such systems only increased to a point where automation alone wasn't sufficient anymore - integration between the automated components was expected. It can be seen in the natural progression of the vernacular from Automated Library System (ALS) to the Integrated Library System (ILS) (Kinner, & Rigda, 2009). Somewhere along, a big "mental shift" happened in libraries' thinking - the realization that technology could be leveraged not only to optimize the internal operations but also to drive innovation and deliver value to the users. As libraries demanded more of the vendors, the vendors responded by opening up the "black boxes" to give libraries some control over what and how things could be developed. Libraries, in turn, began responding to the local needs by hacking and developing tools on top of ILSes, where feasible.

But, libraries' future is not just in ILSes anymore - a remarkable array of new services are being developed. From generic institutional repositories to specialized subject-based data repositories, from offering mediated access to commodity collections to opening up access to troves of unique special collections - in every facet of the new and emerging programs, one can see the influence of technology driving the future. Though vendors have been great collaborators and partners in working with the libraries to support and sustain traditional library operations, it is imperative for the libraries to take control of their future and make investments in technology to support new and emerging services. Tyler Walters and Katherine, urge research libraries to "Be a doer, not a broker" and to "bring these services in-house (e-publishing services, hosting and curating digital archives, datasets) and seize the moments of opportunity as they arise" (Walters, & Skinner, 2011). Another important way in which developers (within libraries) can be a great asset is by looking out for solutions to solve what were once traditional library problems. Dan Chudnov expressed this sentiment eloquently - "The very notion of what has defined "library automation" for the past 30 years will shrink to mean primarily legacy operations; more and more of our critical systems, standards, and services will come to be supported by solutions developed outside of our community, and customized and optimized within it" (Gordon, 2007). Libraries need to invest in software development activities so that employees can implement this "outside-in" strategy to bring in solutions to solve current library problems from other fields.

THREE CASE STUDIES

This section will discuss 3 short case studies covering the gamut of software development projects - starting with hacking "black box" vendor systems to using APIs to develop custom functionality on top of proprietary systems, and from making simple customizations to open source systems to developing a custom application. It lays the groundwork for the last section, in which the author proposes a framework that IT managers can use to develop a strategy that outlines where the software development resources are best invested for maximum benefit.

One of the two axes that will be part of the matrix, will be introduced in this section – Y-axis or the build-buy axis. The two ends of extremes on this axis are vendor driven solutions (buy) and custom built, in-house solutions (build). That is as we move along the axis, more and more custom development would be involved. We start with a case study (#1) that is closer to the "buy" solution and end with a case study (#3) that is closer to the "build" solution. These case studies are presented from the perspective of a developer and in some cases, manager of a small development team.

Case Study 1

This case study discusses the progression of "hacks" that were developed on a proprietary Integrated Library Systems catalog. The complexity of the implementation gets simpler with each example, even though the impact of the functionality remains the same. Before Library vendors started offering cloud based platforms for ILSes, there was widespread dissatisfaction with the way the Online Public Access Catalogs (OPAC) worked. Roy Tennant's quip about "applying lipstick on pig" (Tennant, 2005) summarizes the extent to which the catalogs were broken. During the same time, several innovative projects started looking at enhancing the catalogs or totally rebuilding the functionality from scratch. At Kansas State University, a decision was made to enhance the catalog through various manageable hacks:

1. **Removing the Leading Article:** Catalogs were notorious for choking on the leading articles when searches were performed. Just when majority of Library users were getting used to the google-way of finding things (mid 2000s), library catalogs still suffered from lack of attention given to the user experience part. Asking users to not type in leading articles in their searches was never a good strategy. In spite of hammering the point through library instruction sessions, search logs revealed a big problem with this functionality. Because the focus was on automating functionality for staff, not much attention was paid to how catalogs were built. Customizing the catalogs in the pre-API era required applying band-aid solutions. To fix the leading article issue, the author wrote a simple javascript that would parse the text entered in the search box and get rid of the leading article. Though the solution required only a few lines of code, it had to be thoroughly tested and modified to work across a variety of browsers and platforms. Furthermore, such hacks had to be manually ported to newer versions, and there was no guarantee that the same code could work.
2. **Adding SMS Functionality in the Catalog:** This functionality was added to the catalog when users started using mobile devices to interact with library services. There were two main reasons why this feature was a welcome addition - Library catalogs were not mobile friendly and the wifi/cellular coverage in the stacks was problematic - users were likely to lookup the information elsewhere, but, wanted an easy way to note it down. Offering a link, that when clicked, would send the bibliographic information along with the call number as a text message turned out to a useful solution. The catalog had evolved to using xml and xslt - adding and maintaining this feature was a lot easier using xslt. Porting the code to newer versions was a lot more stable, as, there was less dependence on the user's environment (browser, platform).
3. **Integration With Quasi-Portal:** As campus portal systems evolved to aggregate important student-centered information into one system, Library could leverage this opportunity to push out relevant information pertaining to a student into these systems. One such effort to push out time sensitive information (returns, dues) was undertaken at this University. Luckily, the implementation was much easier, thanks to a well-developed Application Programming Interface (API) by that time. The system would return fines, books due information to the user

upon receiving user's unique ID. The users had to sign into only one campus system, and all the important notifications from various departments, including library, was made available in one system. There was not an issue with porting the functionality to newer versions of the catalog, as the functionality was only tied to the catalog's API. As long as the API remained study, no code had to be re-written.

Team

The author worked in a small team comprising of web development librarian, instruction librarian and a staff specialist to identify priorities, implement the code and publicize the enhancements.

Assessment

All these enhancements were huge successes - the leading article fix was reused in future versions of the catalog and other systems (libx); sms feature was used over 12,000 time in less than 18 months; and traffic from the central portal-like system to the library catalog increased after rolling out the notifications feature.

Discussion

All the three examples were enhancements done to a very mature and well known library service - catalog. The enhancements themselves represent a steady progression and improvement in the product i.e, starting with hacking interfaces that were really not set to be customized to adding functionality in a structured way that vendors facilitated. All the librarians, and staff working at the reference desk were aware of the issues and they developed workarounds that became part & parcel of library instruction. The reason for successes:

1. **Mature Services, Need Already Identified:** The author, as a programmer, focused solely on implementing the solution. Because the author worked in a team comprising of knowledgeable folks who understood the problem, articulated the need, took it upon themselves to publicize the solution, the end result was a huge success.
2. **Structure/Staffing:** Though it was a single programmer, these mini hacks were made possible because of the collaboration between the programmer, web development librarian and others. It was an organic development process that did not rely on any formal departmental structures, but rather, on the notion that things needs to be made easier for the Library users.

3. **Hacks Rather Than Full-Fledged Systems:** The programmer could focus exclusively on adding mini functions rather than developing a full-fledged system. The Library relied on the vendor to deliver core functionality that employees relied on and the development resources could be catered to public facing functionality. As Roy Tenant (2005) had suggested, rather than asking vendors for small enhancements, the library added enhancements themselves and reserved bigger requests for the vendor.
4. **Organizational Barriers:** There was little to no organizational resistance to add these features. Catalog was a well-known entity, and many departments within the Library were accustomed to the issues existent within the catalog at that time - so, any enhancements were welcome. There were no clear stakeholders/ advocates for the catalog within the library - IT, public services, cataloging department - all had various roles but none of them had all the knowledge and expertise to identify and implement these features in the catalog all by themselves. Collaboration was key and the desire to fix catalog issues was so strong in the organization that, not having a strong advocate, did not matter.

Case Study 2

This case study discusses projects that involved customizing open source applications:

1. **Authorization Scheme Built in Dspace:** Dspace was starting to be used as Institutional repository, initially to archive electronic theses and dissertations, but later to archive faculty's creative output. There was a need to identify user's affiliations to academic departments and to provision user's access to pre-defined set of collections for deposit. Dspace lacked this functionality but, because, it was an open source application, developers could look under the hood and add functionality as was needed. A set of java classes were developed that could lookup user's department affiliation from campus's central authentication and authorization system and integrate it with Dspace. When users are signed into their accounts, they had access to their department's collections without having to go through a manual approval process. Porting this feature to newer versions of Dspace turned out to be a nightmare because the code was deeply tied to the rest of the system and any small changes elsewhere warranted changes to this custom code.
2. **Database of Databases in Wordpress:** There was a need expressed to add descriptions to each research database that the institution subscribed to, and to give users the ability to search within the descriptions and narrow down their database selections. A simple solution was created on top of Wordpress, where by, library faculty could add descriptions, tags, keywords to each database.

Users could narrow down the databases by either searching for descriptions or by navigating the tags, and categories. Because of the tags, categories and availability of RSS feeds, the content could be reused and linked to from various other systems without much difficulty.

3. **Bulk Ingest Content Into Dspace:** Though Dspace had the bulk ingest capability, content had to be packaged in a standard way to make this happen. There were several projects where metadata for the content to be ingested was already available in different systems - for example, as MARC records in the ILS, or in MS-Access database, or in excel spreadsheets. The software development team developed a set of scripts that would extract the metadata from these systems, match them up with the digitized files, and package the content in a way that Dspace needed. The team was able to reuse the scripts for each type of data source.

Team

The team comprised of a programmer, systems administrator and a key stakeholder (repository manager, faculty liaison for databases). Whereas the programmer led the actual code development in two cases described above, systems administrator led the code development on the 3rd one. In-house developers were able to mentor systems administrator in the actual code development, thereby increasing the organizational capacity to undertake software development tasks.

Assessment

All the projects were successful judging by whether the original goals of each project were met. The team had good success ingesting materials into Dspace (thousands of records at a time) without having to do it manually or without having to rekey metadata that was already available in other systems. With database of databases, library faculty was able to add meaningful information to the system and users began using tags and categories to narrow down their database selection.

Discussion

A key decision that a development team might encounter during such projects is whether to add functionality to the system itself or to develop that piece of code outside of the system. The decision of course hinges on what other projects are being worked on or other systems are being used locally, but having a dedicated developer who can develop such a strategy always helps. Key takeaways:

1. **Roles and Responsibilities:** Roles and responsibilities were very clear when working with OS projects. Software developers were technical leads whereas repository managers or faculty/department liaisons were project managers for these projects.
2. **Communication:** Because the roles were very well defined, communication was never an issue. It added a few additional steps before the applications could be made live, but, sacrificing speed of development for communication was ok in these cases.
3. **Standards, Policies, and Governance:** A lot more time was spent bringing the right set of stakeholders to the table, creating working groups to evaluate viable options, and making the final decisions. Some of the questions that had to be considered before selecting an open source application included - the type of adoption that application had in libraries, number of contributors to the code, frequency of code contributions to the application (active, passive), code contributors' engagement with the community, and type of skills needed to support the application.

Case Study 3

This case study discusses the applications that were built in-house:

1. **GRA Croplands Research Database:** This database of literature about greenhouse gases and croplands supports the Global Research Alliance (GRA) Croplands Group's mission of reducing greenhouse gas intensity and improving overall production efficiency of cropland systems. The database contains literature about greenhouse gases and many different crops located in various climates. In addition to journal articles, the content also included conference papers, white papers, videos, data sets, and other useful research files. The database served as a place to preserve grey literature that might be difficult to find on the Internet or that might disappear over time (Olsen, Baillargeon, & Maringanti, 2012). The project team started with a small amount of data to understand challenges involved in editing the data, in identifying and correcting any copyright issues and identifying efficient solutions. In the first phase of the project, features that benefited both the end users and the staff were added to the system. Simple user interface enhancements, such as, listing the controlled vocabulary options as drop downs, cut down on data entry mistakes. Several tools were made available to staff to prepare data for ingestion. The technology stack used to develop the pilot project included Apache, PHP, MySQL and Solr.

2. **Workflow Management System:** Institutional Repository (IR) at Kansas State, K-REx, initially began as a platform for students to electronically deposit their theses, dissertations, and reports. After a few years, library started capturing faculty research and publications in the IR. Based on initial pilot projects, it was clear that libraries would have to devote staff resources to do the submissions and also to process the submissions. Each submission had to go through a set of standard steps and individual staff members were responsible for each step. The standard steps included - contacting the faculty member to get permission to archive their research in the IR, check for copyright permission with the publisher, add metadata and finally submit it for ingestion into the repository. A simple tracking system was needed to track each submission as it went through these steps, one-at-a-time. What started as a tracking system evolved into a complete Workflow Management System (WMS) that had a range of features in it - library staff could do most of their work related to the IR submissions in this system and, at the end, simply submit the record to IR without ever logging into IR. The system was developed using Apache, PHP, and MySQL.

Team

In both the cases, the programming team comprised of IT manager and programmer, worked very closely with the project partners. In the first case, the project partners were librarians who wanted to expand their department's outreach efforts by collaborating with other departments on campus. In the latter case, the project partners included repository manager, staff and librarians across a few departments within the library.

Assessment

The GRA croplands research database has been a huge success. More and more data is being added to the system, even after the original creators left the University. Debbie and Jenny, who worked with programming team on the WMS, wrote - "The workflow management system has been a great success, allowing easy handoffs between several individuals in two different departments and expanding to provide greater efficiency as processes develop. The system was designed with tools to simplify operations, such as the RefWorks interface, and the ability to add new features as needed, such as the publisher data. This flexibility provides the means of increasing both the capacity as well as the efficiency of the overall operation" (Madsen, & Oleen, 2013).

Discussion

Both of the above examples demonstrate the importance of having programming expertise within the Library. One was more focused on improving staff workflows (WMS) whereas the other project created a unique opportunity for the library to be an equal partner with the a respected faculty member on campus. It increased the profile of the library on campus and created more opportunities for the library to partner with faculty on campus on more innovative projects.

The 3 case studies follow a distinct pattern in terms of a direct correlation between the depth and complexity of the coding that was required and the size of the software development team. That is, most of the minor enhancements that were developed on top of the vendor systems happened when the software development team size was small (only 1). Gradually, as more resources were added to the team (with an additional programmer and a systems administrator), the development team could undertake complex projects and pursue innovative projects that needed custom applications to be built. Key lessons that resonate across all the case studies include:

1. **Communication:** It does not matter how talented the developers are - IT staff can no longer rely simply on their technical expertise (Trubitt, & Muchane, 2008). Communication is the responsibility of the software development manager and key library faculty who collaborate on projects. The more a developer's time could be dedicated to the development activities (and not administrative duties), the more projects could be finished in a timely manner. It does put responsibility of advocating for the projects, and championing the outcomes onto others, but it plays to the strengths of individuals.
2. **Culture:** The more the interaction between the IT staff and librarians the better. By working with each other, it helps to close the gaps in terminology, and understand motivations behind each type of position. IT specialist need to recognize that the time spent in meetings are important as bulk of the project's success depends on buy-in, relating to strategic goals and ensuring that right amounts are resources are allocated for the project's continued success. Librarians need to recognize that software development is not a commodity, it is a creative and intellectual process, and IT specialists need to be recognized and acknowledged for the work they create.
3. **Team Size and Structure:** Not one model or method will work in every case. Successful projects depend on the ability of the leadership to discern the right structure in each case. For example, grouping all the programmers in one group has merits but care needs to be taken so that each programmer spends enough time interacting with staff outside of IT to learn relevant subject matter.

SOFTWARE DEVELOPMENT DECISION MATRIX

The case studies discussed above were presented from the perspective of a developer. An organization can inventory the IT projects on the build-buy spectrum and assess its current IT strengths and plan future projects. For example, if the projects are more leaning on the buy end of the axis but future projects point to build approach, then managers need to think about creating support systems for build approach. If more IT projects are on the build end of the axis and the future projects point to buy approach, then the organization may need to hire for different skillsets i.e, rather than hiring software developers, the organization may need to hire system analysts. Langer built on the work of others and outlines reasons on when to support buy approach (cost, time to market, political environment, staff skillset, architectural differences) and when to support build approach (availability of software developers, adapt to changing business needs, competitive advantage, poor quality of prior packaged software). While these reasons give a good insight into when to choose either of the strategies, they do not complete the picture in a business context. Whether the build or buy decision needs to be made at the strategic or operational level (Inman, et al, 2011), analyzing it in the context of business functions is critical for IT managers. To do this, we will now add a second dimension to the decision making paradigm – the second axis called the internal-external axis. The two ends of extremes along the X-axis are internal facing applications and external facing applications. By internal, these applications are primarily geared to automate a functionality that would help library employees in their day-to-day operations. External facing applications are the library online services that users can interact with directly without engaging with any library employees.

Marty Cagan introduces a simple terminology to differentiate between internal and external applications - IT software and Product software. IT software, being internal focused, doesn't have the same set of expectations that Product software carries. For example, if there is an issue with IT software, employees can deal with it. But if there is an issue with the Product software then it reflect very poorly on the organization. She summarizes the difference between these two softwares as - "The truth is that most product software has a much higher bar in terms of the definition, design, implementation, testing, deployment and support than is necessary than most IT software. It's also true that salaries usually reflect this. Finding people with the necessary product software experience is much harder than finding IT experience." Given this reality, it is imperative that Product software projects are approached in a much different way than the traditional IT software projects. One of her recommendations is - "If you can outsource or buy off-the-shelf any of your true IT software (internal-facing software) you should do so, so that you can put your best people, time and mind-share on the customer-facing software" (Cagan, 2008).

It is useful to refer to two related concepts in this regard - Ledeen's "Core Vs Context" and Langar's "Driver/Supporter". These concepts introduce vocabulary that parallels the IT and Product software definitions. Ledeen discusses "core vs context" as one of the criterion to employ while choosing between the build and buy approach. He suggests that "Core activities are those that contribute directly to the organizations differentiation and value creation. Context is everything else." (Ledeen, 2014), in other words, core is "Product software" whereas context is "IT software". Langar employs his "driver/supporter" theory to decide between build and buy approach - "to summarize Driver/Supporter, there are essentially two types of generic functions performed by departments in organizations: driver functions and supporter functions… drivers are defined as those units that engaged in frontline or direct revenue generating activities. Supporters are units that did not generate obvious direct revenues but, rather, were designed to support frontline activities." (Langar, 2016).

For academic libraries that are planning to get into software development, a simple framework is proposed that will outline how to think about prioritizing projects based on available development resources. It is by no means a prescriptive model, but a model that can be used in the planning process to answer questions regarding important software development investments.

Figure 1. Two dimensional model

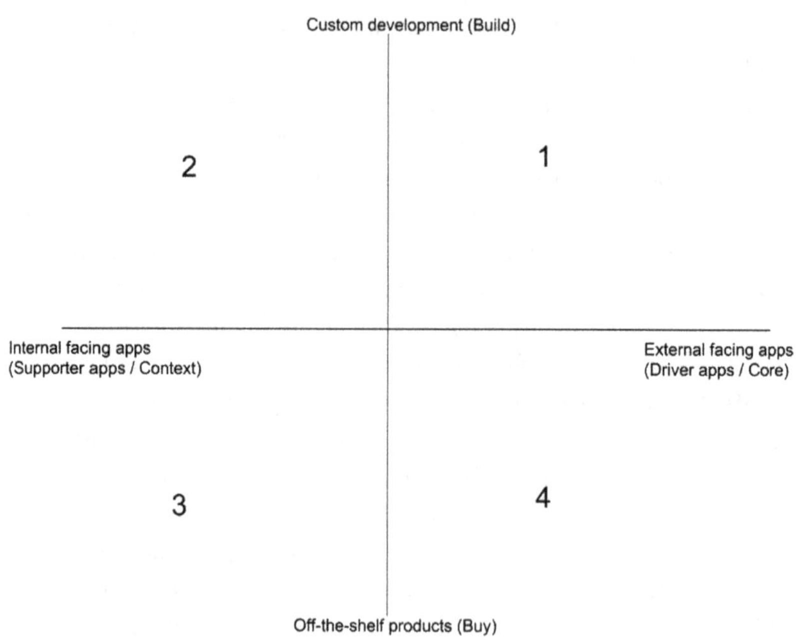

The two-dimensional model shown in Figure 1 is one possible way to map all the software development projects that are undertaken in the Library. The two ends of extremes along the X-axis are internal facing applications and external facing applications. Borrowing Ledeen and Langar's terminologies, internal facing applications can also be labeled as "context" or "supporter" applications, while external applications can be labeled as "core" or "driver" applications. The two ends of extremes on the Y-axis are completely vendor driven solutions and custom built, in-house solutions. That is as we move along the axis, more and more custom development would be involved. There are four quadrants in the figure, numbered from 1 through 4.

IT leadership and management can use this matrix to audit their current application stack inventory and overlay their software developments projects on top. It can give a visual representation of where they are investing most of their software development (human) and financial (operating or capital IT expenses) resources. IT leaders need to engage library leadership in discussions related to future library priorities and develop a robust application strategy. This is important because IT is still not well integrated into the functioning of research libraries (Roger, 2016 & Hinchliffe, 2016). According to recent S+R report (Roger, 2016), several IT structural models exist within academic libraries. It shows how IT is sometimes is still nascent and libraries are struggling to accommodate IT. It is in this context, that IT managers or directors need to engage library leadership very effectively. Without getting into the nuts and bolts of software development, library leadership can advise IT leaders on how to redistribute resources (or add resources) based on strategic goals. IT leaders can help develop key drivers for each quadrant that can guide the strategy discussions internally.

This chart would give the leadership a yardstick to measure whether IT projects are in alignment with their definition of IT. If IT is viewed mainly as an internal organization then, it is likely that majority of the projects on the chart might fall on the left quadrants (#2,#3) on the chart. As long as the leadership wants it that way, it is fine. But, if leadership wants IT to lead new public facing initiatives and the chart is leaning to the left side of the chart, then it shows a real need to change the approach of IT.

Key Drivers

Assuming that an IT manager has a finite operating budget, a finite set of software development resources, and a set of business problems to solve, the matrix can help in shaping the local application development strategy:

- **When to Choose Custom Development for External Applications (Quadrant #1 in Figure 1; Product Software):** If no existing product in the market can solve a current business need, or if an off-the-shelf product that meets the needs is prohibitively expensive, then one could advocate for custom developing a solution. It is quite normal for institutions to develop custom solutions in what they may see as emerging areas – these areas are relatively new in that workflows, processes and features may not have matured to the point that vendors could implement a common set of features to address the needs across the board. Custom development of digital asset management systems and tools, and emerging custom library catalogs built on black light before the discovery tools became a norm, are some examples in this category. Put it differently, emerging areas have the potential to change the relationship between libraries and academic units – Langer argues that IT needs to be a "driver" in such cases (Langar, 2016). Research data management, Digital Humanities, Digital Scholarship - all are additional examples of areas where Libraries could take the Product Software approach. Langer's conclusion for implementing driver applications is to handle it in-house i.e, employ custom development (build) and Ledeen also concluded that "custom solution for core" approach has ample evidence in his research (Ledeen, 2014). Key success factors: Success in developing custom products hinges on availability of highly skilled developers, product managers reporting through appropriate lines who can communicate information back and forth between stakeholders, end users and the developers (structure), and support from library leadership (alignment with strategy).
- **When to Choose Custom Development for Internal Applications (Quadrant #2 in Figure 1):** The same criteria used above apply in this case, but managers may impose additional restrictions on the budget for internal needs. Marty Cagan makes a great case for investing important resources in the Product Software side of the house – in similar vein libraries need to avoid spending development resources for internal applications, unless it is absolutely necessary. Rather than look at the internal needs in isolation, libraries need to be willing to look at the overall context (strategy, structure) and change their workflows and processes to accommodate existing off-the-shelf products, if they are affordable. Workflow Management System (WMS) discussed as part of case study 3 in the earlier section, falls under this quadrant. There were no off-the-shelf products that addressed the local needs at that point in time. One point to consider is to collaborate with other institutions before embarking on development projects for internal needs – it

is likely that, such needs may exist for other institutions and it is always better to collaborate and pool resources together, rather than going solo on such projects. The urgency of the need and the scale of the project will dictate whether a community can be created around such a product.

- **When to Buy Off-the-Shelf Products for External Applications (Quadrant #4 in Figure 1):** If off-the-shelf product exist that meet the requirements and is affordable enough, then, libraries should take this route. If they need the ability to customize the product then those requirements need to be reflected in the specifications list. Libraries always need to develop an exit strategy when considering proprietary products – by having a robust exit strategy they can avoid vendor lock-in and will be better prepared to engage with new vendors in the market for possible solutions. If off-the-shelf products exist, but are expensive, and local development resources are not sufficient to undertake the development, then library leadership could either re-allocate resources from other areas or make a case for more funding from campus administration. What approach one takes will depend on the need that the product can fulfill.
- **When to Buy Off-the-Shelf Products for Internal Applications (Quadrant #3 in Figure 1):** In cases where off-the-shelf products are affordable and can meet the requirements then libraries should consider taking this approach.

Figure 2 shows an overlay of the case studies on the matrix along with key decision drivers for each quadrant. IT managers need to identify strengths, prioritize local needs and invest their resources appropriately to derive maximum benefits. Going through the exercise of mapping their current applications onto this matrix would help IT managers visualize their current application portfolio. If most of their budget and local development resources are weighed heavily on the left side of the matrix (internal facing), it is a clear indication that they have to modify their strategy to become more user-centric (external facing).

CONCLUSION

Developing institutional capacity to create in-house tools is an important strategic direction for Libraries. While every tool has a finite shelf life, the knowledge gained by developing tools in-house, can be invaluable. It will help libraries - to be doers than mediators, to think critically about their local resources and to drive key emerging initiatives without being excessively dependent on vendors. All software

Figure 2.

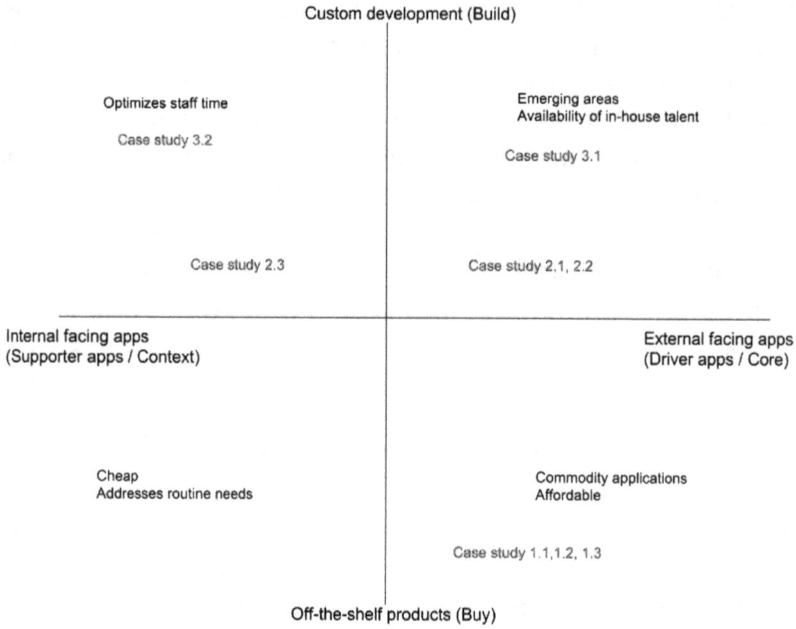

development projects are not created equal – prioritizing projects and committing to invest resources in projects is an important decision that needs to be driven by institutional priorities. Libraries need to develop application development strategy that can help guide decisions on when to develop locally or when to look for off-the-shelf products or some combination of the two. The author proposed a non-prescriptive decision making model in this chapter in the hopes of adding another perspective to this important topic.

REFERENCES

Andrews, M. (2007). Changing Markets, changing relationships. *Library Hi Tech*, *25*(4), 562–578.

Breeding, M. (2006). Reshuffling the deck. *Library Journal*, *131*(6), 40–50.

Cagan, M. (2008, July 6). Moving from an IT to a Product Organization. Retrieved from http://www.svpg.com/moving-from-an-it-to-a-product-organization

Gordon, R. S. (Ed.). (2007). *Information tomorrow: reflections on technology and the future of public and academic libraries*. Information Today, Inc.

Hinchliffe, L. J., & Askey, D. From Invasive to Integrated: Information Technology and Library Leadership, Structure, and Culture.

Inman, R. A., Sale, R. S., Green, K. W., & Whitten, D. (2011). Agile manufacturing: Relation to JIT, operational performance and firm performance. *Journal of Operations Management*, *29*(4), 343–355.

Kinner, L., & Rigda, C. (2009). The integrated library system: From daring to dinosaur? *Journal of Library Administration*, *49*(4), 401–417. doi:10.1080/01930820902832546

Langer, A. M. (2016). Build Versus Buy. In Guide to Software Development (pp. 37-48). Springer London.

Ledeen, K. S. (2014). Build v. buy: a decision paradigm for information technology applications.

Madsen, D. L., & Oleen, J. K. (2013). Staffing and workflow of a maturing institutional repository. *Journal of Librarianship and Scholarly Communication*, *1*(3), 1–12. doi:10.7710/2162-3309.1063

Oakleaf, M. (2010). *The value of academic libraries: A comprehensive research review and report*. Assoc. of College & Research Lib.

Olsen, L., Baillargeon, T., & Maringanti, H. (2012). Developing an open access croplands research database through global collaboration. *Journal of Agricultural & Food Information*, *13*(1), 35–44. doi:10.1080/10496505.2012.639272

Schonfeld, R. C. (2016). Organizing the work of the Research Library.

Tennant, R. (2005, April 15). Digital Libraries: "Lipstick on a Pig." Retrieved from http://lj.libraryjournal.com/2005/04/ljarchives/digital-libraries-lipstick-on-a-pig/

Trubitt, L., & Muchane, M. (2008). In plain English, please: Effective IT communications. *EDUCAUSE Quarterly*, *31*(2), 62.

Walters, T., & Skinner, K. (2011). *New roles for new times: Digital curation for preservation*. Association of Research Libraries.

Chapter 4
Mobile Applications for Libraries

Dana Haugh
Stony Brook University, USA

ABSTRACT

This chapter will detail the use of mobile applications in libraries. It will begin by briefly exploring the history of mobile application development, its inception, and progress to its relevance and use within libraries as a means of improving access and resource delivery for patrons. The prevalence of mobile devices, both inside and outside of the library, has affected the way individuals locate and use information. Libraries play an essential role in delivering resources to enhance the way users retrieve information, and therefore it is important to facilitate learning and scholarship through meaningful experiences in a variety of areas and mediums. A mobile application, not just a mobile-friendly website, can appeal to an increasingly digital population of library users in an environment that is both familiar and modern.

INTRODUCTION

Deciding to invest in, and potentially develop, a mobile library application is a tremendous decision, often invoking feelings of both exhilaration and anxiety. Some may question the need for a library application, as well as the decision to spend valuable time and funds developing a mobile presence when monographs, serials, and other resources demand so much of a library's finite budget. However, many librarians would agree that a library's collection means little if it's not easily discovered and accessible. A collection can be expansive, well-rounded, and comprehensive, but if it's not easily searchable, what value does it truly hold for a patron or researcher?

DOI: 10.4018/978-1-5225-2676-6.ch004

Every year information technology becomes more sophisticated; search engine algorithms are faster than ever, delivering results at six-tenths of a second. Library technology is forced to keep up with commercial search engines or run the risk of becoming dispensable. Library mobile applications can offer users another, possibly simpler, path to connect them to the information they need. Mobile applications offer a direct connection to users, eliminating navigation barriers and valuable page-loading time, effectively lessening the gap between what's visible, and invisible, in a collection.

But why develop a mobile application? Why isn't a mobile-friendly website enough? The first reason is relatively straightforward: an overwhelming majority of Americans use a smartphone. According to a study by the Pew Research Center (2017), approximately 95% of Americans in 2016 owned a cellphone, with 77% of that share belonging in the smartphone category. The percentage was even higher for Americans aged 18-29, amounting to 92% smartphone ownership. The same study also found that about half of Americans own a tablet computer. So, while a mobile-friendly website is best practice, there is a slight barrier to entry: requiring a user to perform a search for the library's website or enter a URL. This seemingly small barrier has the potential to dissuade patrons from even attempting to access a library website. If they do make it to the website, the site itself may not be compatible with the user's device, which can lead to a frustrating mobile experience. Creating a native library application takes away this barrier, giving users access to what they need in a familiar format. With one tap users can land on a simple, easy-to-use page of library resources, enabling research to start instantly. Without navigational barriers, engagement increases, which can in turn lead to increased circulation and ROI for resources.

While the decision to invest in a mobile library application may be becoming clearer, the choice to develop the application in-house is probably still intimidating. To take on a project of this complexity requires a person or team of people familiar with mobile development in addition to the time and resources required to develop it. It also demands familiarity with user navigation, user experience, and web design. A mobile application should be recognizable, intuitive, and intriguing. Ideally, a user could open an application for the first time and know exactly where to go and what to do in order to reach the information they need. While this may sound overwhelming, there are many steps one can take to ensure a library application meets all of the needs and wants of its users.

This chapter will explore a brief history of mobile applications and its introduction in libraries in order to provide an understanding of the evolution of mobile application development. It will then advance to some of the differences between paid and homegrown library applications, equipping the reader with a basic understanding of the benefits and drawbacks for each. Finally, the chapter will describe the homegrown mobile library application currently in progress at Stony Brook University Libraries, detailing some of the strategies, task delegations, roadblocks, and general development processes. The chapter aims to educate readers on the history of mobile applications while also providing concrete examples of how and why a library may choose to develop its own homegrown application.

A BRIEF HISTORY OF MOBILE APPLICATIONS AND THEIR USE IN LIBRARIES

In order to garner a better understanding of mobile applications and their eventual place in libraries, this section will outline some of the major events in mobile application development, beginning in 1983. This timeline is meant to deliver quick, relevant facts about application development throughout its relatively short history, highlighting the speed with which the cultural phenomenon has evolved. The majority of these facts were curated from reputable, archived Internet resources, such as company press releases, recognizing the evolution and importance of information dissemination across the digital landscape about a digital technology.

Significant Moments in Mobile Application Development:

1983: Steve Jobs gives a talk at a conference entitled "International Design Conference in Aspen" (IDCA) where he believes "software distribution through traditional brick-and-mortar was archaic since software is digital and can be transferred electronically through phone lines. [Jobs] foresees paying for software in an automated fashion over the phone lines with credit cards" (Brown, 2012).

1993: Apple releases a personal digital assistant (PDA) device called "Newton" which contains basic 'applications' like email, a calendar, and an address book (AVG Technologies, 2015).

1996: The 'Palm OS' is released and recognized as the first PDA device to 'get it right' transforming the concept of a personal device and effectively 'paving the way for an entirely new class of devices' (Dunphy, 2011).

1997: The game 'Snake' is released on the Nokia 6110, securing its spot in mobile game history as one of the original mobile phone games (Nokia Corporation, 2005).

WAP (Wireless Application Protocol) is created, which is "the global standard for bringing Internet content and services to mobile phones and other wireless devices" (Bennett, 2001).

2001: iTunes digital jukebox software is launched and the first generation of the iPod is released (Apple Inc.).

2003: Apple launches iTunes Music Store and sells 1 million songs in its first week (Apple Inc.).

2007: Apple launches iPhone and announces developers can create third-party Web 2.0 applications that will extend the iPhone's capabilities (Apple Inc., 2007).

2008: Apple launches The App Store (9to5 Staff, 2011).

Google launches The Andriod Market, a mobile application distributor for Andriod operating systems (Perenson, 2008).

2009: Apple releases world-wide campaign 'There's an App for That' (AVG Technologies, 2015).

BlackBerry launches BlackBerry App World, rivaling the App Store and the Andriod Market (BlackBerry, 2009).

2010: Windows Phone Store is launched, becoming the 4th largest distributor of mobile applications (Fuld, 2012).

2011: Amazon releases Andriod App store (Tweney, 2011).

2012: Facebook acquires Instagram for a hefty $1 billion, the highest ever paid for an app company (Primack, 2012).

2013: Google announces over 1 million apps in Google Play (formerly Android market); Apple announces 1 million apps in the App Store (Ingraham, 2013).

2014: "Data from Nielsen shows that U.S. Android and iPhone users age 18 and over spend 65 percent more time each month using apps than they did just two years ago" (Nielsen, 2014).

2015: According to the 2015 U.S. Mobile App Report by ComScore, U.S. adults aged 18-44 spend anywhere from 70-90 hours per month on their smartphones. Approximately 87% of time is spent on mobile applications, with the remaining 13% is spent on a mobile browser (Kong, 2015).

2016: Mobile applications continue to outpace mobile websites by a 7:1 margin in time spent browsing. Digital time spent on a desktop has started to decline, from 49% in 2013 to 33% in 2016 (comScore, 2016).

As evidenced in the timeline, after Apple's announcement of the opportunity to augment mobile phone capabilities with Web 2.0 applications the mobile application phenomenon quickly exploded. Apple's now infamous 2009 'There's An App For That' campaign drove the ubiquity of mobile applications worldwide, forcing competitor companies like Android, Blackberry, and Windows to develop comparable capabilities for their mobile devices. But the app craze didn't infiltrate organizations and academic institutions until later. It was a few years before libraries began considering the potential of mobile applications in relation to resources and user accessibility.

In a 2014 study on mobile web adoption in universities, researchers surveyed the top 50 universities in the United States and found that while 80% have a mobile-friendly website, only 34% have a mobile library applications (Torres-Pérez, Mendez-Rodriguez, & Orduna-Malea, 332). Of those with library applications, only seven are available both for iOS and Android, nine are iOS specific, and one is only for Android (Torres-Perez et al., 332). This discovery suggests that while many libraries began considering the possible benefits of library apps, it was yet to be widespread in this area.

MOBILE APPLICATIONS: PAID OR HOMEMADE?

Once a library decides to invest in a mobile application, the next step is determining whether to develop the application in-house or to use a paid platform. This decision often involves examining a number of factors including budget, staff expertise, application needs/wants, and time allocation. Paid applications offer a more hands-off approach and can be especially beneficial for those who do not have the time, staff, or resources needed to support an application. Homegrown applications allow for extensive customization and hands-on access for on-the-fly adjustments as well as complete control over privacy and information dissemination. It's important to look at both the positives and negatives of each development option in order to determine the one that best suits the library and its patrons.

Paid Applications

There are a number of companies that specialize in creating mobile applications specifically for libraries. With services such as complete ILS integration and federated searching, these all-inclusive platforms are both attractive and easy to implement. Hiring a company to create a library application is much like hiring a company for an ILS - the structure already exists, all that's needed is the content. Much like an ILS template, however, a prefabricated application leaves little room for customizations. Basic personalizations like logo, color scheme, and preferred format preference are easily implemented, but there may be other limitations. Of course, this is not necessarily a bad thing. Those looking for a basic application platform that features a library's key resources will probably not see a need for more a customizable interface.

Those who do not have the time, expertise, or staff to manage a library application may also find benefit in outsourcing its development. Paid platforms often offer complete support for technical issues, various operating systems, user training, community forums and other resources specific to the platform. If the application crashes, a phone call is all that's needed to get the issue resolved. Additionally, one need not worry about device and operating system compatibility with a paid application, as most platforms have this component built-in. Paid applications usually offer analytics to help improve user experiences and examine trends on behavior, which is essential when evaluating an application's value in its community.

However, one of the biggest drawbacks for paid platforms is cost. Budget constraints and limited resources mean that it can be difficult to justify allocating a substantial amount of money to a 'nonessential' application. Investing in a prefabricated mobile application undoubtedly makes it easier for libraries to both implement and maintain, but the choice to go mobile will depend on what a library is able to monetarily allocate. Some mobile application platforms like Boopsie encourage libraries to apply for grants if cost may be a factor in their decision, which could lessen the budget burden. The most important thing a library can do is to assess the way users currently access materials and resources. Examining the way patrons use the library is the best way to determine whether or not the return on investment is worth it.

Homemade Applications

If paid applications are too expensive or there's a need for unique functionality and control, developing a library app in-house might be the way to go. Be warned, however: developing an application is not for the faint-hearted. It takes time, skill, and a lot of patience. It usually requires an actual application developer who knows quite a bit about programming. Homegrown applications are the best way to save money on monthly or yearly application subscriptions and, as long as time and resources are available, it can be a gratifying and rewarding experience.

One of the many benefits for in-house application development is the opportunity for complete customization. The application can be tailored to the exact needs of the library and its users in ways that prefabricated applications may not allow. One is given complete control over every aspect of the application's development, from how it looks and acts, to developing the features that will resonate most with the library's target demographic. There is also the benefit of having complete ownership of the project. There is no contract or agreement that needs to be upheld. The information acquired while developing and maintaining the application is solely the property of the library and its staff. This benefit alone can be persuasive enough to sway library users to the in-house development side. Keeping development in-house decreases the amount of people who have, or will eventually have, access to a patron database, private information, and user habits.

A homegrown approach also allows library staff the opportunity to make immediate changes based on how patrons are using the application. Essentially, keeping an application in-house eliminates the middleman - if something needs to be changed or adjusted, it can be done right away without having to go through a ticket system. This is extremely useful in cases where time-sensitive issues arise or links break.

Depending on available resources and expertise, developing an app could take anymore from a couple months to years to complete a finished product. The process requires continuous intensive, hands-on testing as well as trial and error, training, and updates. The community of developers is a large one and boasts a plethora of online resources, tutorials, and support forums for troubleshooting and problem solving, which can be extremely useful during moments of difficulty. Upfront costs may be high due to the amount of work required to get an application developed and running. The library may require a team of IT personnel that is intimately familiar with the nuances and quirks of mobile applications, which can lead to higher staffing costs.

Additionally, programmers must decide which operating system they will develop first. Unfortunately, all mobile devices do not operate on the same system and so compatibility between platforms is often a challenge. The two most popular mobile operating systems are iOS and Android, and the developer must determine which platform will reach the widest audience first. This will depend, once again, on the characteristics of the library's population. If the majority of patrons use Apple products, it may be best to develop an iOS-compatible version first and unveil an Android-compatible version later.

The decision to develop in-house will be a challenging, but rewarding endeavor. It will require many hours of hard work but the end result is one that will bring a library great pride.

STONY BROOK UNIVERSITY LIBRARIES BACKGROUND AND THE CHOICE TO GO MOBILE

Stony Brook University is a public institution located on Long Island that serves over 25,000 students from all over the world. The university is part of the State University of New York (SUNY) consortia and ranks among the top 40 public institutions, and top 100 universities, in the nation. The university comprises three campuses, including one in Manhattan and one in Southampton, with the main campus located in Stony Brook. There are a total of six libraries serving the Stony Brook community, employing 28 faculty-rank, full time librarians and 56 library staff members as of August 2016.

In the Fall of 2015, President Samuel L. Stanley Jr., MD delivered the State of the University Address at Stony Brook and revealed that the main campus library, Frank Melville Jr. Memorial Library, would be undergoing a transformation in two of its reading rooms in order to support the academic community's growing need for digital-ready spaces. Following this announcement, renovations commenced on the Melville Library's Science & Engineering Library (henceforth renamed 'North Reading Room') and the Central Reading Room. A task force of librarians worked to ensure both spaces would be outfitted with over a thousand outlets, dozens of Wi-Fi access points, and more printers. The renovations were completed by the beginning of the Fall 2016 semester, launching the library reading rooms into the 21st century.

Parallel to the major changes occurring in the library's physical spaces, Stony Brook's Division of Information Technology (DoIT) unveiled a new digital initiative during Summer 2016 aimed at better supporting students through technology. The following quote from a news article on the DoIT website explains the program's goals:

Stony Brook University has embarked on a bold initiative called Mobile/Digital Now (MDN) designed to transform the academic experience of students by reinventing physical and virtual learning environments, optimizing wireless access, inspiring instructors to move to digital content, and leveraging mobile access across the student lifecycle. The first phase of this initiative began July 6, when 185 iPads were distributed to incoming Educational Opportunity Program (EOP) / Advancement on Individual Merit (AIM) students as part of an MDN pilot program being led by Vice President for Information Technology & CIO Cole Camplese and his team in the Division of Information Technology (DoIT). The second phase began in August with DoIT teaming up with the Division of Intercollegiate Athletics to disseminate iPads to student-athletes from the football, men's basketball, women's basketball, women's soccer, men's soccer, and volleyball teams. (Perniciaro, 2017)

This initiative was designed to enhance a student's academic experience by supplementing traditional classroom learning with digital tools and learning environments. Specifically targeted at EOP and student-athletes, this program augments learning by leveraging mobile technologies, giving oft-nomadic students greater possibility of success in their scholarly endeavors. After learning of this initiative, the University Libraries immediately set to work brainstorming ways in which it could collaborate with DoIT to offer library support for students on their mobile devices.

Recognizing the limitations of mobile-friendly websites, the University Libraries decided to develop a native library application compatible with iOS devices that could be pre-installed on the iPads disseminated to students through DoIT's program. If successful, the Libraries would develop the application to be compatible with Android and other devices, as well. The application would provide instant access to essential library information like personalized account details, hours and locations, research databases, and library chat.

Although the library's website is mobile-friendly (which enables users to access the same information regardless of their device) the experience can still be cumbersome. A mobile-friendly website, as explained earlier, is simply the desktop version formatted for a smaller screen. This means that all of the information remains visible on a mobile device unless there is code in place to prevent certain items from showing on a screen smaller than 'X' pixels. Ensuring a website is mobile-friendly is highly recommended, but it doesn't mean the experience will be seamless. Loading times for mobile devices may be longer when attempting to access a mobile-friendly website, which could mean the difference between using a library database or using a commercial search engine for research. An application removes the "excess" information, the kind that often overpowers a mobile-friendly version of a website and that may not be pertinent to users looking for specific information. It's a platform specifically designed for mobile devices, which means it behaves in the way a user has come to expect mobile apps to perform - simply and immediately.

The prevalence of mobile devices, both inside and outside of the library, affects the way individuals locate and use the information a library offers. Therefore it becomes essential that a library is able to deliver tools in ways that enhance a user's information retrieval process, not inhibits it. A mobile application, not just a mobile-friendly website, appeals to an even greater audience of information seekers, offering another avenue for accessing a library's many resources. It is because of this that the University Libraries ultimately decided to begin development on a mobile application, to be installed on iPads through DoIT's MDN initiative.

University Libraries' Mobile Application Team and Workflow

Once the University Libraries decided to development a mobile application, the Associate Dean for Library Technology set to work building a team. The University Libraries has a small team of library IT professionals focused on library-specific technology, which made the recruitment process relatively easy. The team was officially formed in early 2016 and consists of four people: a Senior Programmer Analyst, a Web Services Librarian, and two student workers who study Computer Science full-time at Stony Brook University. The team reports to the Associate Dean for Library Technology, though the student workers rely on feedback and guidance from the Senior Programmer Analyst and the Web Services Librarian.

The Senior Programmer Analyst and Web Services Librarian are both full-time employees. The two students study full-time at Stony Brook University and dedicate approximately 15-20 hours a week during the semester to developing the mobile application; they spend fewer hours working on the application during midterms and finals so that they can focus on their studies. The students are granted slightly more freedom than traditional 9-5 'work hours' as they can develop the application remotely. This means that they are not required to come into the library during set hours and can work on the application from their dorm rooms at any time of the day (or night). Regular in-person team meetings are scheduled every two to three weeks to monitor progress on the application and the team corresponds through email on a regular basis.

The Senior Programmer Analyst is responsible for overseeing the backend of the application's development, including the API integration, catalog & database integration, application building, and troubleshooting. The Web Services Librarian is responsible for front-end development, which includes graphic design, interface strategy and functionality, streamlining user experience, and front-end troubleshooting. The two student workers are ultimately responsible for building the application, from initial setup to design integration. As of February 2017, the application is still in development, though some preliminary design elements are being integrated.

As mentioned earlier, the application is being developed initially for iOS mobile-operating systems. This is to coincide with Stony Brook University's "Mobile/Digital Now" initiative, which is currently distributing iPads to students. During the 2016 fall semester, approximately 71% of the library's mobile website traffic was accessed on an Apple device (iPhone or iPad). This makes it slightly easier to justify unveiling the initial iteration of the application as an Apple app. Its success (or failure) will determine future iterations for Android devices.

Currently the student workers are developing the application using a programming language called Swift 3. The programming language is open-source, meaning it's freely available for use. Users can access the source code on GitHub and the Swift website features many helpful resources for getting started. Swift 3 was designed as a friendlier version of C-based languages, which makes it an ideal language for programming. Currently, the application has four working main sections, which are detailed below.

1. **Home:** The home screen currently has three sections, horizontally organized. The top section features an image of the University Libraries logo, the phone number for the main reference desk, and an email address connected to the library reference team. Below that, there is a list of all the University Libraries with their corresponding hours for the day. Each library can be clicked on, which will in turn open a pop-up featuring more information for that library (phone number, address, and interactive map). On the bottom of the app is a static menu bar with four sections: Home, Databases, Catalogs, Guides.

2. **Databases:** The 'databases' page features a list of databases, pulled directly from the library's A-Z list on Springshare, accessible through Stony Brook University. There is currently a section where users can search by subject or database type.
3. **Catalogs:** The 'catalogs' page features two integrated catalog search bars for searches specific to library collections. There are two catalog search bars as the University Libraries has two separate Aleph accounts - one for the main campus and one for the Health Sciences campus.
4. **Guides:** The 'guides' page consists of research and subject guides created by the University Libraries subject-specific library liaisons. There are currently sections to search by class, subject, and type. These guides are populated from LibApps (powered by Springshare).

Ideally, the next iteration will feature a 'My Account' section as well as a 'Library Chat' function, which would greatly enhance the application's appeal. The team's initial goals were to provide upfront access to the most important research tools in the library, which is why the categories mentioned above were implemented first. There have been some slight setbacks regarding integration with EBSCO products, however as of right now they have been resolved. The application's color scheme is consistent with SBU-branding, using approved fonts, colors, and photos also represented on the library website. The application is meant to look clean and simple, and so the use of white space and flat graphics are present throughout. The application is currently set to launch in June 2017.

MAKING CONCEPT A REALITY: HOW TO APPROACH MOBILE APPLICATION DEVELOPMENT

If a library is fortunate enough to have a team of IT specialists working in-house, then one needn't worry about this part of the operation. However, if the library has a slight deficiency in tech savvy programmers, establishing a team of developers (whether in-house or freelance) should be the first order of operation. Academic libraries may have a slight advantage in recruiting a team as their campus may be populated with aspiring application developers and programmers. But as long as one can find individuals with the right criteria and skillset, all libraries can put together an effective team.

Here's a list of criteria to consider when scouting for mobile application developers:

1. **Experience:** Look for someone with concrete, demonstrable experience in mobile app development. Spend time considering their portfolio of evidence - it's okay if they've never developed a library-specific app before, but some experience with app development is definitely necessary for a successful project.
2. **Drive:** If they've passed the first test (experience), the next characteristic to look for is drive. Are they motivated to finish the task? Do they have other engagements? Will this project benefit them in any way (adding to their work experience, etc.). Candidates with motivation for a project are essential, as app development is an iterative, sometimes lengthy, process.
3. **Design:** Perhaps slightly less important than the first two, front-facing design (in most cases) comes into play toward the end of development. Ideally, finding a candidate with experience in graphic design and user experience is recommended, as the front-face (what is displayed to the user) is important in success.
4. If a library can a few people that meet these qualifications, they will be well on their way to developing a valuable library resource.

Functions and Features

Perhaps just as important as finding a development team is composing a list of functions to offer in the mobile library application. One of the best questions to consider when devising this list is: what functionalities do patrons want or expect to see? The answers to this question will provide valuable insight into how the application will be developed. Carefully consider the application's intended audience: is it primarily for students, children, or adults? Will it offer resources for all types of users or only ones for certain demographics? Start by taking formal and informal surveys (perhaps offer library swag for participation) and be sure to incorporate their suggestions into the development plan. It will make the design more effective and will also ensure patrons know the library is working for them. Talk to colleagues and staff members and find out which apps they enjoy to using, which ones they don't like, and ask what types of features they would love to see in a mobile library app.

Another important tool in the development arsenal is the library's website. Consulting the website analytics will unlock the secrets of seemingly 'invisible' patron behavior and will show exactly how and why patrons are using the site. It will display statistics like what types of devices patrons use, where they are navigating, where they drop off, and the amount of time they spend on pages. Through website analysis one can draw usage conclusions and determine the best ways to streamline user search and exploration. It will also enable developers to predict the type of mobile app behavior patrons are likely to engage in, which will in turn, feed design strategies and feature implementations. Remember, a mobile application is an *abridged* version of a website. It's meant to act as a conduit for the library's resources, not a replacement for a website.

So, what does a dream mobile library application look like? It's different for each library of course! Some might have interactive, GPS-enabled maps, showing the patron's exact location in relation to the library; or an icon for chat reference, available directly through the application; or a My Account button that enables a user to renew or request books and pay their fines. Explore other apps and seek out inspiration to get the ball rolling and a core needs/wants list will develop.

How Do You Start?

1. Develop an actionable timeline and stick to it.
2. Utilize open-source coding projects like MIT's mobile project on Github and seek inspiration from other library apps.
3. Create a wire-frame and a general application map.
4. Start programming.
5. Once you have a working prototype, test it.
6. Create a small test group and get feedback.
7. Tweak and adjust based on feedback.
8. Do a Beta release (soft release).
9. Once the kinks have been ironed out, LAUNCH IT!

Remember, this is an abridged version of your website, meant to complement it. Don't try to cram everything on the website into the application. Keep it basic and streamlined. Consider what translates best into a mobile environment and work from there.

REFERENCES

9to5 Staff. (2011, October). Jobs' original vision for the iPhone: no third-party native apps. *9to5Mac*. Retrieved from https://9to5mac.com/2011/10/21/jobs-original-vision-for-the-iphone-no-third-party-native-apps/

Apple Inc. (2007, June). *Innovative new way to create applications for iPhone.* Retrieved from http://www.apple.com/pr/library/2007/06/11iPhone-to-Support-Third-Party-Web-2-0-Applications.html

Apple Inc. (n. d.). *iPod + iTunes Timeline.* Retrieved from https://www.apple.com/pr/products/ipodhistory/

AVG Technologies, (2015, February). *A history of mobile apps* [Prezi Slideshow]. Retrieved from Prezi website: https://prezi.com/rwc6qmvqkrt-/a-history-of-mobile-apps/#share_email

Bennett, C. (2001, November). A brief history of WAP. *InformIT*. Retrieved from http://www.informit.com/articles/article.aspx?p=23999

BlackBerry. (2009, April). *RIM launches BlackBerry App World*. Retrieved from http://press.blackberry.com/en/press/2009/pressrelease-2223.html

Brown, M. (2012, October). The Lost Steve Jobs Speech from 1983; Foreshadowing Wireless Networking, the iPad, and the App Store. *Life, Liberty, and Technology*. Retrieved from http://lifelibertytech.com/2012/10/02/the-lost-steve-jobs-speech-from-1983-foreshadowing-wireless-networking-the-ipad-and-the-app-store/#

comScore. (2016). *comScore 2016 U.S. Mobile App Report* [SlideShare Slides]. Retrieved from http://www.slideshare.net/comScoremarcom/comscore-2016-us-mobile-app-report

Dunphy, C. (2011, March). Palm: the rise and fall of a legend. *Maximum PC*. Retrieved from http://www.technobuffalo.com/2011/03/31/palm-the-rise-and-fall-of-a-legend/

Fuld, H. (2012, March). After 16 months Windows phone has 70k apps how long did it take iOS and Android. *Inneractive*. Retrieved from http://inner-active.com/2012/03/25/after-16-months-windows-phone-has-70k-apps-how-long-did-it-take-ios-and-android/

Ingraham, I. (2013, October). Apple announces 1 million apps in the App Store, more than 1 billion songs played on iTunes radio. *The Verge*. Retrieved from http://www.theverge.com/2013/10/22/4866302/apple-announces-1-million-apps-in-the-app-store

Kong, V. (2015). *The 2015 U.S. Mobile App Report by ComScore* [SlideShare Slides]. Retrieved from http://www.slideshare.net/VictorKongCisneros/the-2015-us-mobile-app-report-by-comscore

Nielsen. (2014, July). *Smartphones: so many apps, so much time*. Retrieved from http://www.nielsen.com/us/en/insights/news/2014/smartphones-so-many-apps--so-much-time.html

Nokia Corporation. (2005, June). *Snake creator receives special recognition from mobile entertainment forum*. Retrieved from http://company.nokia.com/en/news/press-releases/2005/06/16/snake-creator-receives-special-recognition-from-mobile-entertainment-forum

Perenson, M. (2008, October). Google launches Android market. *PCWorld*. Retrieved from http://www.pcworld.com/article/152613/google_android_ships.html

Perniciaro, K. (2017). *Mobile/Digital Now Vision Aims to Transform the Stony Brook University Experience*. Retrieved from https://it.stonybrook.edu/news/articles/mobiledigital-now-vision-aims-to-transform-the-stony-brook-university-experience

Pew Research Center. (2017). [Charts illustrating mobile phone ownership and device ownership from 2004-2016] Mobile Fact Sheet. Retrieved from http://www.pewinternet.org/fact-sheet/mobile/

Primack, D. (2012, April). Breaking: Facebook buying Instagram for $1 billion. *Fortune*. Retrieved from http://fortune.com/2012/04/09/breaking-facebook-buying-instagram-for-1-billion/

Torres-Pérez, P., Méndez-Rodríguez, E., & Orduna-Malea, E. (2016). Mobile Web Adoption in Top Ranked University Libraries: A Preliminary Study. *Journal of Academic Librarianship*, *42*(4), 329–339. doi:10.1016/j.acalib.2016.05.011

Tweney, D. (2011, March). Amazon launches its own Android app store. *Wired*. Retrieved from https://www.wired.com/2011/03/amazon-android-app-store-2/

Section 2

Services and Workflow Processes

New technologies have changed the way people interact with information and space—as well as expectations of the library as a service provider. This section details how new technologies are harnessed, adapted, and developed to create efficient workflows for library staff as well as provide new means of accessing library services for users.

Chapter 5
Intrapreneurship and Enterprise 2.0 as Grounds for Developing In-House Digital Tools for Handling METS/ALTO Files at the University Library Belgrade

Nikola Smolenski
University of Belgrade, Serbia

Milena Kostic
University of Belgrade, Serbia

Adam Milorad Sofronijevic
University of Belgrade, Serbia

ABSTRACT

The chapter is based on experience of authors who work at different positions at University Library ''Svetozar Markovic'' in Belgrade, Serbia. This library has been aiming at creation of efficient, creative work environment in the last decade and one of the main pay-offs has been the development of a unique set of digital tools for handling METS/ALTO files. The chapter will present both managerial background and ICT related details that encompass this complex process. It will also aim at providing examples of good practice in implementation of Enterprise 2.0 and fostering of intrapreneurship that may be employed in other library environments with notes on specifics of the University Library Belgrade and its relations to more general managerial issues and challenges that may be useful for other librarians.

DOI: 10.4018/978-1-5225-2676-6.ch005

INTRODUCTION

This chapter provides information on the relationship between the concepts of Enterprise 2.0 and Intrapreneurship and how they can successfully be used for the development of in-house digital tools in a context of a library.

First, we introduce the University Library of Belgrade, the scope of its activity and the relevance of the aforementioned concepts. In the second section, we provide some background information on the concept of intrapreneurship and how it can be successfully applied to the current managerial issues in libraries. We present the case study of the University Library in Belgrade which shows how an Enterprise 2.0 concept was implemented via intrapreneurial activities with the resulting recommendations regarding organizational culture, organizational structure, management style, and organizational rules and regulations. The third section deals with the different groups of library stakeholders and explains the importance of the development of digital tools for handling METS-ALTO files for various stakeholder groups. METS and ALTO are XML standards maintained by the Library of Congress and METS-ALTO files are current industry standard for newspaper digitization projects. The fourth section describes how intrapreneurs at the University Library have handled the METS-ALTO challenge through the use of Enterprise 2.0 concepts. Finally, the fifth section portrays the creation of the in-house digital tool for handling METS/ALTO files used for the presentation of digitized materials at the University Library Belgrade.

THE UNIVERSITY LIBRARY BELGRADE

The University Library "Svetozar Markovic", the main library of the University of Belgrade, is the largest, oldest and, as of 2016, the most influential higher education library in the Republic of Serbia. It coordinates the network of academic libraries in Serbia. It employs 92 librarians and support staff members while additional 146 librarians are employed at 31 faculty libraries of University of Belgrade. This workforce meets information needs of 90,000 students and 7,000 researchers, professors, and associates at the University of Belgrade. The Library collection is comprised of1.5 million printed documents and gives access to 30,000 electronic journals and 40,000 electronic books. The Library also promotes the usage of open access data. Interlibrary loan and collaboration with libraries worldwide; providing access to almost any digital document and to the majority of the printed ones.

The University Library operates a library system called Cobiss that automates acquisition, cataloguing, and circulation operations. An Online Public Access Catalogue (OPAC) caters to users in the framework of the system and is equipped with a federated search of library consortia for Serbia and in the region. A Local Area Network (LAN) in the main library building is connected with the Academic Network of Serbia and provides high speed Internet connection grounding Information and Communication Technologies (ICT) for the implementation of other technologies. Users have access to Wi-Fi throughout the main library building. Library 2.0 services are well-developed, with more than 14,000 users networked through social networks such as Facebook and Twitter. As of 2016, a new library website is in use. It offers personalized access to data for three major user groups: students, researchers, and librarians. The University Library hosts Phaidra, the long-term preservation digital repository for the University of Belgrade, which also serves as an open access repository of doctoral dissertations.

In addition, the University Library hosts numerous cultural and scientific events in its art center, one of the most well-regarded venues for exhibiting modern art in Serbia. Exhibitions of printed collections and virtual exhibitions are held regularly. Specialists from all scientific areas give lectures in the Knowledge Center of the Library and a number of virtual lectures are organized using teleconferencing equipment.

The University Library was the coordinator of Tempus project "Building cooperative academic library network in Serbia" (2002–2004) and it also coordinated Tempus project "New library services at Western Balkan Universities" (2010–2012). Tempus is the European Union's programme which supports the modernization of higher education in the partner countries of Eastern Europe, Central Asia, the Western Balkans and the Mediterranean region, mainly through university cooperation projects. The Library was a partner in two CIP ICT PSP projects as of May 2012: Europeana Libraries (2011–2012) and Europeana Newspapers (2012–2014). CIP ICT PSP is the European Union's programme that aims at stimulating innovation and competitiveness through the wider uptake and best use of information and communication technologies (ICT) by citizens, governments and businesses. As of 2016 the Library is a partner in the European Commision's Horizon 2020 READ project and several other international projects. It participates in various projects on digitization and metadata aggregation, partnering with institutions from Serbia and across Europe. In line with these projects, Library staff have developed expertise on various technical aspects of digitization and metadata models.

A new, more flexible organizational structure was introduced in 2008 in order to establish a diversity of activities, many of which are project based. Working processes are executed by task-driven employees who are not restrained by organizational unit differences. Moreover, objectively driven management fosters the formation of working groups consisting of staff from different departments. Even though organizational culture has changed, it has taken time for all Library employees to accept the new values and standards. As of June 2012, several subcultures have been identified as regards age, skills, education levels and exposure of employees to working in international environment. Examples of such varied subcultures encompass among others younger employees that have good IT skills and mid-level of formal education valued ability to get work done, flexible working hours and possibilities for learning, while employees with highest educational background that were exposed to working in international environment developed value system that seemingly was emulating the one of libraries in first world countries. In order to play a proactive role in the changing environment, the University Library management has employed novel techniques and has fostered usage of new technologies since 2012, including Enterprise 2.0 concepts and intrapreneurship.

Enterprise 2.0 describes the use of Web 2.0 tools and approaches by organizations in order to improve internal functions including communication, collaboration, and innovativeness (McAfee, 2009). Enterprise 2.0 flattens the organizational structure provides better prospects for ideas coming from the bottom of the organizational chart. When implemented properly, it empowers employees at all levels and undermines the information dominance of any specific group. In libraries, Enterprise 2.0 should not be confused with Library 2.0, a concept that describes the use of Web 2.0 technologies in libraries for fostering communication and collaboration between patrons and librarians. These two concepts have a lot in common, since the underlying technologies are the same Web 2.0 technologies. Therefore, knowledge and experience gained in the implementation of one might be valuable for the use of the other.

Intrapreneurship is the practice of intrapreneurial skills and approaches within an organization (Pinchot, 1985). This concept is studied and described in many industries, but library research has almost never dealt with it. Therefore, any application of this concept in libraries has been based on intuitive decision making by intrapreneurs and managers. Intrapreneurship in organizations establishes growth and profit (Antoncic & Hisrich, 2003), which in libraries may lead to a higher level of stakeholder satisfaction and funding increases. The level of intrapreneurial activity in an organization is influenced by factors originating in the organization itself and the environment. In order to foster intrapreneurship, management needs to manipulate the factors it can influence: communication between employees, formal control, organizational values, empowerment of employees, and information gathering. Managers also need to understand and acknowledge environmental factors that might be outside their scope of influence.

Internal research into Enterprise 2.0 implementation and intrapreneurship at the University Library Belgrade was conducted by some of the authors of this paper starting in 2009. This research has provided quantitative and qualitative data supporting the relationship between these two concepts (Sofronijevic et al., 2011). Web 2.0 tools are used for fostering collaboration between employees who already collaborate closely at the Library. These include the Google Apps platform, which has been activated under the unilib.rs domain name. Gmail with a proprietary domain and Google Calendar are among the most successful parts of the adoption. Furthermore, a blog and forum technologies are used for internal communication between employees. This has proved very useful as the volume of internal e-mail exchange in organizational units has decreased significantly.

A more recent survey (Sofronijevic, 2011) showed that there is a high level of awareness of Enterprise 2.0 issues among librarians in Europe. However, the implementation of Enterprise 2.0 is not consistent, with some examples of implementation and numerous initiatives at various stages. In many libraries, there is just a general idea of the need for implementation. The qualitative phase of the research showed that successful implementation is always related to high levels of intrapreneurial activities. Also, top management support for intrapreneurship has been identified as the key element for the long-term success of Enterprise 2.0 implementation.

INTRAPRENEURSHIP AND ENTERPRISE 2.0

Background

Intrapreneurship as a concept was introduced in the 1970s. It is first mentioned by Norman Macrae in an article published in The Economist in 1976 and in a doctoral dissertation by Robert A. Burgelman in 1983 (Small Business Notes - History of Intrapreneurship, Kautz, n. d.). The term is defined as the application of entrepreneurial skills and entrepreneurial approaches in the context of a company ("Intrapreneurship," n. d.) Employees act as entrepreneurs or use the company resources for entrepreneurial enterprise. Gifford Pinchot, author of the book "Intrapreneuring", has owned the copyright of the term intrapreneur since 1985 and has influenced the definition of the concept intrapreneurship[1]. An intrapreneur is a person who focuses on innovation and creativity, who turns ideas into profitable enterprises while working within the established organization (Churchill, 1992).

Intrapreneurship is a process which takes place in the entrepreneurial organizations. Stevenson and Jarillo (2007) define it as a process in which individuals strive to use opportunities regardless of resources they control. Hisrich and Peters (1998) talk about the spirit of entrepreneurship in an existing organization, whereas Vesper (1990) discusses work on different new tasks and a break from the common practice in order to use available opportunities. Sharma and Chrisman (2007) define intrapreneurship as the creation of a new organization by the already established one or as a trigger to revision and innovation in an organization. Antončić and Hisrih (2003) define intrapreneurship as entrepreneurship within an existing organization, which refers to the behaviorist intentions and behaviourism of an organization as an exception to the regular activities. This process can take place in organizations, regardless of their size, and does not bind only to the new business ventures, but also to other innovative activities and innovative orientations such as developing new products, services, technology, administrative techniques, strategies, and competitive benefits.

In a dynamic, global atmosphere that generates huge amounts of information and many opportunities, only the distribution of authority based on employees accepting responsibility for specific business sectors and the willingness of employees to engage independently in necessary business activities, which management in a given timeframe definitely would not be able to define, can bring positive results. Therefore, improvement of conditions conducive to the development of intrapreneurship is one of the most important roles of management.

Modern librarianship is characterized by the application of information and communication technologies and their rapid and dynamic development which began in 1990s with the third industrial revolution. The most important factors that determine library business today include diversification of user requests, globalization of business in library services provision sector, an unprecedented requirement for efficient and effective operations set by the funding bodies, and the need for lifelong education and innovation, not as an exception but as a rule. In order to conduct business successfully, libraries and librarians are increasingly turning to techniques and methods used for management of the profit sector. A contemporary market in which offers of funding bodies, donors and sponsors are small and the demand for funding through a variety of innovative projects is big, binds managers of modern libraries to study and apply methods and techniques for approaching investors used by entrepreneurs for years. The differences are obvious and reflect primarily the fact that those who invest in libraries do not want profit but instead want more positive results of cost-benefit analysis on a social level.

The level of knowledge and skill needed to successfully run a library certainly surpasses the capabilities of any one manager. Libraries are increasingly turning to hybrid or project-based organizational structures to achieve growth and business improvement, which requires implementation of creative tasks. The trend of management liberalization, which refers to the change of organizational culture followed by bigger delegation of authority and empowerment of employees, will continue.

The complexity of working conditions, dynamics, everyday changes in technological advances, and the changes caused by social innovations represent a source of information that must be processed by library managers and applied within the life cycle of the given information. With time, this has become impossible, especially in the context of constant staff problems which accompany libraries' human resources (HR) at University of Belgrade. The problems are caused by the simple HR laws in force on the HR managers market, with just a limited number of able managers available and seemingly an unfailing demand generated by the for-profit sector. For example, a young programmer might start working for the library and weeks, or even days, after being hired, transfers to a more profitable job at a commercial IT company. Therefore, library management needs to share the requirements for information processing and decision-making with the staff in an appropriate way. A similar problem occurs in the for-profit sector. The solution is the proper conditions created to encourage the phenomenon of intrapreneurship.

Case Study of the University Library Belgrade

Practical work has established a high level of intrapreneurial activities at the University Library Belgrade. The employees propose changes to work processes or introduce new services, collect information that will be used in developing new services and changing work processes, and work to develop and design new services and improve and acquire new expertise. Internal research has shown that managerial improvements to the working conditions can contribute to an increase in intrapreneurial activities. Can this trend of increasing intrapreneurial activities be connected with the implementation of the Enterprise 2.0 concept? There are two answers to this question. We will look into the attitude of the staff based on the internal research and we will outline some thoughts based on study of the formal organization of the University Library System. By analyzing staff attitudes we can conclude that attitudes related to the implementation of the Enterprise 2.0 concept are more prominent.

Intrapreneurial activities at the University Library Belgrade were conducted to implement Enterprise 2.0 concepts, increase efficacy and productivity of work, and surpass limitations imposed on staff by the formal organization and difficult financial situation. With the perceived and real support of the management, Enterprise 2.0 concepts were implemented via intrapreneurial activities.

Communication was the first field enhanced by the implementation of Enterprise 2.0 at the Library. The planned introduction of Web 2.0 technologies in organization units had a positive effect, including an increased level of cooperation between the staff and resolution of structural gaps that had prevented the flow of information. The existing means of communication were improved. Horizontal communication was improved via organizing educational activities on the topic of new technologies and brainstorming sessions on solving work related problems with the participation of the staff from different organization units.

Selection criteria were established in the formal organization. These criteria should help management to make decisions regarding the choice of initiatives in the field of information technology. Some criteria are related to the level of necessary financial resources such as computer resources and the number of working hours.

The third area that was positively impacted by was the field of collecting information. "Hard" and "soft" methods of stimulating the staff were equally represented and applied. The former refers to the obligations of reporting to the superior managers about the relevant issues in scientific-technical business context, primarily in librarianship, with proposals for the implementation of specific activities. The latter would include the selection of an idea of the month, where authors would be rewarded with souvenirs.

Areas where management assisted to the fullest extent have given impetus to the intrapreneurship and its orientation towards the implementation of the Enterprise 2.0 concept. Verbal and moral support management concretized through a call for participation in formal meetings where intrapreneurs had the opportunity to demonstrate the benefits of innovations that were developed in their own working practices.

Resulting Best Practices

This section will outline general recommendations that foster intrapreneurship and the implementation of Enterprise 2.0 concept in libraries developed through the described activities at the University Library and the collaborative experiences of the authors with other institutions in Serbia and abroad. Good practice recommendations for applying Enterprise 2.0 concepts can be divided into several groups including organizational culture, organizational structure, management style, and organizational rules and regulations.

The first group of recommendations is related to organizational culture. Organizational culture has many elements and layers that affect various aspects of the business. However, it is slow and difficult to change. It is necessary to assess which elements of the organizational culture are suitable for Web 2.0 technologies and intrapreneurial activities and persistently promote and develop them. Organizational culture should be improved according to the long-term plan of library reorganization. In large libraries in developed countries this takes the form of a development strategy or an agenda for a given period. Recommendations for good practice should include two sets of basic guidelines. The first projects organizational culture by highlighting the desirable characteristics that encourage intrapreneurship and the application of the Enterprise 2.0 concepts in the library. The second includes recommendations for the application of management methods and techniques and the creation of organizational measures that could produce such an organizational culture.

The organizational culture that encourages intrapreneurship should have a system of values that emphasizes diligence, dedication to work, and a respect for both the general objectives and interests of the organization, but also those objectives and interests that are specifically related to entrepreneurs. Above all, the organizational culture should reward initiative; the desire to learn and gain new experiences, skills, and knowledge; a willingness to take risks; and readiness for argumentative and critical discussion of the presented solutions and proposals.

Organizational structure can play an important role in encouraging or inhibiting intrapreneurial initiatives including the implementation of Enterprise 2.0 concepts in the library. An important aspect of the organizational structure is its hierarchical height, or the number of hierarchical levels that exist in an organization. Each new level in the hierarchy creates further delay in the information flow and represents a possible congestion in the communication between the top management and the rest of the staff. Other organizational structures can also have a big impact on intrapreneurship and application of the Enterprise 2.0 concept in the library. For example, a matrix organizational structure is more favorable for intrapreneurship than the functional one.

The majority of libraries have a functional organizational structure, which involves specialized teams and hierarchical reporting. As a result of the increasing importance of project financing, they might be in the phase of transformation toward a matrix organizational structure. The matrix organizational structure is adapted to the method of carrying out project tasks and their execution in the framework of cross-functional teams. The matrix organizational structure disrupts the hierarchy of the functional organizational structure; groups and teams of staff from various functional organizational units form teams to work together on specific project tasks. This organizational structure is flexible but requires a high level of cooperation and communication among staff. In libraries, specialized working groups in the functional structure are usually composed of experts in the field of metadata, experts who work with users, and experts in the field of information and communication technologies. In the matrix structure, they leave their organizational units and form a contemporary organizational unit responsible for the implementation of a project, for example, digitization and presentation of a specific library collection.

Management style can influence intrapreneurship initiatives in the library. It can change within the limits defined by an organizational culture, organizational structure, and organizational rules and regulations. If these categories provide a good basis for a management style favorable to intrapreneurship activities, then their absence could lead to significant opportunity costs. Best practice for providing information to library stakeholders, such as founders and funding bodies, includes not only traditional methods of library evaluation, but also the assessment of opportunity costs. Library business activity should be altered in accordance with these opportunity costs so that the library can provide optimum results. Management should encourage entrepreneurs by recognizing the activities of intrapreneurship beyond what is prescribed by organizational rules and regulations. This can be used as a tool for fine guiding entrepreneurs to specific fields of action, such as the application of Enterprise 2.0 concept. Such management activities should include primarily non-material incentives and rewards. Also, it is important that the management adequately encourages leadership and intrapreneurship. These two types of staff behavior are very similar and often overlap. However, there are situations in which there is no overlap and where the successful operation and implementation of the Enterprise 2.0 concept in the library must be encouraged and coordinated with activities of intrapreneurs and leaders. The management style can play a crucial role. It is especially important to properly position entrepreneurs and leaders and allow both to perform in their field of interest and according to their abilities. It is also important to reduce competitiveness. The management should include a clear component of authority while demonstrating openness to cooperation and new ideas and presenting a positive attitude towards initiatives of staff and their needs, goals, and desires. Practice has shown that, in situations where it is necessary to encourage entrepreneurship, the most effective sources of authority are the knowledge, skills, abilities, professional success, and leadership potential of managers. Authority based on legitimacy and tradition does not have a big impact on intrapreneurs. Therefore, management style should seek to reduce these sources of authority and to emphasize authority based on knowledge.

Organizational rules and regulations are an important segment of organizational arrangement and the business environment. This category can be divided into two parts. Some of the rules and regulations that are binding for employees are created outside the organization, for example, general laws and regulations and specific laws and other regulations applicable to libraries only. The organization cannot have strong influence on the adoption and change of these laws. The other group represent the rules and regulations which are established by the organization itself and are under its authority. The separation line between these two kinds of rules and regulations is not always clearly delineated. Organizational rules and regulations should allow and encourage the flow of information and ideas in the organization, both vertically and horizontally, while reducing the time and the selection of the most desirable reporting forms and procedures. In coordination with the library management style, organizational library rules and regulations should provide sufficient autonomy for staff and opportunities for their empowerment so that existing and prospective intrapreneurship activities can develop. Organizational rules and regulations should represent a framework that allows orderly business and equal treatment of employees and the valorization of their contribution to achieving organizational goals.

STAKEHOLDERS AND METS/ALTO FILES

In order to understand the implementation of digital tools for handling METS-ALTO files and their production and use, we will examine various stakeholders and their relevance to the topic.

Stakeholders are all those who have interest in the library business process. In addition to its collective meaning, the term also applies individually to various interest groups in the library business process. The interests of stakeholders vary from material interests, such as staff salaries, to user interests. Interests are never one-sided, as employees also have interest in maintaining a successful library business process. Library users may also have material interests such as a wish to lower the cost of the annual library fee. That is why we note that identifying and defining library stakeholders is one of the most complex tasks in library management.

The application of Web 2.0 technologies, as defined by the Library 2.0 concept, erodes the differences between library users and library staff; users are included in the library business process. To make a clear distinction between groups of library stakeholders, we will outline the differences between the library stakeholders who are legally bound to the library in terms of business activities and those who are not.

On the one side, there are library staff who are legally bound to the library and receive material compensation for work done, volunteers who are also legally bound to the library but do not receive any material compensation, and users. On the other side, there are those who are not legally bound to the library and can receive non-material benefits or indirect earnings (for example, if they use library computers available to the public to do some private business). This main definition already describes three important stakeholder groups: library staff, volunteers and users. To illustrate the complexity of the topic we will define further divisions of these groups into sub-groups with prominent differences. These subtler divisions can be very useful when considering different aspects of the application of the Enterprise 2.0 concept and for understanding various aspects of in house development of digital tools for handling METS-ALTO files.

Library Staff Stakeholder Sub-Groups

Library staff can be divided into management and those who do not participate in managerial activities. The problem of applying Enterprise 2.0 concept in any organization, including libraries, lies in the fact that this application must involve a larger number of staff in managerial tasks. Enterprise 2.0 blurs the line which separates those who participate and those who do not participate in managerial activities, both formally and informally. This affects the development of tools for handling METS-ALTO files at the point of the organizational decision to develop the tools in-house or by outsourcing or to acquire a fully developed product. The decision-making process involves information on budgeting possibilities, but also on the capacity of employees to develop digital tools in-house or to oversee the outsourcing. A complex bond which implies understanding of genuine work capacities between those who may be developing the tools in-house and those who are decision makers is necessary. Such understanding and bond requires special relations that may be developed in a long run and based on the use of Enterprise 2.0 tools. It is important to note that managerial activities traditionally refer to planning, organization, management and control and that the application of the Enterprise 2.0 concept involves all staff into some aspects of these activities.

Library staff can be also divided into other stakeholder groups. These include groups that proactively embrace new technologies and recommend them by giving advice or by their own example of good practice and those who stick to traditional technologies. It is also important to differentiate between groups of library staff who are inclined to intrapreneurial activities and those who are not. With this in mind, we can highlight the importance of intrapreneurial activities in the in-house development of digital tools for handling METS-ALTO files. These activities may be initiated by the employees who are skilled to develop such tools, but also by those who wish to collaborate and see an opportunity in presenting this activity to the management. In both cases, it is up to the management to foster these activities and provide crucial support once such initiative has been defined. It is important to understand the differences in the motivations and intentions of all three groups of employees in order to grasp the process in its full complexity.

Library Users' Stakeholder Sub-Group

Developing digital tools for handling METS-ALTO files for stakeholder groups that include different library users is critically important. Stakeholder groups are interested in this process because searchable text documents are much easier to use than non-searchable documents. These groups are mostly indifferent to the process of tool development and are more interested in the output in production and presentation of METS-ALTO files. Volunteers are motivated to collaborate in the process of in-house development of digital tools for the purposes of gaining experience and as a major upgrade to their personal curricula vitae (CV). The accompanying opportunities for supplementing library resources must not be underestimated since educated volunteers can provide significant work input, especially regarding IT tasks in the library.

Other Library Stakeholder Sub-Groups

In addition to the groups concerned with library operations, it is important to define other stakeholder groups that have a significant direct or indirect impact on the library business process and implementing the Enterprise 2.0 concept. These groups are primarily related to the library profession and include fellow librarians employed in the same type of library (academic and public libraries, school libraries, specialized libraries such as libraries of state and religious institutions). They may also include all librarians as a stakeholder group, librarians with library and information education, retired librarians, teachers and associates in higher education and secondary education institutions, directors of libraries with over a hundred employees, and directors of all other libraries. Each of these groups can be examined within local, regional and international frameworks. There are different motivations in different stakeholder groups regarding the in-house development of digital tools for handling METS-ALTO files. Institutional and personal collaboration and re-use of systems developed other institutions are some of the motivators igniting the interest of these stakeholders.

It is necessary to also define stakeholders which are not directly related to librarianship. First and foremost, there are decision makers responsible for library funding. Depending on the type of library, these stakeholders could include members of local authorities for public libraries, university management for academic libraries, management of institutions or organizations for specialized libraries, and members of school boards or school administrators for school libraries. The interests of these stakeholder groups regarding the in-house development of digital tools for handling METS-ALTO files varies and may be related to budget savings that may arise from this approach or possibilities for new services that may be offered to users if this process is successful. It is important to understand the motivations of these stakeholders and provide detailed information on the process of developing digital tools for handling METS-ALTO files since their role in funding the overall library operations may be crucial for providing quality services to users.

Other stakeholders include the staff of other organizations that conduct business with libraries. These groups are providers of goods and services such as electricity and heating, office supplies, computers and other IT devices, catering, cleaning, and other services. An example of a concrete stakeholder may be a group of entrepreneurs – the owners of small and medium-sized enterprises in the field of information and communication technologies. Their interest in the development of in-house digital tools for handling METS-ALTO files may be very diverse and thus, a more detailed analysis of these will be necessary in the future.

When considering different stakeholders, we must not leave out the groups whose members do not directly influence the library business process, but whose collective and long-term indirect influence can be very important. First and foremost, the potential library users whose tax provides public financing for libraries. In case of local public libraries those are members of the local community, in case of a national library or a state-funded academic library, this would include the general public. Then, there are groups of people connected with the members of the aforementioned groups, such as students' parents who predominantly finance the education of students, providing them an opportunity to use the library. Their long-term interest in the in-house development of digital tools for handling METS-ALTO files may be significant because of enormous advantages that searchable text offers to users. Therefore, it is important for long-term library operations to inform these stakeholders on the possibilities that arise from an in-house project to develop digital tools to handle METS-ALTO files and the advantages that searchable texts offer to users.

INTRAPRENEURS HANDLING METS-ALTO CHALLENGE

Libraries in developing countries and transition economies seek ways to skip the development process and align their practices with those of libraries in developed countries. This often seems like an impossible task, primarily due to the great differences in financing and the accumulated backlog in investment. This lack of resources also leaves a gap in human resources development, especially in regards to work experience, using different technological solutions, and the creation of working groups and teams. However, in practice it turns out that even these obstacles can be overcome by the cooperation of entrepreneurial employees and management. To illustrate this claim, we present some additional elements for the case study of the University Library Belgrade.

The University Library Organizational Culture

The University Library in Belgrade serves the needs of the University of Belgrade, and the total number of registered users is around 9,000. Financing of the Library has not been stable for years. The annual budget usually does not exceed EUR 500,000. There is a regular lack of resources to meet the basic inputs into the business process. Due to the long global economic and social crisis, Library employees are happy and feel privileged to receive salaries on a regular basis and have a relatively secure job. Years of uncertainty and turbulence in the political, economic, business, and technological sphere have influenced the wider social environment of the organization, which has a great influence on the organizational culture in the library, to develop a range of subcultural models that include different ideas about socially desirable values. The attitude towards entrepreneurship, free initiative, willingness to take risks and other elements of the cultural pattern that are relevant to entrepreneurship also vary greatly over the entire range of these subcultural models.

The University Library Sub-Cultures

As a result, the Library has formed a few specific subcultures, mainly related to organizational units, some of which involve groups of employees belonging to different organizational units. Some of these subcultures are typical of other libraries in Serbia and the region of Western Balkans, like the subculture developed around the cataloguing department with characteristics encompassing pride in being a librarian, precision, and 100% accuracy of work done, but also resistance to change. Another subculture that is not specific for this library, but usual in most large libraries in Serbia is related to the lending department, where characteristics of self-perceived fairness to users, strict following of the rules in conduct of users, and resistance to change are praised. Similar subcultures can be detected in some other industries in Serbia and it seems that it is at least partly related to context of the developing economy, since its inherent conservativism may be a way for employees to handle the changing environment.

Implementation of Web 2.0 Technologies by a Subculture at the University Library

The most interesting variation of organizational culture is represented primarily in the information technology organizational unit, which contains elements favorable to the development of intrapreneurial activity. This subculture is favorable to change and risk taking and easily embracing new technology, but also informal communication both among employees and with users. It is not surprising that high levels of these activities have been recorded in previous years. Despite a constant lack of resources, this increase has led to the successful implementation of some elements of the Enterprise 2.0 concept in the Library. Conversations with employees and management showed that the intrapreneurship activities focused not only on the use of Web 2.0 technologies, but also on a whole range of other activities. It is interesting to point out that some of the business activities of entrepreneurs in the Library were implemented mainly due to the communication potential and possibilities for cooperation that were provided by Web 2.0 technologies. This fact indicates their great value because their application does not require a lot of resources. Web 2.0

technologies for business purposes have been implemented for several years. The technologies that are applied cyclically have been changing in accordance with the entrepreneurial activities.

An example of this cycle could begin with the employees' introduction to a new technology that could be successfully used to enhance the mutual cooperation of library staff. The application of the new technology begins and some employees promote the benefits of it. The cycle approaches an end when the use of new technology does not become part of the regular work duties, but part of the management. In this example, many employees do not use it and still communicate and collaborate via other technologies such as e-mail, which has remained the default communication form. The use of Web 2.0 technology continues, but at a smaller scale, because the employees who use it simply do not have time to use multiple channels of communication. The cycle truly ends with the start of the new cycle, a new attempt to introduce more advanced Web 2.0 technology into regular work processes. The crucial moment in this scenario is the lack of active and decisive management support to introduce Web 2.0 technologies across the organization. The existence of several organizational subcultures certainly makes this more difficult, most of these subcultures are not favorable for the development of intrapreneurial activities. Therefore, the first task of the management in this situation was to work on changing the organizational culture or impose a unique organizational culture.

The Organizational Process for Tackling METS/ALTO Challenge

One of the concrete challenges addressed by the use of Enterprise 2.0 and intrapreneurial behavior was the need for searchable texts. The first step in the process of developing solutions for this problem involved joining a proposition for the European Union funded Competitiveness and Innovation framework Programme focusing on information and communication technologies policy support (CIP ICT-PSP) project dealing with refinement of newspaper digitized pages (www.europeana-newspapers.eu). This proposition turned out to be successful and resulted in a 3-year Europeana newspapers project that brought METS-ALTO files that allow searches of text while simultaneously displaying text preview as a picture to the users. This was the first example of these types of files for the University Library Belgrade and Serbia. The files were made out of digitized pictures of newspapers from the University Library Belgrade collection, but there was still no means for presenting them or making such files available in the Library. By exchanging information through the Enterprise 2.0 system, employees were able to be very efficient and filter out the necessary information. The first task was to identify a programmer willing to work with the library and create an in-house developed tool. The next step was to organize a new work process and add design and texts to the provided IT solutions. Managing an IT project is difficult in itself and balancing the intrapreneurial activities of employees while maintaining efficiency was possible only by using Enterprise 2.0 technologies that allow for transparency and 24/7 communication between management and employees. Free software was pinpointed and used to build in-house digital tools for handling the METS-ALTO files.

DIGITAL TOOLS FOR HANDLING OF METS/ALTO FILES

Presentation of digital materials is a challenging task for libraries and other institutions that preserve and promote heritage. There are different approaches to evaluating digital libraries' interfaces accompanied by an array of literature presenting various stances and experiences. The University Library Belgrade has more than eight years of experience in presenting digitized materials. Users praise the use of full text documents more than the use of scanned images. An important milestone in the development of the digital library at the University Library Belgrade was in 2013, when the first METS/ALTO files were acquired within Europeana newspaper CIP ICT-PSP project. The full potential of these files could be unleashed only through a proper user interface which was not available at the University Library Belgrade when the METS/ALTO files were acquired for the first time. Through an exciting and sometimes difficult processes of in-house development, an interface was created and implemented in 2015. In order to present the features of this interface we will give a short overview of the key terms that will appear in the chapter and are crucial for the understanding of the tools and processes described.

Optical character recognition (OCR) is a complex technology which accomplishes the mechanical or electronic conversion of scanned images of handwritten, typewritten or printed text into machine-encoded text. Using OCR, library staff can process scanned books, screenshots, and photos with text and extract editable documents like TXT, DOC, or PDF files which can be electronically searched, more compactly stored, displayed online, and used in machine processes ("Optical character recognition explained", n. d.). The most advanced OCR systems can handle almost any type of image, even the complex ones such as scanned magazine pages with images and columns or photos taken with a mobile phone. There are several equally important steps in the OCR process and each is accompanied by a set of related algorithms. Every step must interact with the given image correctly, otherwise the whole process fails (Optical Character Recognition (OCR) – How it works, Nicomsoft, n. d.). METS (Metadata Encoding and Transmission Standard) established in 2001 is an XML-based open standard. Its schema is hosted (Metadata Encoding and Transmission Standard (METS) Official Web Site, Library of Congress, n.d.) at the Library of Congress (LOC) and it is maintained by METS Editorial Board. METS files are used to describe digital objects which should be preserved for a long time. They can include different kinds of metadata, both descriptive and administrative. METS files may be linked to any digital object.

ALTO (Analyzed Layout and Text Object) is also an XML-based open standard whose schema is also hosted (ALTO: Technical Metadata for Optical Character Recognition (Standards, Library of Congress), Library of Congress, n.d.), at the Library of Congress (LOC) and maintained by ALTO Board. An ALTO file usually contains the content of a single page and it describes the layout of a printed page to re-build the original page including styles, layout, and block type information. It may contain tags which provide more information about the content (e.g. named entities).

The benefit of the METS/ALTO files is that they are widely used in libraries and by content providers which means they represent a standard for digitization. In addition, they secure the long-term sustainability of digital objects which can be handled easily and exchanged. They support article and chapter segmentation. PDF, EPUB, DAISY and other formats can be created from METS/ALTO files (METS / ALTO introduction, CCS Content Conversion Specialists, n. d.).

Document Search and Display

The infrastructure that makes up our document search and display system consists of a Windows server that is the repository for the METS/ALTO files and hosts their viewer—BnLViewer, a web server that hosts the search interface, and a backend Lucene/Solr server used to search the documents.

BnLViewer

The BnlViewer is a rich, interactive viewer for METS/ALTO files developed and maintained by the National Library of Luxembourg and can be seen at the following link http://sourceforge.net/p/bnlviewer/home/screenshots/ (BNLViewer, National Library of Luxembourg, n.d.). The thumbnails of all pages are displayed alongside the table of contents. The full page is displayed and articles can be selected with a cursor. In the article view, one article is cut out so that it can be presented as a long vertical stripe even if it spans over several columns (or even pages) in the original layout. The text of the article is also presented, as it is recognised by the OCR engine (which explains the errors). When a search is performed, the terms that are found are highlighted on the image and in the OCR text (BnLViewer: A newspaper in the viewer, n. d.).

The BnlViewer is very well received and widely used by researchers who would, in addition to its current functionalities, like to have access to full text data as linked data set, to be able to print individual articles and to have a simple "microfilm-like" viewer for efficient viewing of an entire collection (Maurer, 2013).

Search Interface

The user search interface available at http://www.unilib.rs/istorijske-novine/search has three sections: "search", "advanced search" and "browse". The backend search engine of the interface is Lucene/Solr (Apache Solr, The Apache Software Foundation, n. d.) developed by the Apache Foundation.

"Search" presents users with a text field where they can enter desired keywords. The interface converts user query into an appropriate Solr query (Solr Query Syntax, n. d.) that is sent to Solr server, and displays the results returned from the Solr as a preview, offering the hyperlinks to full documents on BnlViewer. For example, if a user searches for "beograd", the corresponding Solr query is "+text:(beograd)". Supported advanced query options (Search Guide, University Library "SvetozarMarkovic", n. d.) are searching for a phrase, searching with OR, and searching for pages without a phrase; more advanced Lucene performances (Apache Lucene Query Parser Syntax, The Apache Software Foundation, n. d.), such as searching by wildcard or Levenshtein distance[2] are not offered to end users, but are available to the library staff.

"Advanced Search" (Searchable Digitized Historical Newspapers, University Library "SvetozarMarkovic", n.d.) extends the search with the possibilities to search within a single periodical, within a range of dates, and to sort the results in various ways. It is able to construct more complex Solr queries, for example a search for "beograd ILI zemun" in the magazine "Beogradskeopštinskenovine" in the year 1900 is expanded to "+text:(beograd OR zemun) +collection_id:00004 +date:[1900-01-01T12:00:00Z TO 1900-12-31T12:00:00Z]".

"Browse" (Searchable Digitized Historical Newspapers, University Library "SvetozarMarkovic", n.d.), enables users to select a desired periodical and its publication date, which is then displayed in BnLViewer. Information about existing journals and dates is kept in a relational database, separately from the search index.

The interface is available in Serbian, English and German, including localization of the query syntax.

Search Engine Improvements

Lucene/Solr is highly satisfactory for library use as regards its storage capacity (Package org.apache.lucene.codecs.lucene40, The Apache Software Foundation, n. d.) and speed (we observed that a search query usually lasts around 200 milliseconds) of search. However, its support for the Serbian language had to be improved, enabling the search of Cyrillic and Latin texts by using Cyrillic and Latin alphabets. Furthermore, as a number of Internet users in Serbia use "bald" Latin, we wanted to support that as well. This was done by creating a Lucene filter (Analyzers, Tokenizers, and Token Filters, n. d.) that converts Cyrillic and Latin text to "bald" Latin (a filter does not affect display of the searched text). The use of the filter is explained in detail at https://wiki.apache.org/solr/SerbianLanguageSupport.

Currently, a stemmer—a computer program that reduces words to their stems, thus enabling finding various grammatical forms of a word by searching for either one of them--, (Stemming, n. d.) for the Serbian language is being developed, which will further improve Lucene's search capabilities. An experimental stemmer that stems only the most common Serbian names is observed to return 100% more search results in searches for supported names, with no reduction in relevance.

In our Lucene schema (SchemaXml, n. d.), every page is indexed as a separate document. A drawback of this method is that it is not possible to find phrases that span multiple pages; but these are very rare, and it is usually not possible to find them anyway since they are interrupted by page headers and footers. Together with the page text, we store the page number, other relevant information about the document the page is from (such as its document identifier or document date), and the corresponding ALTO file.

Documents are imported in Lucene by a command-line script that scans all the ALTO files in our repository, and submits their content to Solr. The script uses information about the ALTO file from the Lucene database to verify whether the ALTO files were modified in the repository.

Although usually various file types are imported in Lucene through a Solr data import handler (Data Import Request Handler, n.d.), instead of creating a METS/ALTO handler, we have found it simpler to convert ALTO files to raw text and externally submit them as such. During the conversion, the script also joins the hyphenated words at lines' ends.

Document Correction

Manual Correction Tool

In order to increase accuracy of OCR text, we have made a web tool that enables manual correction of ALTO files entitled AltoEdit. The tool has been used to correct years 1914 and 1915 of the journal "Ratnidnevnik" (a war diary of the Serbian army during WWI)—in total, 984 pages of text (Searchable Digitized Historical Newspapers, University Library "SvetozarMarkovic", n. d.). The corrected files return around 10% more search results with no reduction in relevance.

The tool works in the following way: a command-line script modifies ALTO files so that every relevant element without an ID gets one. Another script then imports the content of ALTO files into a relational database, keeping track of the IDs in ALTO files. For correctors, a web interface that can display ALTO files' content line-by-line with the corresponding cutout of the page image is provided. The correctors can then edit the words which are saved in the database; the database preserves history of all edits. Finally, the third command-line script exports corrected words from the database back to ALTO files according to their IDs.

Unfortunately, while using the tool we have discovered certain drawbacks. The database has a relatively complex structure, mimicking all the complexity of ALTO files, but it does not need any of the benefits provided by relational databases. The correctors have also reported that working line-by-line is tedious and that work on whole pages or columns of text would be preferable. It is thus our recommendation for future tools of this type, that ALTO files are kept in a version control system[3] and edited directly, and that correctors are provided with more comfortable interfaces.

Automatic Detection of Rotated Pages

While surveying the corpus we have discovered that a relatively common error is pages turned upside-down. Since this is very inconvenient for the reader, we wanted to see whether it is possible to identify the pages and turn them the right way up. We did this by statistically analyzing the text of the pages in order to find pages with poor OCR text, then by conducting OCR on the pages in various orientations and statistically analyzing OCR output in order to find the correct orientation.

The statistical analysis of the text was done by searching for every word in the text in a spelling dictionary. While this method provided satisfactory results, we have discovered that it reveals too many false positives, as it sees no difference between a word with a single unrecognized character and a completely jumbled word, which occur in a page that is rotated upside-down. We believe that better results might be obtained by using other methods, probably a statistical n-gram analysis.

An experimental tool that can rotate all the coordinates in an ALTO file so that the elements can be set into their correct positions has also been created, although the correct solution to this problem would be to rotate the image and re-OCR the text.

Everyday communication with users revealed that after the first few months of promotion and online availability of in-house developed tools for presentation of full text materials at the University Library Belgrade proved to be reliable and in line with user needs and expectations. In addition, the number of users with positive experience seems to be increasing. Users spread positive experience by word of mouth and informal communication through social media. Availability of full text files has been identified as a key added value in the framework of effectively functional search interface and METS/ALTO viewer.

METS/ALTO is a highly versatile format which can easily be used in various ways and completely fulfills our needs for creation, presentation and preservation of digitized documents. The fact that the format is XML-based facilitates creation of tools for its handling and processing. Its versatility also facilitates inter-library cooperation in digitization and tool creation.

CONCLUSION

The in-house development of digital tools for handling METS-ALTO files has been an important landmark in the operations of the University Library in Belgrade because it has provided an important upgrade to the services and also presented an example of good practice where significant gains have been made with relatively small budget and resources. The importance of intrapreneurial activities and implemented Enterprise 2.0 as a grounding infrastructure for these activities has been depicted in some detail in the previous sections, grounding the case for fostering intrapreneurship and implementation of Enterprise 2.0 in libraries. These concepts also provide a solid base for further improvements regarding handling METS-ALTO files at the University Library in Belgrade. Intrapreneurial activities will be crucial in establishing collaboration based on developed digital tools. Enterprise 2.0 tools used and implemented in the library will lay the groundwork for communication to allow future collaborative activities both in-house and with external partners.

REFERENCES

Antoncic, B., & Hisrich, R. (2003). Clarifying the intrapreneurship concept. *Journal of Small Business and Enterprise Development*, *10*(1), 7–24. doi:10.1108/14626000310461187

BnLViewer. (n. d.). Screenshots. Retrieved 23 Sept 2016, from http://sourceforge.net/p/bnlviewer/home/screenshots/

Churchill, N. C. (1992). Research issues in entrepreneurship. In *Sexton, Kasarda) The State of the Art of Entrepreneurship*. Boston: PWS-Kent.

Content Conversion Specialists. (n. d.). METS / ALTO introduction. Retrieved 23 Sept 2016, from http://content-conversion.com/wp-content/uploads/2014/09/CCS-METS-ALTO-Info_basic_20140909.pdf

Solr Wiki. (n. d.). Data Import Request Handler. Retrieved 23 Sept 2016, from https://wiki.apache.org/solr/DataImportHandler

Hisrich, R. D., & Peters, M. P. (1998). *Entrepreneurship: Starting, Developing and Managing a New Enterprise*. Chicago: Irwin.

Kautz, J. (n. d.) Small Business Notes - History of Intrapreneurship. Retrieved from http://www.smallbusinessnotes.com/choosing/intrapreneurship/inthistory.html

Library of Congress USA. (n. d.). ALTO: Technical Metadata for Optical Character Recognition. Retrieved 23 Sept 2016, from http://www.loc.gov/standards/alto/

Library of Congress USA. (n. d.). Metadata Encoding and Transmission Standard (METS) Official Web Site, Retrieved 23 Sept 2016, from http://www.loc.gov/standards/mets/

Maurer, Y. (2013). *Presentation on BNL viewer*. Amsterdam.

McAfee, A. (2009). *Enterprise 2.0: New Collaborative Tools for Your Organization's Toughest Challenges* (Kindle ed.). Harvard Business School Press.

National Library of Luxembourg. (n. d.). BNLViewer. Retrieved 23 Sept 2016, from http://www.eluxemburgensia.lu

Nicomsoft. (n. d.) Optical Character Recognition (OCR) – How it works. Retrieved 23 Sept 2016, from http://www.nicomsoft.com/optical-character-recognition-ocr-how-it-works/

Pinchot, G. (1985). *Intrapreneuring: Why You Don't Have to Leave the Corporation to Become an Entrepreneur*. New York, NY: Harper & Row.

Solr Wiki. (n. d.). SchemaXml. Retrieved 23 Sept 2016, from https://wiki.apache.org/solr/SchemaXml

Sharma, P., & Chrisman, S. J. J. (2007). Toward a reconciliation of the definitional issues in the field of corporate entrepreneurship. In *Entrepreneurship* (pp. 83–103). Springer Berlin Heidelberg.

Sofronijevic, A. (2011). New Paradigm of Library Collaboration. In S. Gradmann, F. Borri, C. Meghini (Eds.), *Research and Advanced Technology for Digital Libraries - International Conference on Theory and Practice of Digital Libraries, TPDL 2011*, Berlin, Germany, LNCS (Vol. 6966, pp. 519-522). Springer.

Sofronijevic, A., Milicevic, V., Ilic, B., & Seaman, S. (2011). Enhancing Library Business Performance by Implementation of Enterprise 2.0 via Intrapreneurship: The Case of a Serbian Library. *Journal of Academic Librarianship*, *37*(4), 358–362. doi:10.1016/j.acalib.2011.04.010

Solr Wiki. (n. d.). Solr Query Syntax. Retrieved 23 Sept 2016, from https://wiki.apache.org/solr/SolrQuerySyntax

Solr Wiki. (n. d.). Analyzers, Tokenizers, and Token Filters Retrieved 23 Sept 2016, from https://wiki.apache.org/solr/AnalyzersTokenizersTokenFilters

Stevenson, H. H., & Jarillo, J. C. (2007). A paradigm of entrepreneurship: Entrepreneurial management. In Entrepreneurship (pp. 155-170). Springer Berlin Heidelberg

The Apache Software Foundation. (n. d.). Apache Lucene Query Parser Syntax. Retrieved 23 Sept 2016, from http://lucene.apache.org/core/3_6_0/queryparsersyntax.html

The Apache Software Foundation. (n. d.). Package org.apache.lucene.codecs.lucene40. Retrieved 23 Sept 2016, from http://lucene.apache.org/core/4_0_0/core/org/apache/lucene/codecs/lucene40/package-summary.html#Limitations

The Apache Software Foundation. (n. d.). Apache Solr. Retrieved 23 Sept 2016, from http://lucene.apache.org/solr/

University Library SvetozarMarkovic. (n. d.). Search Guide. Retrieved 23 Sept 2016, from http://www.unilib.rs/istorijske-novine/about#search-guide

University Library SvetozarMarkovic. (n. d.). Searchable Digitized Historical Newspapers. Retrieved 23 Sept 2016, from http://www.unilib.rs/istorijske-novine/advanced-search

University Library SvetozarMarkovic. (n. d.). Searchable Digitized Historical Newspapers. Retrieved 23 Sept 2016, from http://www.unilib.rs/istorijske-novine/browse

University Library SvetozarMarkovic. (n. d.). Searchable Digitized Historical Newspapers. Retrieved 23 Sept 2016, from http://www.unilib.rs/istorijske-novine/browse?newspaper=UB_00029

Vesper, K. H. (1990). *New Venture Strategies*. Englewood Cliffs, USA: Prentice-Hall.

Wikipedia. (n. d.). Intrapreneurship. Retrieved 23 Sept 2016, from https://en.wikipedia.org/wiki/Intrapreneurship

Wikipedia. (n. d.). Optical character recognition explained. Retrieved 23 Sept 2016, from https://en.wikipedia.org/w/index.php?title=Optical_character_recognition&oldid=686827150

Wikipedia. (n. d.). Stemming. Retrieved 23 Sept 2016, from https://en.wikipedia.org/w/index.php?title=Stemming&oldid=685786913

ENDNOTES

1. For further reference www.pinchot.com/MainPages/About/Bios/GiffordBio.html
2. Levenshtein distance is the minimal number of operations necessary to transform one string of characters into another, which can be used to search for words similar to each other, since they will have small Levenshtein distance; Wikipedia, the free encyclopedia, "Levenshtein distance", retrieved 23 Sept 2016 from https://en.wikipedia.org/w/index.php?title=Levenshtein_distance&oldid=688663203
3. A version control system keeps various versions of a document as it was changed through time, so that they can be compared, old versions restored in case of an error, etc.; Wikipedia, the free encyclopedia, "Version control", retrieved 23 Sept 2016 from https://en.wikipedia.org/w/index.php?title=Version_control&oldid=690270257

Chapter 6
Developing In-House Digital Tools:
Case Studies From the UMKC School of Law Library

Ayyoub Ajmi
University of Missouri, USA

ABSTRACT

The author describes his experiences working in the Leon E. Bloch Law Library designing and prototyping in-house digital tools to improve communication among internal and external stakeholders. The projects discussed include a custom study room schedule application syncing university calendar to affordable tablets to increase staff productivity, an online data visualization dashboard to help digest large and complex sets of data for better understanding and decision making, and a mobile application to offer students and community an easy access to library resources and services. In addition, the author calls for the need to engage in innovative and experimental practices in libraries by encouraging collaboration with external partners to help develop new services and improve existing ones.

INTRODUCTION

Makerspaces, innovation labs, and Do-It-Yourself (DIY) movements became in the recent years one of the important development in technology for academic and research libraries (Johnson, et al., 2015). Perhaps it is due to their ability to engage and allow for hands-on exploration and participatory learning. In their short existence,

DOI: 10.4018/978-1-5225-2676-6.ch006

however, they have demonstrated how libraries can reach new constituencies by redefining themselves as community spaces and intellectual hubs and not just a print warehouse.

In the age of information abundance, libraries learned to adapt to cultural, technological and educational shifts to meet the needs of their communities. By bringing innovation into libraries, users now have a place to build, learn, and experiment in a new collaborative and engaging environment. However, innovation in libraries should not be limited to physical spaces and services we provide to our users. Libraries should also adopt innovation into their operations and practices by building, learning, and experimenting with new services and workflows that can support their communities and increase staff productivity.

In this chapter, we describe three prototypes launched with the help and in collaboration with computing and engineering students. Among the projects highlighted are: a custom study room schedule display, an online data visualization dashboard, and a mobile application. While these prototypes are still in their early development stages, they nevertheless demonstrate how working with partners outside of your library and school can open the door to new opportunities for professional and personal growth and success.

Bringing innovation to your library is not clear or easy path. Engaging in developing new, untested and unproven services is often risky (Bieraugel, 2015). In this chapter, we share the experience we gained through successes and failures while exploring the projects libraries can engage in without necessarily benefiting from an institutional "top-down" approach to innovation but rather a "bottom-top" push for the sake of our users and profession.

ABOUT THE LEON E. BLOCH LAW LIBRARY

The Leon E. Bloch Law Library is located within the University of Missouri-Kansas City School of Law, the urban law school of the University of Missouri System. It supports the School of Law's mission of providing students with a comprehensive and affordable legal education. It aims at improving the legal information and technological literacy of law students and faculty while also providing access to its legal resources to members of the public. The law librarians are heavily involved in the educational programs by supporting the pedagogical needs of law school faculty curriculum and teaching in the first-year program and upper-level advanced research courses. Facing a rapidly changing landscape of library services and infrastructures, the library created in 2013 a new librarian position, the Digital Communications and Learning Initiatives librarian, to be responsible for the law school's website and intranet, its digital collections, and facilitating students, faculty and staff access to various educational technologies.

Although the law librarians have a strong relationship with the university library system in term of continual collaboration on ideas addressing common challenges, the Leon E. Bloch Law Library is autonomous from the main library and is governed entirely by the Dean of the School of Law and the Director of the Law Library. Its budget is part of the law school's budget and the Dean and the Director of the Law Library determine library policies with the advice of the Faculty Library Committee.

The UMKC School of Law declared 2016 the Year of Technology highlighting several initiatives and programs to support and train tomorrow's lawyers by introducing them to top of the line technologies, new technology-based courses, and opportunities to engage in events and conferences that connect our faculty and students with legal technologists, other law schools, and cities.

As early as 2014, the library helped establish the first Law, Technology, and Public Policy class in collaboration with Brooklyn Law School and MIT Media Lab. The course gives students a hands-on experience with technology and law by working on real projects. It brings together law students, and students from the management and engineering schools, city officials, and the civil society to develop and prototype projects aiming at improving the way citizens interact with Kansas City's government and communities. The library is also involved in organizing and hosting several conferences introducing students and new graduates to emerging law fields and concepts such as electronic discovery, open data and sharing economy to prepare them to face the 21st century's challenges requiring new technological thinking and ability to work collaboratively across disciplines.

INNOVATION IS A NECESSITY

American legal education and the legal profession still haven't recovered from the 2008 financial crisis and its impact on declining job opportunities for new law graduates (Joy, 2014). According to the American Bar Association Employment Summary Report of 2012, only 56 percent of the class of 2012 had long-term, full-time employment requiring bar passage nine months after graduation (Joy, 2014). Strong competition among law graduates for fewer employment positions still remain an issue and is expected to persist for the years to come despite the declining number of applicants to law schools. The number of students entering the American Bar Association approved law schools over the years of 2012, and 2013 have declined by 10 and 14 percent respectively from the years prior (Joy, 2014). The UMKC School of Law is not immune from those challenges. As of 2016, the number of applicants for the 2016 entering class was down by 12 percent compared to applicants in 2015 (UMKC School of Law, 2016) and only 62 percent of 2015 graduates secured a long-term, full-time employment requiring bar passage nine months after graduation (UMKC School of Law, 2016). This situation left law schools facing increasing criticism and bad publicity for the past several years arguing that pursuing a law degree is "either a costly, risky proposition or simply a bad idea" (Joy, 2014).

However, higher education is facing more than just workforce shifts and economic instability. Other issues such as growth of technology, changing student demographic, competency based education, assessment, accreditation, and cost are threatening the future of higher education and the traditional educational delivery (Bryan & Holly, 2015).

For academic libraries, these challenges mean large-scale reorganization and resource reallocations take place (Mathews, 2012). Unless librarians engage in new opportunities to advance teaching, learning service, and research, libraries are vulnerable to "becoming just another campus utility like parking, dining services, and IT rather than the intellectual soul of the community" (Mathews, 2012). Whether libraries are still needed always come up when facing growing and changing demands. Long before the internet and web 2.0 revolutions, when "paperless society" and users being "able to search the library files electronically and receive a printout of specific information or facsimile copy of a desired document" was perceived as "extreme and painful", libraries back then recognized the need to adapt and innovate by using technology to their benefit to "provide more responsive service" (Drake, 1979). Today the challenges are different but the fear is the same: how to justify the existence of libraries when struggling to meet the expectations of our users. Today, library users expect a Google-like search capabilities to retrieve information across all formats and sources then access it with iTunes-like interface anytime, anywhere, on any device (Mathews, 2012).

Instead of chasing the next feature or service, libraries should take time to "zoom-out" (Mathews, 2012) and innovate to become more effective in gaining new users and retaining existing ones (Bieraugel, 2015; Bieraugel, 2015; Bieraugel, 2015). According to the 2016 NMC Horizon Report, among the trends to drive technology decision-making and planning in 4 to 5 years is the advancement of cultures of innovation among higher education institutions (Johnson, et al., NMC Horizon Report: 2016 Higher Education Edition, 2016). This trend reflects the role of the university in fostering innovation, creativity, and entrepreneurial thinking not only in the curricula but also for institutional leadership to stimulate top-down change (Johnson, et al., NMC Horizon Report: 2016 Higher Education Edition, 2016). Many of today's high profile companies have seen their debut in university dorms and classes. In the same manner, non-profit higher education institutions are credited for most of the learning tools now promoted by for-profits and education technology startups such as online education, MOOCs, adaptive learning, and competency-based education among other learning tools (Bryan & Holly, 2015).

The argument for innovation in higher education is often hard to make. It is difficult to move away from the comfort of what is known and adopt new approaches that are yet to be proven as effective (Bryan & Holly, 2015). Drake (1979) relates the barriers to innovation in academic institutions and libraries to psychology, organizational factors, perceptions of the future, and economic factors. For library staff, resistance to changes coming from other people who don't speak their language, may be based on fear of change, threat of being manipulated, conflict with their interests, constrain to their freedom of choice, or failure to see the value of the innovation (Drake, 1979). Many of the challenges depicted 37 years ago are still present today. Many of our users and staff are still wary about any new technology or policy changes that might threaten their established ways of doing things.

Other organizational factors constraining innovation in academic libraries presented by Drake (1979) are the difficulty to measure their successes and contributions in social values produced by access to information and knowledge. Unable to provide the needed justification for capital investment, the value of librarians is perceived in the salary paid rather than the value produced (Drake, 1979).

In the absence of a "top-down" process for innovation through policies, leadership, resources and procedures, individuals and groups create a "bottom-up" push acting alone and often without explicit permission experimenting within their immediate environment and users (Bryan & Holly, 2015).

At the UMKC School of Law, our experience can be described in what Bryan and Holly (2015) described as "an innovator's way of being":

What is that innovators do?

- **Grab and Apply What They Can:** Innovators leverage existing, new, proven or unproven methods or tools to improve practice, solve persistent problems or create a new offering, service, solution, product or idea.
- **Do Not Shy Away From Choices:** Innovators make important choices and trade-offs throughout their process.
- **They are Inspired by Their World and Use It:** Innovators identify tools, ideas, strands or practices from other fields and apply it to a new context.
- **Try, Try, and Try Again:** They don't view innovation as "right or wrong," "a failure or success," instead all approaches are considered, tested, prototyped and learned from. (Bryan & Holly, 2015)

COLLABORATION WITH GREADUATE STUDENTS

Student workers have always been part of academic libraries. Their duties have been traditionally limited to support roles such as shelving books, answering phone calls, or staffing the circulation desks when libraries are facing staffing shortage. However, many academic libraries are using the untapped resources of skilled student workers by expanding their roles into positions with greater responsibility and requiring far more training such as graphic design and web development (Draper, Oswald, & Renfro, 2007).

Before reaching out to graduate students from the engineering and computing school, we used to handle all the development needs internally at the law library or with the help of the main campus programmers. However, it is difficult to justify the time and the expenses needed when working on experimental projects. We faced this limitation in 2015 when we decided to investigate the potential of wearable devices in academic libraries by acquiring the newly released Google Glass. However, without developing custom applications for the device to make a good use of its advanced capabilities we were limited to hands-free videos or the out of the box applications. This experience, made us realize that if we want to continue to investigate new technologies to improve the services we provide to our users, we must look for resources beyond the wall of our library and find new opportunities to collaborate across disciplines with external partners.

In spring 2016, we opened our first position of Web and Mobile Applications developer in the university's careers network targeting graduate students enrolled in the Engineering and Computing School. Among over 50 applicants who expressed their interest in this position, we selected two graduate students to work on new and experimental projects to help us improve access to our resources and to investigate new ways of accessing and sharing information.

Our initial objective was to work on small projects that can be completed or near completion within one semester. However, graduate students are more likely to seek internship during their final semesters to help them secure a job after graduation. Therefore, we couldn't engage on long-term projects requiring longer commitment.

The potential high turnover, besides not necessarily understanding all the coding and programming aspects of our projects, left us aware of the importance of documentation as an essential part of managing our projects and establishing traceability regarding what has been done, who has done it, and when it has been done.

Once a student joins our team, they are granted access to an online collaboration platform in which they can access all essential information regarding a specific project and quickly understand what has been done prior. The same platform is used to store all project-related documents such as meeting minutes, wireframes, tutorials, usability testing results, and source code.

Our students maintain flexible work schedules based around their classes. However, they often work remotely from home or from other locations on campus. Due to the nature of the projects and the convenience provided by online collaboration platforms, we don't see the need of having the students work exclusively at the library. We have weekly meetings where we all meet to discuss on-going projects and pending items. When needed, we work together to brainstorm new ideas or work on design and coding challenges.

The students report to the Digital Communications and Learning Initiatives Librarian who is assisted by one staff member represent the ad-hoc committee in charge of this initiative.

STUDY ROOM SCHEDULE DISPLAY

The Leon E. Bloch Law Library provides several individual and group study rooms to students on first-come first-served basis. While reservation is not required, the rooms are often reserved for orientations, meetings, make-up exams, or other collaborative purposes. Traditionally, the library's administrative assistant is to take reservations, usually over the phone, and makes sure the weekly schedule is printed and posted in the study rooms. However, when a meeting is canceled or updated, the schedule often remains outdated. In addition, students are in the habit of just using the room when it is vacant without paying attention to upcoming meetings posted on the schedule. It is on the next user to ask for the room to be vacated or simply move to a different room.

The goal of this project is to prototype an efficient system to manage the library study rooms while providing an agreeable experience to our users.

Conference room signage is common in large facilities such as hotels and conference centers. They provide an easy and attractive way to display information specific to each room. However, the price tag associated with them is often prohibitive. Recently, several affordable alternatives are now available to users based on low cost tablets and ready to use mobile applications. Several free and paid applications are available for Android and iOS that work with popular calendars such as Google Calendar or Microsoft Exchange Server. These applications can be installed in many tablets to meet the functionality and budget needs of all users.

However, our school uses a proprietary schedule calendar that can't work with off-the-shelve scheduling applications but require a custom-built application to feed the occupancy status back to a tablet. Due to the nature of the content displayed requiring minimal processing power and bandwidth, we prefer to use generic Android tablets instead of high-end alternatives such as Samsung Galaxy Tab or Apple's iPad.

Equipped with this initial understanding of our needs and options, we developed this list of features and requirements:

- Possibility to sync data with the school's calendar
- Display occupancy status in real time
- Access upcoming event
- Security measures to prevent tempering with the application

The work on the Study Room Schedule Display started in spring 2016 with one graduate student. His task was to deliver a working prototype of a mobile application that sync and display a study room schedule on an Android-powered device by the end of the semester.

The first document delivered by the student was a detailed scope of work describing the time and resources for this project. The initial estimated time of accomplishment of the programming portion of this project was 78 hours comprising the preliminary research and requirement analysis of the project, design and branding, development, and initial testing.

Since we anticipated using Android devices exclusively for this project, the development was done on Android Studio, the official integrated development environment for Android platforms. The development and initial testing was done on a $50 Android tablet (Dragon Touch Y88X Plus 7'') running on version 4.4 KitKat of the operating system.

AdAstra, is an online scheduling software provided by the university and popular among higher education institutions. This system syncs automatically with the university course schedules and offers a secure access to its Application Program Interface (API) allowing a seamless integration with third-party applications.

We kept the interface design to its minimum while focusing on having a better user experience. The home screen of the application offers access to all its features: real-time occupancy status, upcoming reservations, monthly schedule, reservation request form, and access to the secured admin section (Figure 1).

The secured admin section is used to customize the application to each study room. An authorized user can assign the tablet to a specific room, enable or disable the reservation feature, update the contact information and change the schedule synchronization interval (Figure 2).

The students worked ten hours per week exclusively on this project. With the estimated time of accomplishment of 78 hours, we were expecting to have a working prototype before the end of the semester. However, we neglected to take in consideration time off during semester breaks and exam periods. In addition, students approaching graduation are more likely to be actively looking for job opportunities

Figure 1. Home screen of the study room schedule application

Figure 2. Secured admin section of the study room schedule application

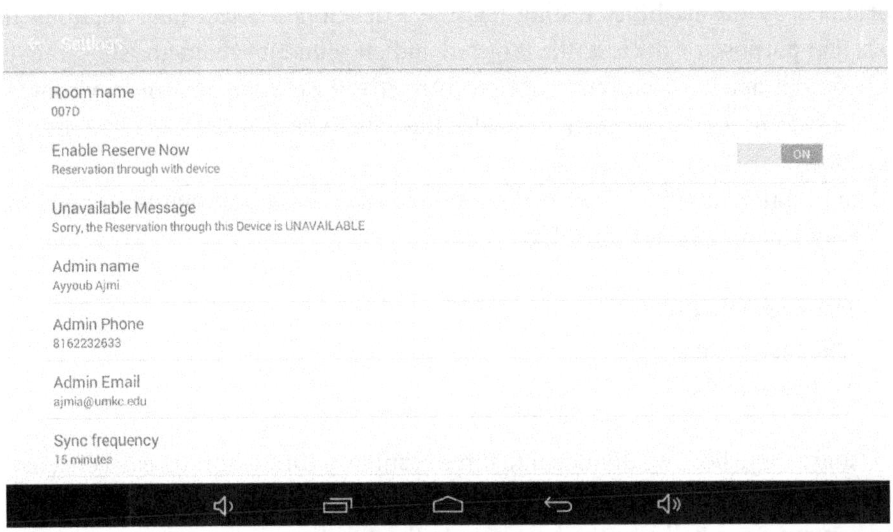

requiring them to take additional time off. With a little delay, we had a working prototype of the room schedule application on the final week of spring semester.

During the programing period, we were testing the application and sharing feedback with our student developer. This quick and ongoing testing, addressed on the Lean Startup methodology as part of the "build-measure-learn" process help organizations expedite product development by presenting new services or ideas to users for feedback and gradually building upon them (Bieraugel, 2015). In our situation, we felt confident that the working prototype, while not perfect, was good enough to be tested among our students and staff allowing us to quickly discover programing bugs and usability issues.

While most students leave the school in summer to takes a break or an internship, others return for classes. This group, while not big enough, it represents a good sample of our student body to invite to the first usability testing.

Our partner for library-related surveys and usability testing is our main library Usability Testing team lead by an outcomes and assessment librarian. The team derived from librarians and library specialists performed several Key Task Assessment, Heuristic Evaluation, and surveys to help the library make informed decisions regarding the design of its online resources and purchase of new furniture among other tasks where direct feedback from end-users was necessary. Due to our time constraints and limited number of students available to test the application in summer, we performed a popup usability testing right were the end-users are instead of a traditional usability study requiring to watch and record users performing specific tasks on the application.

Helped by the usability testing team, we developed a test plan detailing the goals and purpose of the test, the targeted audience and its characteristics, the test methodology and the list of tasks to be performed by the participants, the environment and logistics needed to perform the tasks, the data to be collected, and the research questions.

Our usability test was based on three simple and measurable questions regarding the Study Room Schedule Display:

1. Is it easy to use?
2. Is it easy to read?
3. Would you use it?

Using a large box, we divided into three sections with a whole on each one, users can use two set of ping-pong balls we painted green and red. If their answer is no, they can put a red ball into the hole near to the question, if the answer is yes, they can use a green ball.

We placed a short description of the project near the box and installed the tablet running our prototype application at the faculty and staff break room for one week.

We did the same usability testing the following week with the students at the student lounge (Figure 3).

Figure 3. Pop-up usability testing at the faculty and staff break room

The staff and faculty group seemed more engaged with the tablet, actively testing all its features and answering the survey questions. Few members also left additional suggestions and comments in the box or shared them directly with us.

While the students answered the survey questions, few tested the reservation feature. This behavior is also reflected on their answers to the survey and later when we installed the first tablet.

In total 24 users took the time to try the Study Room Schedule Display and answer the survey questions. While these numbers don't represent an ideal sampling of the population, received valuable feedback and understanding of what to expect.

Regarding the legibility of the system, 80% of participants found it easy to read. While 79% of students found the system easy to use compared to only 72% for staff and faculty. However, 88% of faculty and staff expressed their wiliness to use the system while only 63% of students will do so.

The most shared comment was regarding the small size of the tablet, a seven-inch tablet manufactured by Dragon Touch. Besides its small size, we also could not find a wall mount that fits this size. As we planned to have a real-life test of the system on the study rooms, we had to make sure it can be securely installed to eliminate any risk of injury or theft. After the users' feedback, we resumed the development on an 8-inch tablet also manufactured by Dragon Touch for less than $100. This new tablet features a larger display area and runs on a newer operating system (Android 5.1 Lollipop). We also found several wall-mounts and secure kiosk displays that fit this size.

At this time, we hired a new student to work on this project. Although, we made sure the original developer leaves the files and documentation to help the new developer understand the design and programming processes that took place, they nevertheless, needed to communicate with each other directly to exchange ideas and tips about the project.

Our goal during summer was to finish the programming and continue to improve the design while also requesting the installation of a tablet in one of the study rooms at the library.

Powering the tablet was the main issue we faced during the installation. After surveying the space, the facilities department suggested to power the tablet over Ethernet cables. With this method, we can run a network cable from the nearest network switch directly to an adapter then to the tablet using a regular USB cable. It is safer and inexpensive than running a power cable through the ceiling and walls. The end result is a clean installation with the visible part is the tablet inside the secured wall-mount. However, the work order had to be transferred from facilities to the networking department which resulted in a huge delay and an unwanted scrutiny from the campus information services department. However, with approval from the library director, we moved forward with the testing and installation of the tablet. While we couldn't power the tablet over Ethernet, we used the nearest power outlet and concealed the USB cable along the door frame (Figure 4). Not exactly the installation we hoped for, but we knew it will be temporary just for the time to test the prototype by the library users during fall semester.

Having the tablet installed in a permanent location away from our constant supervision proved to be very helpful. In the first week, we discovered that students bypassed the security feature of the application. While not necessarily harmful, it shows a serious issue with the application that can be used by ill-intentioned users to access secured content or simply use the tablet to access or display inappropriate material. Another issue we encountered during this test was regarding the performance of the tablet itself. We often found the tablet in sleep mode or the application not syncing to the schedule. While we couldn't determine the exact cause of this behavior, we identified few possibilities to investigate.

After reviewing the code to make sure it is not causing this sporadic behavior and testing the application with different versions of Android, we decided to use the built-in Power Off/On feature of the operating system to reboot the tablet daily. Shutting down apps and processes improves the device's overall functioning. In addition, we added a new feature to automatically relaunch the application every 60 minutes making sure it remains connected and synced to the school's calendar all the time.

Figure 4. Installation of the tablet using external power source and concealed USB cable

The question is how many development hours we can put on this project. There is always a room for improvement. But our goal was to build a working prototype to test the possibility of using a custom-built application running on affordable tablets.

Our push to move forward with the installation of the tablet in the library resulted in an opportunity for the law school to embark in an official pilot project for a conference room schedule display with the outcome being an approved standard solution for hardware and software that can easily be replicated throughout the campus. However, the campus preferred solution is to outsource this service and delegate all installation and support responsibilities.

While having a custom-built application can make sense in the library with limited number of study rooms, it can represent many logistic, technical, and security challenges when dealing with hundreds of rooms throughout the entire campus.

After a year of building, learning and measuring the success of the study room schedule application we wrapped-up this pilot project and shared our findings and recommendations with the campus to decide whether we can deploy and sustain this project.

DATA VISUALIZATION DASHBOARD

In 2015, the Leon E. Bloch Law Library revived a long defunct national survey of law school information technology staffing and services survey created by E. Ann Puckett, former professor and director of the University of Georgia School of Law Alexander Campbell King Law Library (Watson & Reeves, 2011). The survey in its original format gathered data about full-time employees assigned to law libraries and law schools and their responsibilities on administering various information technology related tasks and services. The survey results show the trends in IT administration from the perspective of law libraries over the years. Our interest in this survey stems from our desire to understand and assess the organization of our information technology infrastructure, as we were in a transition to a shared services agreement with our campus IT department.

While the survey deployment and making sure we get an acceptable participation rate was a challenge, we underestimated the time and effort needed to review and make sense of the large amount of data we received from over one hundred law schools.

This project started in summer with a goal of presenting the survey results in a visual format to help us understand the results and identify new patterns. The set of data was based on the results of the survey we conducted in 2015 as well as results from prior surveys which we received from our colleagues at the University of Georgia School of Law.

The following is the list of features we provided to our developer:

- Create an online dashboard
- Present each question on an appropriate graph
- Compare results by year

While building this system is not technically challenging for the graduate students who are familiar with big data analysis as part of their field of study, they nevertheless has to work on a short deadline as we planned to use the dashboard in a poster session on the same topic presented during the American Association of Law Libraries (AALL) annual meeting.

There are several online data visualization tools available enabling users to convert a set of flat statistics to many charts, graphs, maps and other visually appealing graphics. However, these tools, especially the free ones, are often limited to a single set of data manually provided by a user. In our case, we wanted to give users a great flexibility on viewing data while easily adding new results as they become available.

The dashboard was build using PHP, MySQL database, and Highcharts JS. Highcharts JS is a Javascript library used to generate interactive charts free of charge to non-profit organizations and for personal use under Creative Commons (CC) Attribution.

Before exporting the data to the online database, we had to make sure both survey results of 2010 and 2015 are identical and free of any duplicate entries. We also standardized the naming of the participating schools used a consistent state coding to generate an accurate geographic distributions of data.

The online dashboard included answers to all questions except any Personally identifiable information.

The choice of graphs used was based on the type of questions and information to display. Based on the addresses, we generated map chart grouping schools by their US District Courts affiliation. The chart also displays the number of schools participating in the survey from each state (Figure 5).

Other graphs used in the dashboard are bar chart to illustrate the average number of full time employees supporting IT services, and pie chart to illustrate the number of schools considering entering a shared services agreement. In each graph we added a an option to display the results by year. The year value is dynamically generated based on when the data was collected making sure new dates are added automatically to the charts.

Figure 5. Map chart used to illustrate the geographic distribution of schools by District Courts

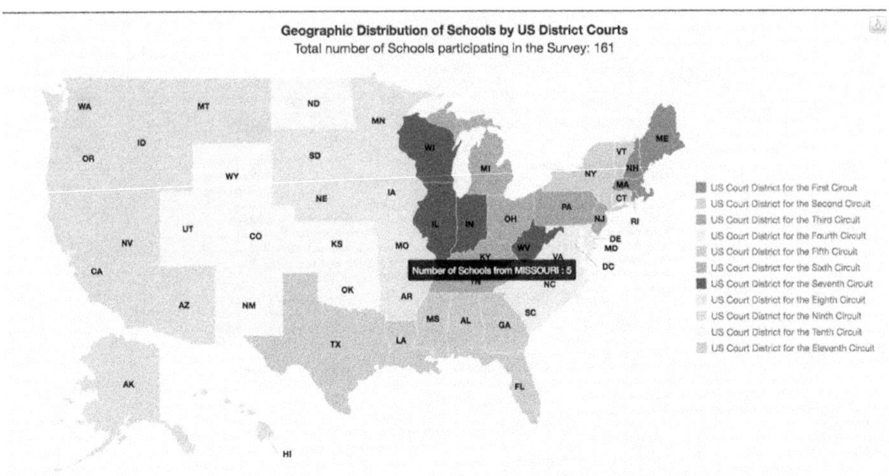

The last section of the dashboard is regarding the question of responsibility for specific IT domains and functions. For this question, we identified 31 domains and services that can be managed by law libraries, law schools, campus, vendor, other entity, or a combination of multiple stakeholders. To better illustrate the large information in this question, we chose a stacked bar chart showing the percentage of schools for each domain and for each stakeholder (Figure 6).

As we are looking to continue to administer this survey in the future, we made the last section of the dashboard available to participating schools only in order to incentivize others to participate on the survey. For this purpose, we added an email field to automatically check if the user is a member of a participating school. If a user is from a law school that has never participated in the survey in the past, they receive a message inviting them to take the survey.

This project was finished ahead of the schedule allowing us ample time to test and improve on it before sharing it during the AALL annual meeting.

Working on the dashboard was straight-forward as expected. The bulk of the work was already done as the results of the 2015 survey were published as an infographic using the same charts but generated manually from an Excel sheet. However, our goal was to be able to repurpose the dashboard to illustrate different set of data. Using the same source code, with some minor adjustment, we were able to create another visualization dashboard for a survey we use to track students' progresses in a variety of lawyering skills. The survey features around 200 questions and having a visual representation of the results make this complex set of data more accessible and easy to comprehend (Figure 7).

Figure 6. Stacked bar chart used to illustrate the ownership of various IT domains

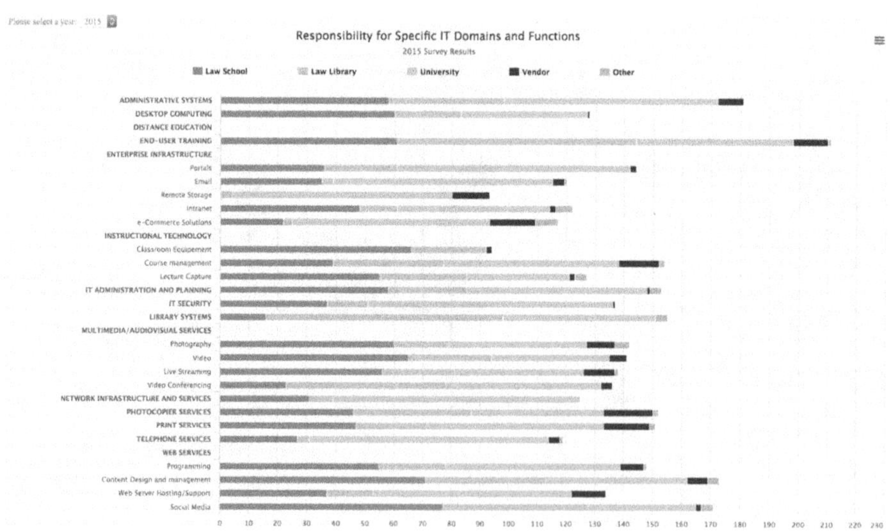

Figure 7. Stacked bar chart illustrating negotiation skills for entering students as part of the Practical Skills Self-Assessment Tool

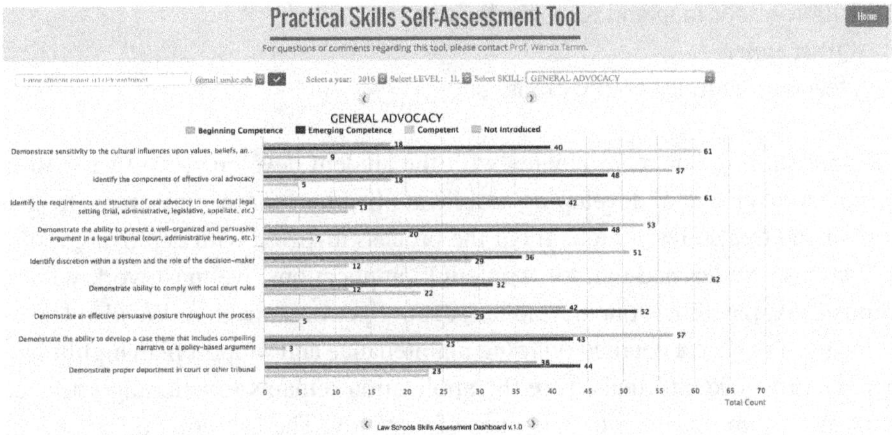

Since this survey tracks students during the first and third year of their legal education, we don't have yet enough data to fully evaluate the dashboard. However, from the initial feedbacks we received, we think that it can also be helpful to students as a self-assessment tool.

LIBRARY MOBILE APPLICATION

Having a mobile application for your library is very tempting. However, with Web 2.0 tools and the proliferation of responsive design, it is hard to support the necessity to build a mobile application if the same information is already accessible from a web browser. In addition, distribution platforms such as Apple's App Store can reject an application if it lacks the engagement or if it is not utilizing the features unique to mobile devices (Apple, 2016).

The Leon E. Bloch Law Library mobile application is one of the first projects we started hoping to have working prototype in one semester. The goal was to give students and community users access to the law library resources directly from their mobile devices.

Based on our understanding of how our users interact with the library, we developed this list of features we wanted to provide through the mobile application:

- Access the library catalog and research guides

- Library and reference hours
- Computer lab occupancy status
- Library floor map and resource locator
- QR scanner
- Beacon proximity notifications

Before sharing our requirements with the student developer, we met with the department in charge of developing mobile applications for the university, to share our plan and to also learn more about the process involved with deploying mobile applications. We learned that for Apple iOS applications, we must work with the campus as Apple allows one developer account per organization. We also learned that we need to have a detailed ongoing maintenance and support plan highlighting the steps to be taken to make sure the application remains functioning after each operating system update, which happens frequently. The last point discussed was the copyright of all graphic and third-party coding elements used in the mobile application.

The estimated time of accomplishment of this project is 130 hours comprising the preliminary research and requirement analysis, design and branding, development, and testing. As with all our projects, we scheduled weekly meetings to discuss the progress and walk through any issues or challenges we might face. During the early meetings, we mainly discussed the feasibility of the features and we decided which one we should tackle first.

As of 2016, 65% of mobile devices in the U.S. run on Google's Android operating system while 31% run on Apple's iOS (Kantar Worldpanel, 2016). These numbers are different regarding adoption of mobile devices in higher education. But, nevertheless, they show what platform we should focus on. However, building native applications for each operating system can be difficult and lengthy. Thankfully, there are other alternatives to design hybrid applications to run cross platforms using web technologies such as HTML, CSS, and Javascript.

Based on the requirements of this project, the developer suggested to use Ionic Framework which offers a ready to use front-end design built on top of AngularJS and Apache Cordova as the foundation of the application. Hybrid applications combine the flexibility of web-based layout rendering and access to native features in mobile devices. The result is a single application that run on most mobile devices.

As we started working on the application, we quickly realized that this project won't be as easy as we anticipated. Our goal from the beginning was to provide a unique mobile experience to our users without having to duplicate content and services already available through the library website. However, without having access to third-party application program interfaces (API) in the case of the library catalog or the absence of customizable API for the library research guides, we were limited to mobile friendly features which are already accessible from a web browser. Another feature we quickly abandoned was the reference desk live status. While the library is open for an extended period of time during regular sessions, the reference desk is only staffed from 10 a.m. to 4 p.m. Having the status of the reference desk in the mobile application would be a helpful feature. Especially for members of the public who wish to represent themselves before a court and need assistance from the law librarians.

Inspired by the computer lab widget, which displays the occupancy status on the library website by monitoring the logon sessions, we wanted to duplicated the same feature at the reference computer. However, we omitted the simple fact that reference librarians do not necessarily use the computer while helping patrons. This is the first lesson we learned with this project, which is to engage all stakeholders early in the design process.

The features that we managed to implement without any major difficulties were the library hours which was built using a JavaScript code that compares the current date and time to an existing list of holidays and special opening hours, the resources locator which provides users with a call number and a floor map when searching for specific resource in the library, and finally a QR Code Scanner which is available as a plugin for Cordova platform.

Perhaps the only feature that can provide a unique mobile experience to our users is the near proximity notification based on iBeacon technology. iBeacon is a communication protocol developed by Apple in 2013. iBeacon compatible devices transmit low energy signal over Bluetooth to nearby mobile devices. This technology allows mobile applications to trigger specific actions when near a beacon (Wikipedia, 2016).

The beacon device we used is manufactured by Estimote. It features a waterproof silicon enclosure housing a small computer accompanied by accelerometer, temperature sensor, and a 2.4 GHz radio using Bluetooth 4.0. Estimote Beacons are energy efficient and can last over 3 years on a single battery (Estimote, 2014). We decided to implement this feature in the library mobile application in order to push targeted notifications to users. In retail, proximity notifications are used to promote sales, locate products, and provide a customized shopping experience. Libraries can also benefit from this new communication medium by using near proximity communication to promote events and services, and share location-based resources. The default range of a beacon in real life situation is between 40 and 50 meters. In order to avoid overlapping the signal in the library, we had to adjust the strength for each beacon separately. We also had to control the interval of each notification. Users will not mind receiving a notification welcoming them when they enter the library. But it can be an annoyance if they receive the same notification each time they pass through the same location in a short period of time. In addition, we had to think of an easy way for our staff to update the notifications as needed. The solution we came up with was a web-based interface to manage signal strength, title, description, and type of action for each message we send.

The signal transmitted by the beacon includes a unique identifier. When a mobile device intercepts a signal, the application compares it to the parameters saved on the web interface and decide on the action to trigger based on the identity of the beacon received. For example, if a beacon is configured to send a notification message once a week when a mobile device is within 10 meters, the application will only trigger the notification when within the range and will only do so once every seven days.

We installed the first beacon in the main floor of the library to promote general library news and events. The second beacon is installed in the ground floor of the library and is used to promote resources for first year students. The third beacon is installed outside of the library near the Professional and Career Development Center allowing us to reach students outside of the library with general information and events (Figure 8).

During our testing, we found that the signal strength of Estimote Beacons can vary depending on the location and the environment surrounding them. The signal can also travel between floors when using high broadcasting frequencies. Therefore, we limited the signal strength to few meters to keep the notifications relevant to the locations.

Another challenge we faced with the beacons is the interval of notifications that each user might get. Storing the phone and the beacon unique IDs on our server can

Figure 8. Example of push notification received when in proximity of a beacon

allow us to easily control the interval of notifications. However, for privacy reasons, we decided to store the data directly on the mobile devices.

We started working on the library mobile application in spring 2016 and by the end of summer we had the Android version ready for testing while we were still struggling to fix the proximity notification intervals for the iOS version. We also faced other issues after the release of iOS version 10 which resulted in unstable performance of the application.

Without having a fully working prototype for both platforms Android and iOS in a reasonable time we were unable to do any usability testing or move forward with this project.

CONCLUSION

The projects mentioned in this chapter fit with the strategic goal of the law library to build a solid communication platform capable of disseminating all type of information with internal and external stakeholders. While our approach in bringing these projects to life was unconventional, because we relied heavily on internal resources, the risk associated with developing them was minimal.

However, when we started prototyping the mobile and web applications in collaboration with the computing and engineering students, our understanding of the users' needs and expectations were just assumptions. It's by presenting a minimum viable product and gathering feedback we tested our hypotheses and decided where to focus our energy and resources.

The Study Room Schedule Display project which was initiated to find a better way to help library staff manage the library study room schedules and it received a positive feedback from those who will benefit from it. The prototype demonstrated the viability of this solution and its potential to improve the staff productivity. While scaling, this project will require an ongoing maintenance and improvement, we still have to decide whether this is something that the library can sustain or not. The lack of feedback regarding library mobile application and the development hiccups we faced demonstrated that our assumptions and guesses regarding users' need to access the online resources through their mobile devices were false. One of the most common startup mistakes addressed by Mathews (2012) is the inability to validate their ideas early on. Building a working prototype and test our hypothesis allowed us to quickly discover that our concept was not viable. While the mobile application in its current version might not be feasible, there are several elements of it that we might reuse with other projects such as the near proximity communication using the iBeacon devices.

Another lesson learned from these prototyping projects is the need to have an ongoing communication among the library stakeholders earlier in the process. New concepts must grow organically by letting potential users help nurture them rather than "cooking them up" in closed offices and meeting rooms (Mathews, 2012). In the mobile application for example, we focused on building the technology using the near proximity sensors to facilitate communication with our users while we neglected feedback from those who will create the content itself. For the application to succeed, we must plan and create new promotional content regularly. The proposed system doesn't fit with any existing workflow we have at the library. In the other hand, the study room schedule display is based on an existing calendaring system that we are already using. In this situation, the technology doesn't require an additional effort or learning new processes which increased its chance of success.

Finally, innovative ideas require trial and error. While the concept can be common among startups and private institutions, it is not always the case with publicly-supported ones (Coffin & Morril, 2015). Therefore, having the management trust is very important to create an environment that fosters innovation. We have been very fortunate to work with supportive managers that bring life into new ideas by facilitating access to resources and adding the weight of their own experiences to the development processes. Our colleagues have also surprised us by engaging and embracing our embryonic culture of change and sharing their innovative ideas and honest feedback with us.

We hope to continue experimenting with new ideas and processes to improve our services and empower our users one innovation at a time.

REFERENCES

Apple. (2016). *Common App Rejections*. Retrieved 10 16, 2016, from https://developer.apple.com/app-store/review/rejections/

Bieraugel, M. (2015). Managing library innovation using the lean startup method. *Library Management*, *36*(4/5), 351–361. doi:10.1108/LM-10-2014-0131

Bryan, S., & Holly, M. (2015). *Building a Culture of Innovation in Higher Education: Design & Practice for Leaders. EDUCAUSE*. EDUCAUSE.

Coffin, A., & Morril, S. (2015). Promoting Innovation: The WiLs Model. *Collaborative Librarianship*, *7*(1), 22–29.

Drake, M. A. (1979). Managing innovation in academic libraries. *College & Research Libraries*, *40*(6), 503–510. doi:10.5860/crl_40_06_503

Draper, H. L., Oswald, T. A., & Renfro, M. (2007). Student Workers: Cross Training in the Academic Environment. *Journal of Access Services*, *5*(1/2), 133–137.

Estimote. (2014). *Beacon Tech Overview*. Retrieved 10 2016, 17, from http://developer.estimote.com/

Joy, P. A. (2014). Law Schools and The Legal Profession: A Way Forward. *Akron Law Review, 47*(1).

Kantar Worldpanel. (2016). *Smartphone OS sales market share*. Retrieved 10 2016, 17, from http://www.kantarworldpanel.com/global/smartphone-os-market-share/

Mathews, B. (2012). *Think Like A Startup: a white paper to inspire library entrepreneurialism.* Virginia Tech.

The New Media Consortium. (2015). The NMC Horizon Report: 2015 Library Edition.

The New Media Consortium (2016). NMC Horizon Report: 2016 Higher Education Edition.

UMKC School of Law. (2016). *Admissions Facts at a Glance*. Retrieved 09 2016, from http://law.umkc.edu/prospective-students/jd-program/admissions-facts-at-a-glance/

UMKC School of Law. (2016). *Employment Summary For 2015 Graduates*. Kansas City: UMKC School of Law.

Watson, C. A., & Reeves, L. (2011). Technology Management Trends in Law Schools. *Digitalcommons*. Retrieved from http://digitalcommons.law.uga.edu/law_lib_artchop/21

Wikipedia. (2016, October 18). *iBeacon*. Retrieved 10 18, 2016, from https://en.wikipedia.org/wiki/IBeacon

Wise, N. (2016, April 11). *Sonic Foundry Announces Finalists in the 12th Annual Enterprise Video Awards*. Retrieved from http://www.sonicfoundry.com/sonic-foundry-announces-finalists-12th-annual-enterprise-video-awards/

Chapter 7
MyLibrary at Brooklyn College: Developing a Suite of Digital Tools

Colleen Bradley-Sanders
Brooklyn College, USA

Alex Rudshteyn
Brooklyn College, USA

ABSTRACT

The Office of Academic Information Technologies (AIT) at Brooklyn College is based in the college library and has a history of successful innovation in developing in-house digital tools for the use of students, faculty and the library staff. In tight budgetary times developing software solutions in-house has not only improved services at lower cost than commercial products but also tailored them to the library's needs. There is some discussion of earning income from selling one of the tools to other libraries, however commercialization is not a prime motivator in the creation of the software. This chapter explores one aspect of the work done by AIT, the development of a set of digital tools called MyLibrary Suite.

INTRODUCTION

Brooklyn College (BC), founded in 1930, is one of the oldest of the senior colleges in the City University of New York (CUNY) system, the third-largest university system in the United States, and has full-time equivalent enrollment of 13,000, of whom 2000 are graduate students. The Brooklyn College Library, the most advanced in the CUNY system, is the academic, cultural and technological hub of the college. Students, faculty, staff and members of the surrounding community enjoy access

DOI: 10.4018/978-1-5225-2676-6.ch007

to the 1.5 million print materials housed at the library, more than 83,000 electronic books and journals and over 300 online databases. The library provides access to a wireless network and has more than 500 computers for public use. Additional services include, but are not limited to, the 24/7 Library Café, which houses a Starbucks and a 85+ computer facility, the New Media Center which manages the second floor computer lab, Woody Tanger Auditorium, group viewing and listening rooms, laptop and iPad loans; software skills courses taught by Academic Information Technologies (AIT) staff; and the Faculty Lab, which provides faculty training and development and manages multimedia classrooms. Library faculty are actively involved in supporting and encouraging faculty, staff and students as they contribute works to the CUNY institutional repository, Academic Works.

With such a large facility to service, the near-constant budget concerns of a public institution, and the ever-expanding role of technology in libraries, the AIT unit of the Brooklyn College library almost inevitably became more than a faculty support team and administrator of computer systems. This chapter discusses how and why AIT created a suite of digital tools for the benefit of library faculty, staff and students, shared some of the tools with other campus departments and libraries at other institutions, and learned some lessons along the way. It briefly touches on commercialization of software.

MERGING THE LIBRARY WITH ACADEMIC INFORMATION TECHNOLOGIES (AIT)

In the early 1990s, when developing a master plan for renovating the campus, senior administrators at Brooklyn College decided the new library would become the core location for the "transmission and retrieval of knowledge" on campus (Higginbotham, 1997). This decision was part of a trend discussed by Mary K. Bolin in her 2005 article in which she reported on the growing discussion about mergers of libraries and computer centers in the 1990's. Given the wide range of what constitutes an academic library, she focused her study on a group of similar institutions (land grant universities) while noting that such changes were occurring at all types of colleges and universities—large, small, public, and private. Bolin's description included that 88% of the universities she studied retained the traditional structure in which the library and computer centers reported separately to their respective administrators. She also noted that her study results seemed to "confirm Mech's assertion that the merged organization is a phenomenon of smaller institutions, and that when it does occur, the top administrator of the new organization is generally a librarian" (Bolin, 2005). This is what happened at Brooklyn College, where AIT reports to the chief librarian.

Columbia University and the University of Southern California both have smaller student bodies than a typical land-grant university, and like other institutions in the 1990s and early 2000s, they merged their academic computing and library units. In separate articles for a special issue of the *Journal of Library Administration* in 2012, the stories of the respective mergers are told.

The University of Southern California merged its academic computing and library functions in 1997 into an Information Services Division (ISD), hoping to try new ways of providing services and perhaps provide a model for other institutions. After ten years, a new Provost determined that the merger was not effectively serving the patrons of the library or the IT unit. It was a difficult merger on the library side, with library faculty feeling undervalued. While the merged entity supported innovative work from the information technology (IT) staff, software developed by the team was "never fully developed for use by our community" (Quinlan & McHarg, 2012). In 2006, the two units were separated.

The IT/library merger at Columbia University had a more successful outcome, and the two units remain a single entity in 2017. Columbia has since the 1970s combined certain technology and information services functions; by 2007, various mergers and restructuring efforts resulted in a new organizational structure, at the heart of which was the belief that "academic computing would be the foundation of new library services and that the integration of academic computing units and skills into the traditional library organization was critical to our ongoing success" (Renfro & Neal, 2012) Collaboration and creative thinking on meeting the needs of students resulted in a refinement of a traditional "information commons" model for campus computer labs, and today Columbia has a Digital Humanities Center, a Digital Social Sciences Center, a Digital Music Center, and a Digital Science Center. Significant lessons learned by Columbia include the need for flexibility and lack of territoriality among the staff, the vital importance of institutional support for hiring quality technical staff, and having enough technologically proficient library staff to support a work environment open to innovation. At Brooklyn College, to achieve the goal of merging the library with AIT, some restructuring of the IT services was required. As the Provost and Vice-President for Administration and Finance explored the possibilities, they learned that the expertise needed to create the hub was already in place within the library. Dr. Barbra Higginbotham, chief librarian, was already working on a variety of academic computing projects with Dr. Howard Spivak and strongly supported the idea of transforming the role of the chief librarian into the Executive Director of Academic Information Technologies. She stressed the library faculty's technological savvy and pedagogical experience, and their ability to understand faculty needs. To achieve the desired goal, obstacles had to be removed, including the organizational structure that had the library and academic computing reporting to different vice-presidents. The newly unified entity also had greater staff, equipment and budgetary needs, which were met with the support of the Provost, Vice-President for Administration and Finance and the Assistant Vice-President for Information & Technology Services. The restructured IT responsibilities at Brooklyn College resulted in the educational technology group, audio-visual services, and the faculty training and development lab being placed in the library, under the leadership of the Chief Librarian and Executive Director of AIT (Higginbotham) and head of Library Systems (Spivak). A few years later, with the creation of a 24/7 computer lab, the Library-Café, the hiring of additional staff and an expansion of services offered, another reorganization of AIT took place, and the new structure is reflected in the current organizational chart (Figure 1).

Placing academic computing under the auspices of the library prior to the construction of the new library building allowed the college time to observe the results of the experiment; a few years later, when the administration was ready to solicit designs for the new building, the accomplishments of the unified library/AIT unit (including curriculum innovations) persuaded the college to place the administrative computing offices within the new library building, permitting both computing units to take full advantage of the synergies between them, as well as features of the new

Figure 1. Organizational chart for the library

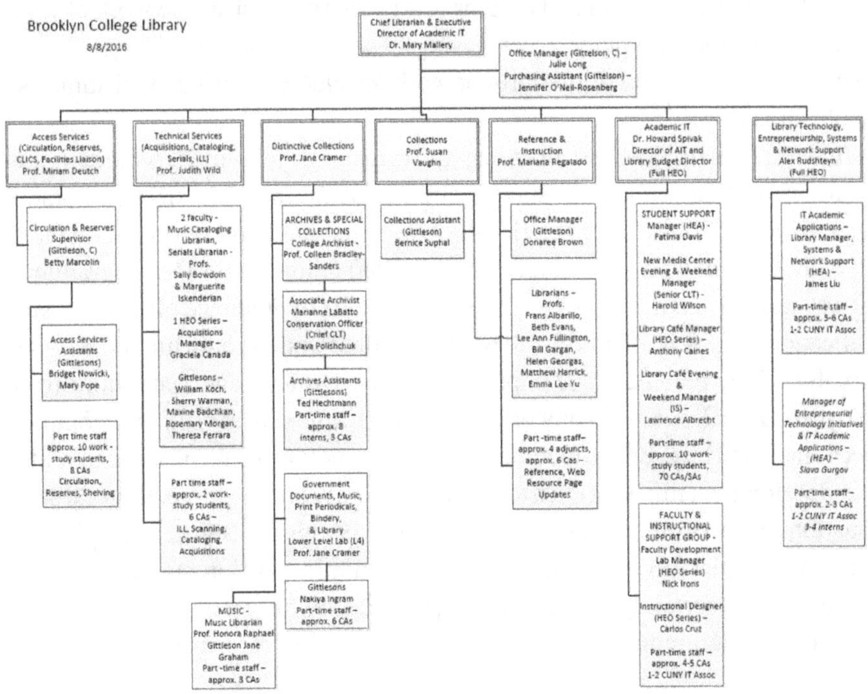

building, including a Faculty Training and Development Laboratory and multimedia classrooms (Higginbotham, 1997).

Strong leadership is required as we approach the new frontiers technology invites us to cross. Unless we strengthen our efforts in academic computing, we cannot keep pace with developments that would enable us to enhance instruction and research. We therefore explored options and configurations consistent with available resources. And we found both the talent and the structure right here on campus – in the Library.[1]

Over time a strong culture of collaboration developed between AIT and the library administration, aided by the leadership of Professor Stephanie Walker (chief librarian 2007-2015) in recruitment and retention of talented AIT staff.

FULL-TIME PROJECTS, PART-TIME STAFF

Although Professor Walker persuaded the college that promotions and raises for some non-faculty positions were essential, and included the heads of both AIT branches (Student & Faculty Services, and Network Services) on the Library Senior Management Team, the structure of the unit was not initially ideal for consistent, timely development of software tools. In addition to serving as the Project Manager on the work of mostly part-time programming staff (often consisting of computer science students), the Associate Director of AIT also supervised the work of varying numbers of senior Computer Science majors as they undertook required senior projects, some of which laid the groundwork for elements of the MyLibrary suite of applications.

While AIT knew that best practices in software development included system analysis and design prior to the start of any coding, in the real world best practices are not always followed, and the first tools were created without this crucial step. Lack of system analysis and design meant limited guidance for the programmer on what was wanted and needed from the tool. This lack of guidance often necessitated modifications—a waste of time for all parties. Student workers have limited knowledge and real-world experience, and supervisors have less leverage than with full-time employees. Other limitations of working with part-time staff, or students completing projects, included inadequate documentation of a project from inexperienced students, longer development times for each tool, and temporary halts to projects due to student graduations or part-time staffers finding full-time positions elsewhere. Asking a new programmer to pick up someone else's project in mid-development is not an ideal practice, and has certainly added to the time needed to fully develop some tools. As the full-time programmer who eventually brought Web Information Management

System (WIMS) online said upon starting work on the partially completed SRMS/ WIMS project, “Never give a full-time project to a part timer,” he lamented, “I wish I had worked on this from the start” (Gurgov, 2016).

DEVELOPING MYLIBRARY

MyLibrary is a single-sign-on portal created to manage user accounts, groups and permissions for all MyLibrary applications. Some have been used by other departments on campus and others have been shared with other CUNY campuses. The most popular modules in the suite of applications are: WIMS (Web Information Management System), TIMS (The Inventory Management System), Timesheet Management system, Find-a-Book, Room Scheduler, and Laptop Loan.

The earliest tools in MyLibrary (SRMS/WIMS, Room Scheduler and Timesheet Management System) were developed in response to suggestions and requests from librarians and supervisory staff, while later applications were initiated by AIT. An ongoing budget crisis at CUNY has forced AIT to be more careful with its budget and staff resources. As a result, the later tools in MyLibrary (Find-a-Book, Inventory Management System, Laptop Loan and Book Scanner) all benefited from the system analysis and design process. Due to the personnel structure of AIT, and the sources of the original ideas for various tools in MyLibrary, development on different tools often occurred simultaneously. Faculty and staff requested AIT to develop the following tools:

- Subject Resource Management System (SRMS, 2002-2006)
- Web Information Management System (WIMS, 2007-present)
- Room Scheduler (2004)
- Timesheet Management System I (2004-2008)
- Timesheet Management System II (2014-present)

SRMS

As in many academic libraries, timely and effective Web resource management was a challenge at Brooklyn College library. Web page maintenance was subject to postponement in favor of more pressing projects, and technical know-how (or lack of it) also affected how often pages were updated; while some librarians marked up and even uploaded their own pages to the library servers, others collected links and relied on support staff to create the actual pages. Once created, updating pages – link-checking as well as selecting new resources – required a significant amount of continued attention. Duplication of effort where single (usually subscription) resources appeared on many different pages made updating especially tedious. Trial databases were sometimes not placed on subject pages where they would have been most effective. Removing trial databases from a list was another challenge. In addition to concerns about timeliness and accuracy, lack of uniformity of language, style, and presentation of resources on library web pages could drastically impact a user's experience. These factors meant that updating and managing the library resource web pages was an uneven endeavor at best, and an onerous and therefore neglected one at worst.

The library's first website in the mid-1990s consisted almost entirely of a list of licensed resources (http://library.brooklyn.cuny.edu/pages/nostalgia/), with subject-related resource pages following in the late 1990s (Figure 2). At the time, AIT lacked the time and technical staff for more effective web page maintenance.

In response to the library's need to better manage its subject guides—but not having the funds to pay for Aleph's expensive E-Resource Management System—AIT and a team of library faculty from the Information Services (IS) unit began working on a tool called the Subject Resource Management System (SRMS), which debuted in 2005. The idea of a database-driven solution originated in 2002 with one of the subject librarians, and was initially worked on by a Computer Science student doing a senior project. He gathered information from the librarians as to what they wanted to be able to do, and researched existing software options. The beta version of Source Finder, a database-driven resource management system developed by the Preston Library at the Virginia Military Institute, provided a model.[2] The idea behind the database was straightforward: each resource would have a single instance within the database, but would be displayed on multiple web pages. Thus, updates to a resource would appear immediately and simultaneously on all relevant subject Web pages. In addition, the exigencies of the database would impose some uniformity on the look and terminology used on our subject web pages.This database tool controlled the "Resources by Subject" section of the library web site, permitting librarians to easily update resources themselves, without needing HMTL programming skills. The SRMS tool evolved over time into the Web Information Management System (WIMS), a key module in the MyLibrary suite of applications developed by AIT to aid and simplify the day-to-day tasks of the library faculty and staff.

Divided into public and administrative views, updates to a resource from an administrator are instantaneously applied to all related public pages. Expired resources are hidden from view. To facilitate solving technical problems with electronic resources, WIMS also stores vendor contacts, as well as licensing information. As a security measure, each librarian or staff member has his/her own username and password. Users with regular levels of access can only see and customize their own assigned pages, unless they are designated as administrators. Administrators can

Figure 2. Early library webpage
(Circa 1998)

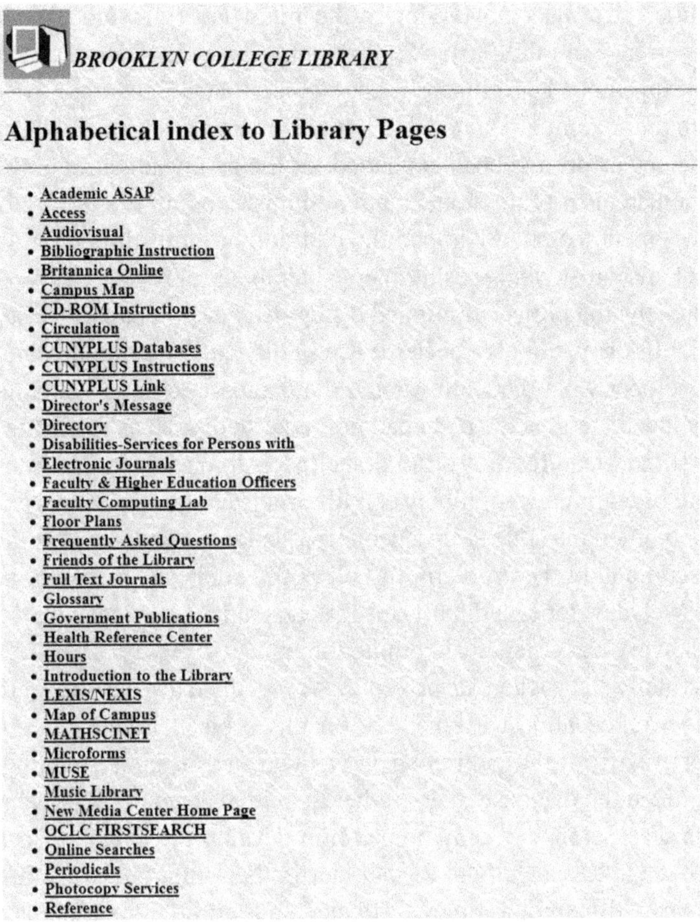
BROOKLYN COLLEGE LIBRARY

Alphabetical index to Library Pages

- Academic ASAP
- Access
- Audiovisual
- Bibliographic Instruction
- Britannica Online
- Campus Map
- CD-ROM Instructions
- Circulation
- CUNYPLUS Databases
- CUNYPLUS Instructions
- CUNYPLUS Link
- Director's Message
- Directory
- Disabilities-Services for Persons with
- Electronic Journals
- Faculty & Higher Education Officers
- Faculty Computing Lab
- Floor Plans
- Frequently Asked Questions
- Friends of the Library
- Full Text Journals
- Glossary
- Government Publications
- Health Reference Center
- Hours
- Introduction to the Library
- LEXIS/NEXIS
- Map of Campus
- MATHSCINET
- Microforms
- MUSE
- Music Library
- New Media Center Home Page
- OCLC FIRSTSEARCH
- Online Searches
- Periodicals
- Photocopy Services
- Reference

create, delete, and update any information in the entire database. Functions available to librarians in this module include: adding new resources, customizing subject resources, search engine, back-up, managing librarian information, adding new subjects, and logs. AIT staff also developed a method of supplying static pages to replace the dynamic pages in the event of network issues. Most importantly, WIMS allows global changes and on-the-fly updates while preserving individual database descriptions and modifications tailored for given subject pages.

Despite the promised convenience and efficiency of a database, there was some early resistance to the idea based on concerns about autonomy and control over intellectual content. Over time, everyone came to understand that library faculty would control content, while the look and layout of pages would be automated and uniform. All library faculty were invited to give input early on and throughout the project.

Meanwhile, the project moved slowly: the initial part-time student worker lacked the time, experience and skills to tackle a project that was considerably more complex than it first appeared. Unfortunately, the subject database project was seriously stalled when the student graduated and left for greener pastures. By then, however, enough time and effort had been expended for the practical nature of the database to become apparent to professionals and administrators in the library beyond the initial development team. AIT hoped the addition of a full-time programmer/web development specialist would result in considerable progress.

Unfortunately, the project continued a sluggish pace, in part because it was not given special priority, but also because it was difficult to communicate clearly to the Web developer what the team wanted the database to do. As a result, the new database included features the team had not requested, such as super-high levels of security, and lacked features truly desired, such as customizable resource descriptions. The problem of communication between librarians/content providers and IT staff/techies is a common one, due to the specialized language and needs of the different groups. To compound the problem, in Fall 2003, after only a few months on the project, the Web developer suddenly left for personal reasons, leaving the database project in the very early stages of completion.

Success finally came when the project was reassigned to a part-time programmer in AIT who worked almost exclusively on this project. Equally important, this programmer was from the beginning very interested in understanding what the librarians wanted the database to do, rather than in his own ideas of what it should do. In-depth discussions not only helped him develop the database structure, but also allowed the library faculty to further clarify their thinking about functionality. Though this part-time programmer graduated and left after six months, there was only a small hiccup in progress since the project was passed to the new full-time Web development specialist. Though initially complicated to pick up where the predecessor had left off, the project quickly got rolling again.

As he finished the database and developed both the staff and end-user interfaces, library support staff worked furiously to input over 300+ resources into the database, beginning with the subscription databases followed by Web-based resources from individual subject pages. The data input process turned out to be an important way to test the SRMS. The test phase revealed problems with the stability of the server, non-functional elements of the database, and display problems. As each issue cropped up, the programmer studied and fixed them. Eventually the public side of the SRMS went live for Spring 2006 (Figure 3).

For library faculty who maintained their pages themselves the database was a wonder: there was instantaneous updating across pages and corrections made at a

Figure 3. SRMS

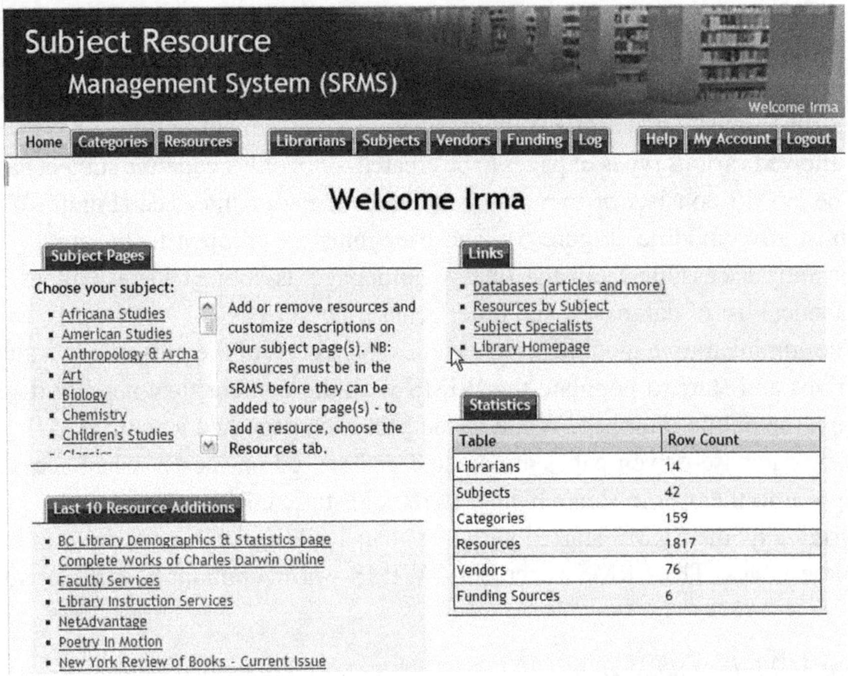

moment's notice. The SRMS proved to be the labor-saving, highly efficient, and very cool technological innovation AIT had hoped it would be. Of course, some library faculty still preferred to rely on support staff—proving the old adage that the more things change, the more they stay the same—and the SRMS has not solved every problem of web page updating. In particular, human intervention was and still is necessary to make sure sites are all still relevant and available (e.g., automated link checkers can only indicate if it is valid, but cannot look at or make decisions about the value of the linked page).

At this point the experience for the researcher was not substantially enhanced beyond finding updated resources. However, the next phase of development was to create a more complex search that would allow researchers to be more selective as they searched.

Now that AIT better understood and appreciated the value of databases for easy site maintenance, the team discussed other areas of the website that could be usefully added to the database, such as the directory, library hours, even information about the library. These goals were accomplished later in WIMS.

WIMS

In 2007, as development continued and system functionality expanded, a name change was needed. With the system now managing much, much more than subject web pages, it became known as the Web Information Management System, or WIMS. It now allowed various types of pages to be created—not only academic subject pages.

The WIMS consists of two major modules: the user interface (Figure 4) and administrative module (Figure 5). The user interface is open to the public and is currently accessible from the library homepage as subject Pages/Guides, our alphabetical list of databases, and other general library pages.

The administrative module is the technical backbone of the project and it allows librarians and staff to populate the WIMS with the content they need to display through the public interface. While in the past each page had a static HTML file, the new database-driven pages are created and served on-the-fly when accessed, yet appear to the user in same manner as the old static URLs.

Originally, the SRMS started with less than 1,000 records, consisting of eight database tables. The SRMS successor—WIMS—now contains more than 4,000

Figure 4. WIMS -public view

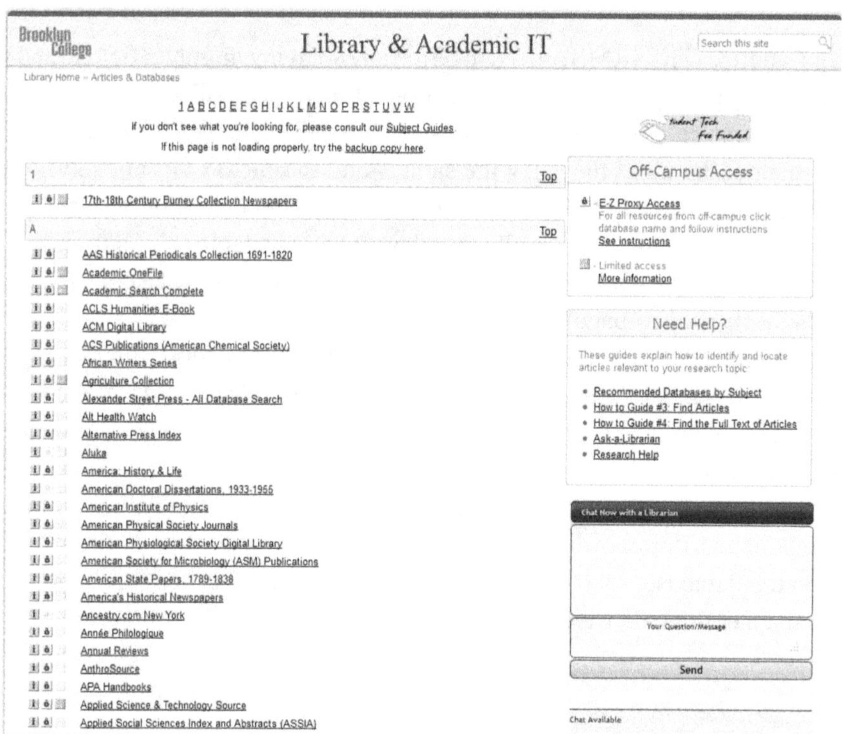

Figure 5. WIMS - admin view

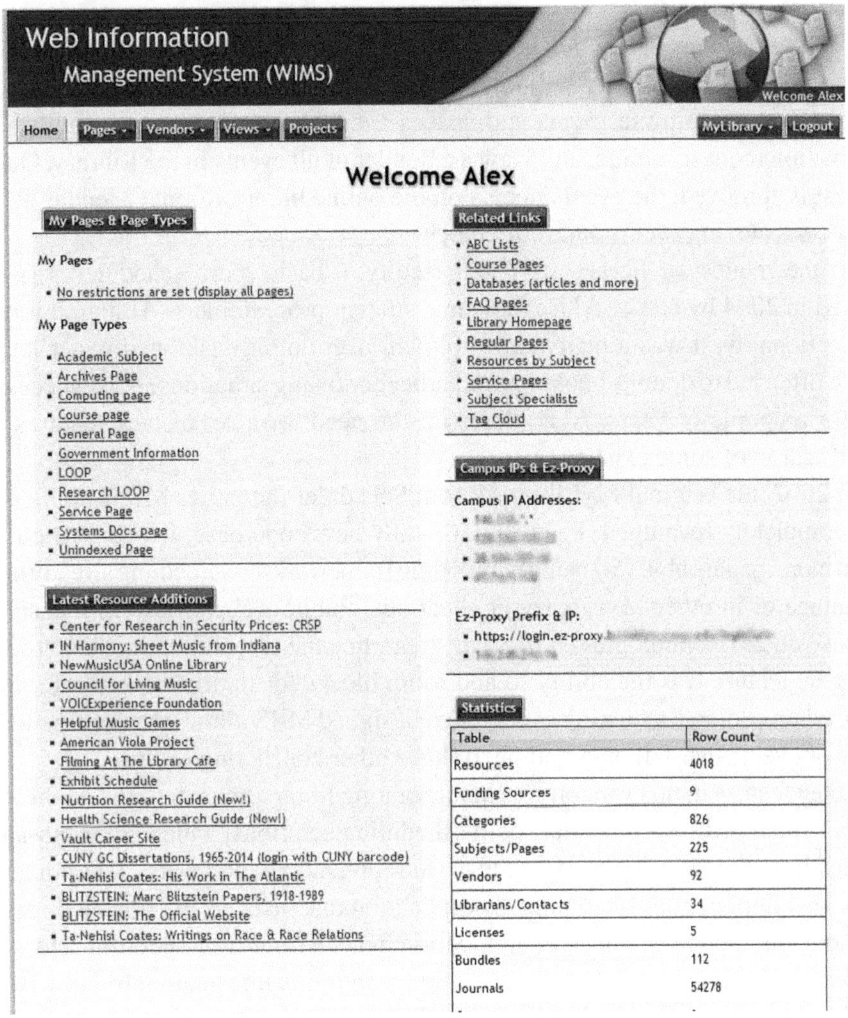

records, with even more tables added. After using the SRMS to only manage academic subject pages, AIT quickly realized that it could be used to produce other library pages as well and soon the entire library website became WIMS-driven. Another WIMS feature in the administrative module—vendor contact information—soon proved to be an extremely useful feature when the college changed and added external IP addresses without informing AIT. After receiving complaints from users unable to access various electronic resources (due to IP-based authentication used by vendors), AIT was able to use the WIMS to quickly locate vendor contact information and inform them of the IP changes. It would have been very difficult to accomplish this using the old-fashioned Rolodex system.

Room Scheduler

The Library Room Scheduler is a web application that allows efficient facility management of the Library building. The college community (including students and faculty) can browse rooms and spaces available in the library, submit room reservation requests online, and view a calendar of all events in the Library. Once a request is approved, the event appears on the online library Room Calendar. It also supports recurring events and room blocks.

At the request of library staff and faculty, a basic room scheduler was first created in 2004 by one of AIT's part-time student programmers. Although limited in functionality, it was a major improvement over an old-fashioned paper ledger, which often led to double-bookings and other confusing situations. After successful use for a couple of years, AIT addressed the need for a set of new features and modification of some existing ones.

In 2007, the original MyLibrary Room Scheduler (hereafter MRS) application was completely revamped. Featuring a totally new code base, it was written in a much more manageable way using new coding frameworks—something already taken advantage of in other MyLibrary applications. Public webpages were redesigned to use Web 2.0 technologies (AJAX) to streamline the reservation request process. One new feature was the ability to add room blocks for multiple rooms at a time. Also, when adding a recurring event, the redesigned MRS allows the user to modify times of events that fall on a holiday or have other conflicting events.

A key feature in this version was incorporating library hours into the application logic. Unlike many commercial room scheduling solutions, which are stand-alone applications, the MRS is part of a suite of web applications, and works in conjunction with other applications, including an application that displays the library directory and hours of operation. The hour application indicates hours of operation and when the building is open or closed. The MRS taps into this information to know when the library is open. In addition to regular hours of operation, the hour application keeps track of schedule exceptions, such as holidays and other scheduled changes. Users trying to book an event on a holiday or another day that the library is closed are instantly notified, and the request is not allowed to go through, unless a manager overrides the system. This relieves the staff of the responsibility of making sure that room reservation requests are not approved for days that the library is closed.

Directory is another MyLibrary module and it describes all rooms and areas available for booking in the Library, its occupancy, equipment available, and even has pictures of each area. Together they help the MRS book rooms in the library.

Reservation requests are always received in a pending state. After submitting a request, an email is automatically generated and sent to the user confirming receipt of the request, as well as to the library unit representing the room requested. The room is not yet booked and is pending approval from the unit manager or unit staff delegated to process reservation requests. Once it is approved, an email is once again generated to notify the user of its approval.

Use of the application and its improvements made room scheduling easy, efficient and hassle-free. It quickly became a very important tool in managing the library's rooms, eliminating entry errors and double-bookings, as well as relieving the staff of the constant hassle of making sure that reservation requests are sent for times when the library is actually open and following up with the patron to notify them of a room's availability.

Timesheet Management System

In a busy workplace, keeping track of employee time and attendance often becomes a real burden for a manager. The Timesheet Management System tracks 100+ library and AIT part-time employees, using a biometric punch clock. AIT modified the system for Brooklyn College's Facilities Department, which plans to use the program to track staff hours. Prior to the development of this module, the manager in charge of the timesheets for the part-time contract employees (who each had varying numbers of contract hours per year) spent approximately one day per week with paper schedules figuring out who needed to work when, and how many hours each person had left on their contracts.

CUNY regulations require all employees to submit a timesheet at the end of each pay period. While timesheets are supposed to be filled out daily, in practice timesheets were filled out every two weeks, just before submitting it to a supervisor for final approval. Once approved, the timesheets were sent to the payroll department. This practice led to complaints from payroll about illegible handwriting and too many corrections on the timesheets, for mistakes such as an employee marking a holiday as a normal work day, or correcting a dispute between the employee and a supervisor about actual time in and time out.

The original timesheet project started in 2004 when the New Media Center (NMC) manager asked AIT to set up digital punch clock software in the NMC in order to maintain better control over part-time employee working hours. In the beginning, AIT installed simple punch clock software on a designated computer called "Punch Clock Station." It presented an employee with simple menu only allowing punch in and punch out. This solution did not really solve all problems. The manager still spent a considerable amount of time comparing dates from the PunchClock software database with actual timesheets submitted for an approval, nor was the issue with bad handwriting resolved.

The need for a better solution forced AIT to step in. Once again using one of the unit's part-time programmers (another computer science student), AIT created an application to handle employee time keeping and timesheet generation. In the beginning, they used the commercially available software Time Clock MTS. This software had an easy to use interface and administrative modules to manage users, adjust times, and generate reports.

Each employee in the system was assigned a PIN number to be used for authentication when punching in or out. To create timesheets that would match the college-approved form, AIT wrote a special module that extracted actual times from the Time Clock MTS database and generated a printable timesheet that met the college requirements.

Although the system worked well, and even the handwriting issue was eliminated, another problem appeared. Some employees shared their individually assigned PIN number with their colleagues to clock in or out on their behalf. Research on how to resolve this problem led AIT to the solution of using a biometric device as an employee authentication method. The DigitalPersona, U.ARE.U 4500 fingerprint reader with a gel pad surface was an inexpensive option, and solved all remaining problems except the fact that the library had to pay a yearly maintenance fee for use of the Time Clock MTS software. At the same time, the library's timesheet system was recognized on the campus as an excellent solution to manage employee work time records and generate timesheets, so the human resource office approached AIT to adapt the library's timesheet solution for some categories of employees outside the library (custodial, facilities, etc.). Creation of such a system was a daunting task that required a considerable amount of time and countless meetings with HR to understand all the rules and union regulations applicable to employees under various union contracts. AIT used this project as an opportunity to develop its own software and eliminate the need for a commercial product.

Developing its own software freed AIT from the limited number of punch-clock stations allowed under the licensing agreement with Time Clock MTS. Moreover, they utilized the U.Are.U software development kit to take full advantage of the newer DigitalPersona-U.ARE.U 5160 fingerprint reader. The common problem with gel pad surface is frequent wear and tear and sensitivity to different types of skin. Users with very dry skin had problems using gel pad readers. The new reader has a glass surface that minimizes wear and tear; it also reads a wide range of fingerprints accurately and rapidly regardless of placement angle.

The use of biometric devices for authentication caused some users to express concern about AIT keeping copies of their fingerprints. In response to this concern, the library opted to store only an encrypted set of key elements of the fingerprint instead of the entire fingerprint.

In addition, when AIT wrote its own punch-clock software they were able to fully control the flow of the program. While TimeClock MTS forced users to select their name from a list, AIT's software expedited the process by removing that step. This has proven to be very effective when multiple employees try to use the punch-clock system at the same station.

The new version of the Timesheet Management System (TMS II), requested by Human Resources, will be utilized by blue-collar and custodial staff, which necessitated programming changes to account for the work hours stipulated by various union contracts.

ADDITIONAL AIT INITIATIVES

As mentioned previously, budget restrictions began to force AIT to more carefully allocate staff time and money, leading them to follow common procedure in software development and utilize system analysis and design in later applications for MyLibrary. The tools described below were all AIT initiatives, proposed in response to perceived needs and created by part-time programmers (computer science students) under the direct supervision of the full-time web programmer. The unfortunate reality is that while many projects started with part-time employees or students, when they left in the middle of a project, the full-time programmer was required to complete the work.

Find-a-Book, 2005

"Find-a-Book in the Library" is another module of the MyLibrary Suite that started as a senior project for a computer science student. It was one of AIT's favorite projects, one that continues to have an impact on all patrons searching for a book in the Library. Brooklyn College Library has 277,650 square feet of space and is home to more than 22 miles of shelving and more than 1.4 million volumes.

To simplify the task of finding a book and allow patrons to spend more time on their studies and other important activities, AIT created an application that is accessed on the web and allows library patrons to find a book's exact location – floor and shelf range. It works with the CUNY online catalog to create a floor map of the library and highlight the shelf on which the book can be found.

While Find-a-Book is a popular app in the MyLibrary suite today, this was not always the case. When AIT released the program as a pilot project in Fall 2005 and installed it on a few lookup terminals in the library, they encountered resistance from librarians. One of the main arguments was along the lines of "I've worked in the Library for 20…30 years and I know where every book is located." While this might be true for an individual librarian, a majority of students often feel frustrated and give up searching for a book in such a large building. Despite the initial resistance, in a very short time the librarians' attitudes toward this program improved. Once they realized the benefits this application offers to its users, AIT was asked to install it on all lookup terminals.

In light of its usefulness and success, AIT continued to improve the Find-A-Book module through a series of modifications. The first release of the program was a desktop application rather than a web-based one. It required an installation on each PC in the Library (primarily look-up terminals) that needed this functionality. It was preloaded with hundreds of images, each representing a floor map with the shelf range highlighted. A shelf range consists of two sets of call numbers, each representing the first and last book on the shelf. Maintenance of this version of the program was problematic. Any change in the call number range would trigger a sequence of events, such as the need to create new maps and updating them on all computers running this program.

In a subsequent version of the program, AIT decided to create a web-based solution to empower anyone on the web to find a book in our Library. This required the use of a browser plugin. The plugin was necessary to replace any call number found on the CUNY online catalog with a link pointing to our web application. While a major improvement, this update was not ideal. Although the floor map images now resided in a single location on our web server, manual installation of the browser plugins on every computer was still required. Moreover, maintenance of call number changes and floor map updates was still an issue.

AIT sought an even better solution—one that would reduce maintenance to as few steps as possible while providing the same or better service to library patrons. Programmers were looking for a way that would allow them to make changes in a single location and have the changes seamlessly propagate to all users. This version would not require any installation or software modification on user devices.

AIT developed a database-driven web application with integration to the CUNY Online Catalog. First, they compiled a list of all call number ranges and added them to a database. Then they developed an algorithm that would find a particular call number range based on a given book's call number, and enabled dynamic floor map creation rather than keep hundreds of old static floor map images. With the help of colleagues from the Office of Library Services (OLS) at CUNY Central, all Brooklyn College call numbers could now link directly to the application, thereby removing the need for any browser plugin installation. With the call number passed directly to the application, it was able to find the corresponding shelf range and dynamically create a floor map with it highlighted (Figure 6). In addition to the floor map, the module displays the image of the book cover, title, author and other details about the book the patron is searching for. These enhancements empowered patrons to quickly find a desired book in our spacious library.

Figure 6. Find-a-Book search results

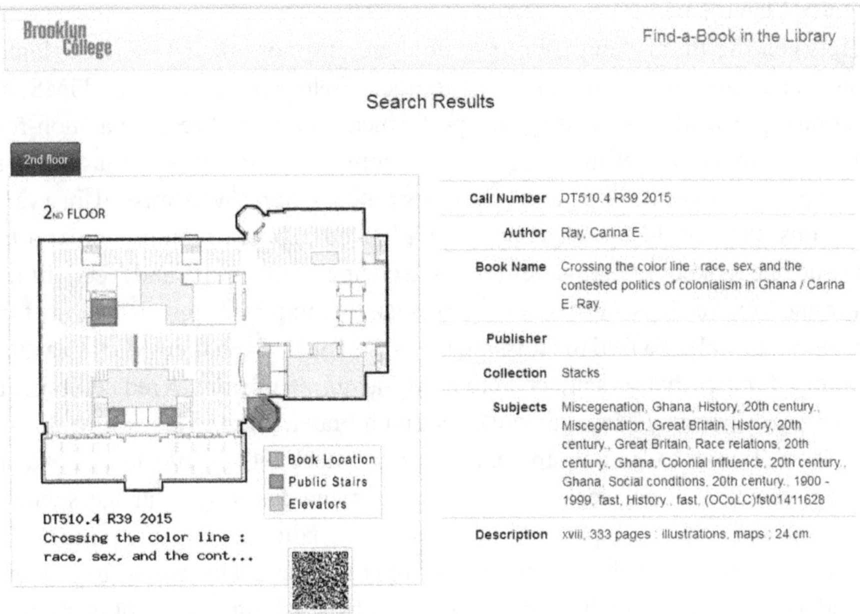

The Inventory Management System (TIMS), 2007-2008

The Inventory Management System is a web application designed to provide a complete up-to-date inventory of hardware, software and supplies. It provides inventory management for hardware and equipment. It allows viewing the current status of an asset in real time. Previously the inventories were done on paper, and a significant backlog in entering the data meant that items noted as "sent for salvage" in prior years often reappeared on the inventory checklist, resulting in time wasted looking for them. The new tool allows users to produce computer-generated reports without trying to decipher handwritten inventory sheets. Adopted by the Brooklyn College Office of Internal Audit and Property Management, this module of MyLibrary has helped to streamline inventory processes, saved hundreds of person-hours of staff time, and reduced error rates dramatically.

Keeping track of and managing the life cycle of hardware and software assets is one of the many challenges facing an IT manager. Under federal regulations governing colleges and universities, CUNY is required to conduct an annual physical inventory of equipment owned by the colleges. To comply with this regulation, all equipment in the Brooklyn College Library and Library-Café is subject to the annual re-inventory process performed by Brooklyn College's Office of Internal Audit and Property Management.

Between the library and Library-Café there are more than 1300 PCs, laptops, printers and other pieces of equipment to track. Before the creation of TIMS, after the annual physical re-inventory was performed AIT would receive a "non-found items" document, sometimes 50 pages or more. It consisted of all tagged assets missed or overlooked during the re-inventory process. Items were missed for a variety of reasons; they could be off-campus, in a locked office, or simply under a table where no one looked. Locating items missed during re-inventory and reconciling the non-found item list was a time-consuming task that required significant effort from managers and staff. To find the missing items, AIT was given the BRO tag (a unique inventory number that was attached to newly-acquired or transferred equipment by the Office of Property Management), a serial number, and the last known location of an item. Trying to find equipment with only these bits of information was like finding a needle in a haystack—time consuming and daunting. Managers with full workloads and various responsibilities found it a challenge to respond promptly to the request to reconcile the missing pieces of equipment. This would trigger email reminders from the property management office asking the equipment holder to reconcile the non-found items list, at which point he/she would have to drop everything and start searching for the missing items. This interrupted the normal workflow and took considerable time.

A second factor in the creation of TIMS was the need to comply with CUNY's Capital Asset Policy and CUNY's Fixed Asset Disposal Policy. These policies require that, all items to be transferred, relocated or salvaged be accompanied by an appropriate transfer form (Figure 7, Figure 8). These forms have to be signed and sent to the Office of Internal Audit and Property Management. Having handwritten transfer forms often proved to be problematic. Differences and idiosyncrasies in each individual's handwriting often left room for misinterpretation of data and as a result there were often discrepancies between the local inventory list and the list maintained by the Office of Internal Audit and Property Management.

Differentiating the letter "O" from the number "0" while interpreting handwriting is a constant struggle. Moreover, people with programming backgrounds would cross each zero with a vertical line to differentiate from letter "O". In one case, all such crossed zeros were completely missing in a serial number and it turned out that the person entering data from the transfer forms to the college's inventory system thought that these zeros were crossed out to correct a mistake.

TIMS is more than just simply an IT asset management system. It is a critical component in the service delivery model that the office of AIT established in the library and Library Cafe. It not only facilitates a complete up-to-date inventory of hardware, software and supplies, but also provides an effective way to follow the

Figure 7. Sample of handwritten transfer form

BROOKLYN COLLEGE EQUIPMENT TRANSFER FORM

Instructions: Complete this form to record the transfer of equipment and / or furniture to a new location. Complete this form if you need equipment to be moved by Facilities Management and attach work order.

Submit to: Property Manager's Office - 2428 Boylan

Print Name of ITS Representative	ITS Representative Signature	Date
Alex Rudshteyn		
Print Name and Dept	**Authorized Signature**	**Date Out**
James Liu, IT		
Print Name and Dept	**Authorized Signature**	**Date In**

					FROM			TRANSFERRED TO (including off campus)			MOVE BY FACIL. MGT.		
Item Description	1. Cond.* / 2. Works**	Serial #	Mfr/Model	Res Tag #	Dept. #	Bldg.	Room	Dept. #	Bldg.	Room	Yes (Y) No (N)	For Salvage	For Repair
Standard Projector - VP6121		213D4F56SFD8	HP VP6121	BRO-0043241	Systems	Library	387	AIT	Library	234	N	–	–
Laser Printer - Administration		DNJ45F11	HP LaserJet P1006	BRO-0051284	Systems	Library	387	AIT	Library	234	N	–	–
LCD Monitor - E173FPC		CN-0F5035-64180-533-4WUS	Dell E173FPC	BRO-0042653	Systems	Library	387	AIT	Library	234	N	–	–
Laptop - Faculty-Loan-Mac-1		W80186CDATP	Apple MacBook Pro	BRO 0053157	Systems	Library	387	AIT	Library	234	N	–	–

The Department head must approve all salvage and off campus transactions. The ITS rep must approve all computer salvage and affix a sticker.

Date Work Completed: ________ Facilities Management: ________ Property Manager: ________ Date: ________

* 1. **All equipment to be transferred as surplus or salvage should be classified as (G) Good, F (Fair), P (Poor), or (J) Junk by user. **2. Indicate Y (Yes) or N (No)**

White Copy - Property Management / Green Copy - Security / Yellow Copy - Salvage Office / Pink Copy - Computer Center or other / Gold Copy - User Department

Figure 8. Sample of TIMS produced transfer form

BROOKLYN COLLEGE EQUIPMENT TRANSFER FORM

Instructions: Complete this form to record the transfer of equipment and / or furniture to a new location. Complete this form if you need equipment to be moved by Facilities Management and attach work order.

Submit to: Property Manager's Office - 2428 Boylan

Print Name of ITS Representative	ITS Representative Signature	Date
Alex Rudshteyn		
Print Name and Dept	**Authorized Signature**	**Date Out**
James Liu, IT		
Print Name and Dept	**Authorized Signature**	**Date In**

					FROM			TRANSFERRED TO (including off campus)			MOVE BY FACIL. MGT.		
Item Description	1. Cond.* / 2. Works**	Serial #	Mfr/Model	Res Tag #	Dept. #	Bldg.	Room	Dept. #	Bldg.	Room	Yes (Y) No (N)	For Salvage	For Repair
Standard Projector - VP6121		213D4F56SFD8	HP VP6121	BRO-0043241	Systems	Library	387	AIT	Library	234	No	-	-
Laser printer - Administration		DNJ45F11	HP LaserJet P1006	BRO-0051284	Systems	Library	387	AIT	Library	234	No	-	
LCD monitor - E173FPc		CN-0F5035-64180-533-4WUS	Dell E173FPc	BRO-0042653	Systems	Library	387	AIT	Library	234	No	-	-
Laptop - Faculty-Loan-Mac-1		W80186CDATP	Apple MacBook Pro	BRO-0053157	Systems	Library	387	AIT	Library	234	No	-	-

The Department head must approve all salvage and off campus transactions. The ITS rep must approve all computer salvage and affix a sticker.

Date Work Completed: ________ Facilities Management: ________ Property Manager: ________ Date: ________

* 1. **All equipment to be transferred as surplus or salvage should be classified as (G) Good, F (Fair), P (Poor), or (J) Junk by user. **2. Indicate Y (Yes) or N (No)**

White Copy - Property Management / Green Copy - Security / Yellow Copy - Salvage Office / Pink Copy - Computer Center or other / Gold Copy - User Department

Table 1. The benefits of using The Inventory Management System

Before TIMS	After TIMS
50-plus pages of "non-found" items after an inventory	Automated up-to-date inventory of hardware, software and supplies; email reminders sent when inventory is low
Hundreds of work-hours devoted to reconciling the missing items list; many hours to write and format inventory report	Automated inventory checking; Missing items spreadsheet compared to TIMS database; Report generated showing current location
Handwritten forms led to frequent discrepancies in inventory lists and data entry errors between the library and Office of Internal Audit and Property Management.	Automate inventory tracking to the fullest: Simplified and more efficient process of equipment transfer and elimination of two points of failure (writing a transfer form and entering data into the inventory system); computer generated forms easier to read
Manual tracking of pending hardware, software changes on PC's and Macs; manual tracking of location	Automated computer discovery WMI (Windows Management Instrumentation) for PC's; System Profiler for Mac systems collect data daily and submit to TIMS queue of pending changes (hardware, software, location); Queue processed daily; report sent to system administrator

proper procedures on handling sensitive items established by the Office of Internal Audit and Property Management. TIMS also allows AIT to provide better technical support and monitoring of the manufacturer and the college's life cycle expectations for the equipment.

Laptop Loan, 2009-2010

When the library and AIT were charged with developing and running the laptop loan programs for both faculty and students in 2009, the first step was to determine what program or tool to use to keep track of loaned equipment (its status and available inventory).

In researching the options for managing a laptop loan program, AIT learned that some schools used CUNY's online catalog or a third-party program to handle the laptop loan program. After closely examining each option and finding serious flaws with them, AIT dismissed both. Option one, use of the existing CUNY online catalog program called Aleph, would require cataloging laptops into the system in the same manner as books. While doable, such an option would put an additional burden on the circulation desk staff who already handled book circulation, interlibrary loan book deliveries, group study room reservations, and over the counter public printing distribution. In addition, the circulation staff does not possess the technical expertise AIT expects for the staff responsible for handling the laptop loan program.

Laptops are checked before a loan and after return to make sure the equipment is in working condition. Basic questions about Wi-Fi connectivity and printing have to be answered as well. Another argument against using the catalog (which requires use of the Aleph program) for the loan program was that if a unit other than circulation were responsible, it would require a great deal of training for a program that is not intuitive. All staff members in the responsible unit would need login credentials with similar rights to the circulation desk staff. The library was not ready for this. Almost all part-time staff members are students who sometimes leave after just one semester; such an initiative would require a great deal of user management in the Aleph system, which is primarily handled by the Office of Library Services at CUNY Central. So using the Aleph system to handle the laptop loan programs was dismissed.

Option number two—use of a third-party application—was not promising, either. Not only was AIT unable to find an application which would handle the laptop loan program the way they envisioned, all off-the-shelf solutions required a great deal of learning, management, and configuring to integrate with existing systems. Another sticking point was that such programs maintain their own inventory system. The library already had TIMS, and keeping two inventory systems in parallel would be a bad business practice.

At this point AIT decided to create an application which would be fully integrated into the MyLibrary Suite and work with the existing inventory management program. In 2010 AIT released the first version of the laptop loan program. Laptops for the students are loaned out from the NMC, located on the second floor of the Library building and laptops for the faculty are handled by the Faculty Training and Development Lab.

The laptop loan program (Figure 9) is closely integrated with The Inventory Management Program (TIMS). Such integration allows staff not only quickly to locate any device but also to know its current status (e.g., available, broken, on loan). The program tremendously improved and sped up the process of the physical inventory, which is done at least once a year.

To use the laptop loan program borrowers must provide two pieces of identification, one of which is school ID. Laptop borrowers sign an agreement, which states the user's responsibilities in case of damaged or lost equipment. To simplify and speed up the loan process, AIT enhanced the laptop loan program with the use of an Ambir DS687 Card Scanner and Topaz T-S460 Model Series SigLite 1x5 signature pad. Use of a duplex ID scanner allows the library to simultaneously scan both sides of ID and print its copies on the user agreement for a reference.

Today the laptop loan procedure consists of the following steps:

Figure 9. Laptop loan management screen

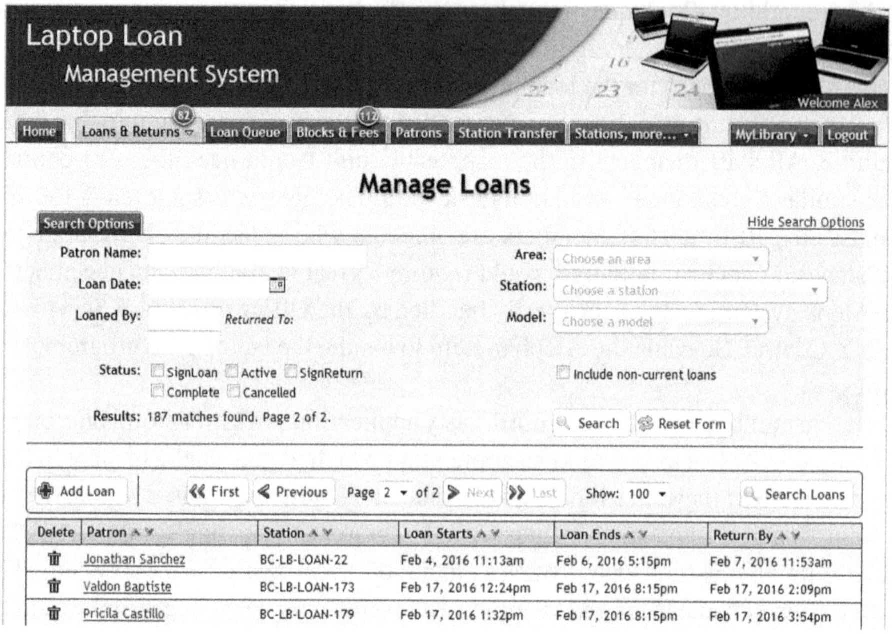

- User comes to the new media center to borrow a laptop (Windows or Mac OS) or iPad.
- Staff member takes a device from storage, turns it on to verify working condition, and uses a handheld barcode reader to scan the inventory tag of the device into the Laptop Loan Program. At this point the equipment status is changed from available to in use. The laptop charger is treated as an accessory and has it own bar code and scanned as an additional item to the laptop.
- User presents two IDs to the staff member.
- Staff member scans two IDs.
- User signs the user agreement.
- Staff member prints receipt and gives it to the user along with a laptop.

Because the Laptop Loan program is integrated into the MyLibrary suite, it uses the Library's calendar program to determine business hours of the library and prints on receipts the due date and time by which equipment has to be returned. When a laptop is returned, its working condition is verified and it is scanned back into the system. At this point, the equipment status is changed to available.

The loan program started with about 29 four-year-old laptops, but quickly gained popularity and now consists of 215 Windows and Apple laptops, plus 5 iPads. The library also loans 85 laptops to Brooklyn College faculty.

Brooklyn College is primarily a commuter school and a majority of students travel to classes. The laptop loan program is a very successful service.

Book Scanner, 2009-Present

After a pilot project with book scanning hardware proved popular with students, but less so with library faculty (due to needing classes on how to use the software on the scanner), AIT considered the possibility of developing its own hardware-independent book scanning software. With commercial book scanners ranging in price from $5500 to $20,000, there was a strong budgetary incentive to come up with a less expensive as well as more user-friendly option. In April 2012, AIT released the first version of the software, which it then modified and improved based on feedback and requests from users. By the summer of 2013, other CUNY campuses (including Lehman College, Baruch College, and John Jay College) had purchased the software, with some requesting functions specific to their campus needs.

The pilot project of using scanners in the library, initiated in 2009, proved to be very successful. The ability to scan various materials to a USB flash drive quickly became popular among the students. Surprisingly, lines started to form to use the scanners during busy times. Library staff also noticed that some users had difficulty using the default scanning software, as it was not intuitive and required a certain level of training. AIT also received numerous requests from librarians for workshops on how to use the standard scanning software.

These factors prompted AIT to consider creating a simple, intuitive program that patrons of the library would find easy to use, although the overall vision was broader. AIT envisioned providing features that commercial scanners were missing. Saving to USB was nice, but the programmers wanted more. Not everyone has a USB flash drive at all times and these flash drives do get lost and run out of memory. AIT wanted to offer multiple ways for patrons to save their scans and more importantly improve ease of use. These were the top priorities when developing book-scanning software in-house.

Using Plustek hardware for the scanners, AIT started the development of the BookScanner software in 2010. Initially it offered patrons an ability to save scans to USB drives, as well as emailing and printing scans directly from the application. While these options proved to be a success, work on further improvements continued. In 2011, AIT introduced a new method for saving scanned documents— online storage. As online storage became more and more popular, the library introduced Google Drive as an option for patrons, and AIT has recently added Dropbox as an additional online storage option.

Another feature designed to appeal to patrons was variety in save formats. PDF is a standard format option for documents, so the software offered it from the start. For those scanning art or other graphics there is a standard image file format—JPEG, which is best for photographs and paintings of smooth variation of color, yet still minimal in file size. AIT also wanted to offer a format that would allow patrons to scan their work into an editable file. This was accomplished by with OCR, or Optical Character Recognition.

The BookScanner was designed for easy maintenance. It comes with a password-protected administrative panel, where all settings are managed from a central location, in an easy-to-use fashion. The BookScanner also collects statistics on the number of scans performed by a particular scanning station along with save formats and save destinations. It is so customizable that other libraries using the software can specify their own logo banner to allow their patrons feel right at home.

By 2016, the library had more than ten new book scanning stations installed throughout the building. To date, Brooklyn College has shared this application in the form of a bundle (Dell Optiplex 9030 AIO Touch and Plustek 4800 Flatbed Color Book Scanner) with more than 17 different libraries, most of which are within CUNY. Some are State University of New York (SUNY) and the rest are privately owned. AIT presented the BookScanner to CUNY's Council of Chief Librarians and CUNY's Systems Librarians in April 2012. As part of the quality control program, AIT loaned the BookScanner bundle to the CUNY Graduate Center Library. It was run side-by-side with a commercial book scanner system (BookScan Station) offered by iVina, Inc.

AIT has received very favorable reviews from end users and continues to work toward improving and enhancing book scanner options, such as the ability to save to Dropbox and the most recent upgrade to the OCR capabilities. Initially offering patrons only a plain text Optical Character Recognition (OCR) of the scans in a form of a text file, user demand for searchable PDF capability at Brooklyn College and from Plustek (who has clients that prefer the AIT software to the Plustek program) led AIT to reexamine the OCR functionality of the BookScanner software. After some research, programmers found a solution that incorporates an open source OCR library, called Tesseract, that will provide users with high quality searchable PDFs. The updated software was released to clients in January 2017.

LESSONS LEARNED AND WISHFUL THINKING

SRMS officially debuted in 2005, well before today's popular library web publishing platforms existed (such as LibGuides and other content management systems).

The parent company of LibGuides—Springshare—was founded in 2007 by Slaven Zivkovic, an ed-tech entrepreneur with a history of library innovations. Zivkovic also worked in libraries—he spent his undergraduate years as a student assistant at his college library. Together with the select group of like-minded "Springys," the crew is creating cutting-edge library web apps and setting new standards for great customer service (SpringShare, n. d.).

Although AIT's pioneering efforts created the right tool at the right time, it has failed to market the tool on a large scale and keep up with its further development and enhancements to meet the ever-growing demands of users. It was and still is very uncommon for a library not only to have its own fully functioning IT group, but to create a product that could be marketable and potentially be sold for a profit. Had AIT, as creators, had more of an entrepreneurial spirit and a College administration with vision and means to provide the unit with necessary financial and staffing support, it would be in the position where the Springshare company is now—offering a great tool to the Library world.

Entrepreneurial efforts were encouraged by Stephanie Walker, Chief Librarian and Executive Director of Academic Information Technologies, with some success (the BookScanner), and sanctioned by the CUNY Office of Technology Commercialization and the Vice President of Finance for Brooklyn College. However, the ability to generate further income through service, improvements and new tools is limited by the size of the staff and the demands of their positions in AIT at Brooklyn College.

Commercialization of tools developed in-house is complicated, and each institution has its own requirements and restrictions, with private schools generally having more freedom to explore the possibilities with regard to profiting from their creations. With public colleges and universities, there are often state and local constraints, and the overall structure of a library, and the relationship of campus IT to that library, determines the ability to produce innovative digital content, applications, and provide additional services.

An example of the constraints can be seen in the development of EZproxy, an outstanding example of an "in-house" solution to a library's service need. Chris Zagar, a community college librarian in Arizona with extensive IT experience, saw a need at his library for simpler access to databases that require user authentication and went to work to create it. Because it was not part of his normal duties, Zagar developed the software on his own time through his company Useful Utilities. The software was soon successful, quickly gaining users such as Harvard, MIT and the State University of New York (SUNY) system, and has a world-wide user community that shares ideas. By early 2008, OCLC had purchased the software, which was in use in over 2200 libraries around the world (Zagar, 2007).

CONCLUSION

Developing in-house digital tools, some of which have been shared or sold to other libraries, has been of great benefit to the Brooklyn College Library in terms of saving money, improving services, and generating some income for the library, but the drive to create the tools was not solely driven by economic necessity. The sometimes-unnecessary complexity (resulting in a sharp learning curve) of commercially available software and lack of sufficient functionality to meet the library's needs were key factors in the decision to create applications in-house. The MyLibrary suite of applications started with a couple of requests from library faculty and staff for a tool that would simplify certain tasks, and along the way has become an integrated suite of applications that enhance the user experience in the library, and makes the daily work of librarians and staff easier and more efficient. AIT learned lessons about staffing and the importance of incorporating the system analysis and design step into all projects. Some projects have been so successful they have been adopted by other campus departments and other libraries, and more tools are in the development stage. Brooklyn College Library and AIT continue to serve as a successful model of partnership between IT professionals and library faculty.

REFERENCES

Bolin, M. (2005). The Library and the Computer Center: Organizational Patterns at Land Grant Universities. *Journal of Academic Librarianship*, *31*(1), 3–11. doi:10.1016/j.acalib.2004.09.004

Gurgov, V. (2016, December). (Personal communication).

Hadro, J. (2008). OCLC Aquires EZProxy. *Library Journal*, *33*(3), 23.

Higginbotham, B. (1997, December) Marriage, Brooklyn Style: How the Library, the Faculty and Administrative Computing Deliver Brooklyn College's Academic Computing Program. *Paper presented at the CAUSE annual conference*, Orlando, FL.

Memorandum from Provost Christopher Kimmich and VP for Administration and Finance Patricia Hassett to Brooklyn College Faculty and Staff. (1994, November 14).

Quinlan, C., & McHarg, H. (2012). The Emerging Library: Structure, Culture, and Lessons Learned from the Dissolution of a Combined Libraries-IT Organization. *Journal of Library Administration*, *52*(2), 147–161. doi:10.1080/01930826.2012.656483

Renfro, P., & Neal, J. (2012). The Integration of Libraries and Academic Computing at Columbia: New Opportunities for Internal and External Collaboration. *Journal of Library Administration*, *52*(1).

SpringShare. (n. d.). About. Retrieved from http://www.springshare.com/about.html

Zagar, C. (2007). Unlocking Library Subscriptions. *Library Journal netConnect.*

ENDNOTES

1 Memorandum from Provost Christopher Kimmich and VP for Administration and Finance Patricia Hassett to Brooklyn College Faculty and Staff, Nov. 14, 1994.

2 Built with a Microsoft Access database, this beta version was called the "Rat Race" in honor of their first-year cadets who are known as "rats." The Source Finder was itself inspired by The Data Genie at California Polytechnic State University, San Luis Obispo. http://www1.vmi.edu/sourcefinder/about.htm

Chapter 8
Developing Unique Study Room Reservation Systems:
Examples From Teachers College and Stony Brook University

Laura Costello
Stony Brook University, USA

Shafeek Fazal
Stony Brook University, USA

ABSTRACT

Room reservation systems are important in an increasingly collaborative library environment. This chapter explores two case studies of libraries experimenting with room-bound, electronic reservation kiosks. Teachers College, Columbia University built a native app to run on room-coded iPads, while Stony Brook University developed custom code to run Steelcase's RoomWizard system in a university environment. This chapter will discuss the particularities and challenges of both systems while addressing the solutions from other libraries discussed in the literature. Room reservation systems are a challenge for libraries of all types and many diverse solutions, from using vendor solutions to creating tools from scratch, have emerged in recent years. This chapter will explore two stories on that spectrum with attention to the potential applications and solutions emerging in this area.

DOI: 10.4018/978-1-5225-2676-6.ch008

INTRODUCTION

Collaborative spaces are an essential part of many academic libraries. Access to technology and growing expectations from patrons have led many libraries to transition from paper-based systems for reserving collaborative group study rooms and other spaces, towards web or mobile reservation systems. There are now many web-based options for libraries, including both open and licensed systems and some of these are affiliated with integrated library systems or other vendor-produced products. These systems must have the ability to conform to each library's specific policies, groups, and specifications, which leads many libraries to create their own customizable reservation systems. This chapter will explore an overview of libraries in the literature creating web and mobile study room reservation systems and focus in on two case studies, from Teachers College, Columbia University and Stony Brook University, of libraries creating and customizing vendor-created room reservation systems for their own requirements.

Most libraries do not have the infrastructure to support the full development of study room reservation systems and onsite display systems, so this chapter will focus on two case studies that have built upon existing software and adapted it to meet the unique needs of the institution. In the case of Teachers College, a native iPad app was built on an open source meeting room booking system and at Stony Brook University, developers made modifications to a vendor-supplied product for booking study rooms.

BACKGROUND

There are several examples of libraries customizing their own web-based reservation systems on top of existing technology using open source software, WordPress Plugins (Smith, 2016), and other tools. There are also examples of libraries taking on this task from scratch with teams of developers and sharing them with the community. Ball State University Libraries built a web system for room booking called OpenRoom (Arthur, Robert, & Bradley, 2010) which later added the capability to book rooms via mobile (Kim, 2013). The Cabell Library at Virginia Commonwealth University also adopted Ball State's OpenRoom (Doherty & White, 2012). Ball State's OpenRoom is a good example of a room reservation technology that was built for a specific library, but was then made open source and adapted to several other libraries. This model represents a good way to mainstream library created technologies to institutions that may not have the infrastructure to support from-scratch development.

These web and mobile systems increase accessibility for patrons reserving rooms in advance, but many room reservation systems also include technologies to benefit the onsite user including electronic displays of events and onsite booking from kiosks or display tablets. This group includes the examples from this chapter's case study, the iPad-based Roomer system from Teachers College and Steelcase's RoomWizard product at Stony Brook University. An example from Tallinn University of Technology Library in Estonia also describes an integrated room reservation system built into an informational kiosk that users could access from onsite (Järs, 2014). Addressing the needs of onsite users is an emerging need in study room reservation systems. Brigham Young University also developed a lower-tech solution to this problem using QR codes linked to specific rooms in the reservation platform so when students scan the code outside the room they are taken to the reservation page for that specific room (Whitchurch, 2012).

There are also examples in the literature of libraries building additional features into their room reservation platforms to enhance user experience. D.H. Hill Library at North Carolina State University created a system called GroupFinder that integrates into their room reservation system (phpScheduleIt) to let groups publicize their locations to other members of the group on the eboards throughout the library and on the GroupFinder site and mobile site (Ryan & Boyer, 2011). Though this system does not allow booking from onsite tablets, it benefits the onsite user by showing them additional information about their reservation and other reservations in the library. Library room reservation systems and the technologies surrounding them are diverse and represent a dynamic market of production that includes vendor-created, open source, and home grown technologies.

CASE STUDY: TEACHERS COLLEGE

Teachers College, Columbia University began planning for an iPad based study room reservation system in 2011. For several years, Teachers College had used the open source Meeting Room Booking System (http://mrbs.sourceforge.net/) for managing web-based reservations. Prior to the project, student workers would print the daily schedule from the Booking System and affix the paper schedule to each study room to facilitate reservations. This process was time and resource-intensive and could not adapt to reservations made after the library opened. The study rooms at Teachers College are unsecured and reservations were generally peer-enforced, but there was no way to create or cancel reservations on the paper schedules after they had been printed, so students had no way to prove that they had reserved rooms same-day or onsite. One of our developers generated a proposal for an iPad-based room reservation systems that would be coded specifically for each room and allow onsite patrons to reserve study spaces while reflecting the current reservations and any last-minute cancellations. This system had the potential to maximize the use of our limited study spaces and facilitate the peer-enforcement that kept the rooms running smoothly. Our students frequently made last-minute reservations and this system would enable them to approach any terminal to see spaces that were available and reserve them on the spot.

A team was created to support the project with a front-end and back-end developer, a librarian project manager, and a designer. This team worked together to build a native iPad app to plug into data from the web-based Meeting Room Booking System. This system was built with the goal of improving the booking experience for the "here and now" patron, onsite users who were looking for open study spaces at the point of need. It also had the benefit of allocating staff resources to other opening tasks and reducing waste from printed paper schedules. The team also crowdsourced the name of the project and, based on feedback, dubbed it "Roomer."

Each iPad must be individually programed to display the room it represents, but our back-end developers built in a system to verify new iPads using both an iPad ID and a room ID so that we would have the flexibility to move and change out the iPads if necessary. The hash signature to verify the new device must include the new ipad key, as well as the ID and room assignment. In order to mount the system to the wall, we purchased metal cases from a company called iPad Wall Bracket (http://www.ipadwallbracket.com/). Recessed wall outlets were installed behind the bracket so the iPads could constantly charge while mounted. The cases are secured with a hex screw and the home screen button is covered so iPad operations can be effectively locked down except for the touch screen-based activity in the Roomer app.

The existing web form shaped the way the Roomer was designed. Users had to authenticate using University credentials to access the web form and we kept that functionality in the iPad format. Due to the location of Teachers College in New York City, unaffiliated walk-ins were a frequent occurrence and it was important to continue to reserve study spaces for student, faculty, and staff use even though this added complexity to the creation of the form. Rooms were automatically sorted in the form by number of participants, so it was important to keep this functionality as well. Teachers College has two large format rooms that can accommodate up to 30 participants, 5 medium sized rooms that can accommodate up to 12 participants, and 5 smaller format rooms for 5 or fewer participants. When users entered the number of participants, the system automatically sorted them into a room based on availability and the size of their party.

User interface was very important to the design and Roomer focuses on the patrons at the point of need. Automatic content scrolling was built into the system so that the current event is always displayed in the default view. Every few seconds, the iPad refreshes to the room it is coded to display and the current date and time. Refresh was also built into the system to ensure that account credentials were protected. Initially, every 10 seconds the system would clear the credentials and return to the default view, but this had to be adjusted after the pilot because initial users frequently took longer than 10 seconds to create their reservations. The team built several new functionalities into Roomer to cater to the point-of-need patron including the ability to view their own future reservations and cancel reservations. Using Roomer, patrons are able to see the future reservations for any specific room as well as toggle between rooms to see their schedules. Patrons can also approach any Roomer terminal to see a full list of available rooms on all floors of the library and book those rooms immediately.

The other important feature added to the Roomer was the ability to request technology to be set up in the room. The Library staff offers setup of projectors, screens, audio, recording, and teleconferencing to users who book at least one day in advance. In the web-based form, booking parties were always shown the options for technology. This system was confusing for users who were simply looking to book space and those who were booking same-day, because the technology would not be available when they arrived. Roomer presents a checkbox for technology on the first page of the dialogue and users are only shown the options for technology if they indicate they might need it in the beginning of their booking and if they are booking one day or more in advance.

The final product in January of 2013 (https://edlab.tc.columbia.edu/blog/8703-Spread-the-News-Roomer-is-Live) with a semester-long pilot room and was pushed out to all study rooms in the summer of 2013. The system is very popular and still in frequent use. Future considerations for the system include a checkout or timeout period to ensure that empty rooms can be recirculated and integrating other content, such as advertising for library events, into the display rotation.

CASE STUDY: STONY BROOK UNIVERSITY

Stony Brook University Libraries got involved with room reservation systems a year ago in 2016. Beginning Fall Semester 2015, the planning stages for a major space renovation project got underway to redesign over 50,000 sq. ft. of space to meet 21st century users' needs for knowledge creation. Design elements for such contemporary learning spaces include access to technology, collaborative engagement, and social interaction spaces. The new space design included 16 technology-enhanced study rooms and given the buzz and anticipated demands for these rooms it became imperative to have some sort of reservation system to facilitate management.

RoomWizard Room Scheduling System

The reservation system in use at Stony Brook University Libraries is RoomWizard from Steelcase. No other systems were considered since Steelcase was selected as the furniture vendor and given budget constraints along with a room reservation system not being a high priority the RoomWizard was a package deal with the media:scape furniture (https://www.steelcase.com/products/collaboration/mediascape/) for the study rooms.

The color touch screen panels were installed at each rooms using Power over Ethernet (PoE) cables and each equipped with dedicated IP addresses to facilitate network access. An administrative console was set up by the Library's programmer to manage all consoles from a single interface. Also, the panel interfaces were redesigned to reflect the University's branding. Using the built-in web server on the RoomWizard, a basic (out of the box) online public facing interface was setup to facilitate web based reservation from any device. Patrons can make reservations both online or in person on the touch screen panel.

Challenges

RoomWizard design is more conducive to a corporate environment, where employees honor each other's reservations, and to a less secured network environment where restricted firewalls and highly secured authentication are not factors to overcome. In Stony Brook's academic environment, serving over 40,000 users, the RoomWizard design lacks essential functionalities and therefore poses many challenges.

Security features on the University's network are of a high caliber and thus the RoomWizard, with minimal embedded firewall security, could not be trusted as a node on the network. As a result all reservation units have to reside privately inside the network. This means online reservations have to be restricted to on campus access only which frustrates users trying to reserve a room from off campus, prior to traveling to campus. In addition, the preferred and more secured method of campus authentication uses shibboleth and the RoomWizard is not compatible with this system. The library programmer had to develop a client based javascript to validate users against LDAP through a secondary workstation. Another issue is the internal system clock does not sync accurately with real time and this causes lots of confusion when patrons show up for their reservations. To correct this the system clock has to be reset manually once a week.

Usage data shows over 47,000 reservations were made since the system was implemented in September, 2016, an average of 6,700 reservations per month. With such high demand for the study rooms the Library had to institute several room use policies to ensure equity in access. The RoomWizard, however, cannot enforce these policies and the Library has to rely on its policy web page to get the message out to users (http://library.stonybrook.edu/research/places-to-study/reserve-a-study-room/). A prime example is the need to impose a 2-hour limit per day on the length of time for reservations for each user, and this is not possible with the out of the box API for RoomWizard. Through some genius coding by the Library's programmer, reservations can now be limited in blocks of maximum 2 hours, however the system cannot restrict the number of reservations to the same user. Therefore, some patrons are reserving rooms for all day with multiple blocks of bookings. Staff have to manually check the system for abusers, deleting the multiple blocks of reservations, and emailing the patrons with a reminder of the policy. Another example of a policy need is for the system to restrict advance registration to a maximum of one week. Fortunately, the programmer was able to code this restriction into the API.

Despite challenges with the system, RoomWizard was a welcome enhancement to the study rooms reservation process, facilitating online and advance reservations. The system, however, is not capable of handling all required functionalities and therefore could not exist as a standalone system. Staff intervention is definitely required, which resulted in the Library using a hybrid automated/manual reservation process. Patrons first make reservations either online or at the touch panel; staff will oversee reservations and "police" abusers as necessary; at the reserved time, patrons will first see staff to check and confirm ID matches reservation; staff will then let patrons into the study room. This process also gives staff the assurance to delete reservations for no-shows after 15 minutes into the reservation, as per policy. This process is not ideal, but has worked fairly well so far.

Looking Ahead

Given the shortcomings of RoomWizard, the Library has dedicated one of its Senior Programmers to investigate solutions to improve functionalities. Alternative reservation systems such as Booked (open source php) and LibCal from Springshare are being investigated for possible use with the existing touch panels. Also, since Stony Brook University is using Google's G Suite, the Google Calendar connector for RoomWizard is being explored to streamline and sync reservations with individual's calendars.

CONCLUSION

The case studies from Teachers College, Columbia University and Stony Brook University demonstrate that the process of developing room reservation systems has both challenges and benefits. In the case of Teachers College, a native iPad app was created to the exact specifications of the institution, but this process required a team of staff developers, designers, and librarians to produce. The infrastructure for creating web and mobile software was already in place and this is not the case in most libraries. Stony Brook University's example built modifications on an existing vendor framework with a smaller team of developers, but is still in the process of adapting this system to meet their unique needs.

We hope that future research will focus on creating better open source resources for libraries and the community to support the modification of those resources. Study room reservation systems are an important part of providing library service to collaborative University practice and as more librarians and developers explore this issue, best practices and solutions will emerge for developing and modifying these products to each institution's unique needs.

REFERENCES

Arthur, W. H., Robert, L. S., & Bradley, D. F. (2010). OpenRoom: Making Room Reservation Easy for Students and Faculty. *Code4Lib Journal,* (10). Retrieved from http://proxy.library.stonybrook.edu/login?url=http://search.ebscohost.com/login.aspx?direct=true&db=edsdoj&AN=edsdoj.f03e86ee6ca54827a209798ccb3ba7e4&site=eds-live&scope=site

Doherty, M. T., & White, E. R. (2012). Room reservations at VCU Libraries How we coped with rapid growth and overwhelming demand for student study space. *College & Research Libraries News*, *73*(3), 142–146. Retrieved from http://proxy.library.stonybrook.edu/login?url=http://search.ebscohost.com/login.aspx?direct=true&db=edselc&AN=edselc.2-52.0-84859732064&site=eds-live&scope=site

Järs, J. (2014). IT-based solutions for users and library staff: case study of the Tallinn University of Technology Library. In *Proceedings of the IATUL Annual Conference* (Vol. 35, pp. 1-5). Retrieved from http://proxy.library.stonybrook.edu/login?url=http://search.ebscohost.com/login.aspx?direct=true&db=lih&AN=97787043&site=eds-live&scope=site

Kim, B. (2013). The Present and Future of the Library Mobile Experience. *Library Technology Reports*, *49*(6), 15. Retrieved from http://proxy.library.stonybrook.edu/login?url=http://search.ebscohost.com/login.aspx?direct=true&db=f5h&AN=90405355&site=eds-live&scope=site

Ryan, J., & Boyer, J. (2011). GroupFinder: A Hyper-Local Group Study Coordination System. *Code4Lib Journal,* (13). Retrieved from http://proxy.library.stonybrook.edu/login?url=http://search.ebscohost.com/login.aspx?direct=true&db=edsdoj&AN=edsdoj.55dd1303be374518a28b212d8abd952e&site=eds-live&scope=site

Smith, B. R. (2016). Book-a-Room Software.

Whitchurch, M. J. (2012). A quick response: QR code use at the Harold B. Lee Library. *The Reference Librarian, 53*(4), 392–402. doi:10.1080/02763877.2012.704573

KEY TERMS AND DEFINITIONS

GroupFinder: (https://www.lib.ncsu.edu/reports/groupfinder): The onsite display developed by North Carolina State University to help students find their group in the library.

Meeting Room Booking System: (http://mrbs.sourceforge.net/): An open source room reservation platform which was used as the scheduling platform for the Roomer iPad App.

OpenRoom: (https://www.bsu.edu/libraries/getopenroom/): The open source meeting room booking system developed by Ball State University.

RoomWizard: (https://www.steelcase.com/products/scheduling-systems/roomwizard/): A meeting room booking system developed by the furniture company, Steelcase. This is the system that Stony Brook University adapted for its study rooms.

Roomer: The room reservation system developed by Teachers College, Columbia University.

Chapter 9
If You Build It, They Will Come:
Creating a Library Statistics Dashboard for Decision-Making

Laura M Horne-Popp
University of Central Missouri, USA

Elisabeth Bliese Tessone
University of Central Missouri, USA

Joshua Welker
University of Central Missouri, USA

ABSTRACT

Like many academic libraries throughout the United States, the James C. Kirkpatrick Library at the University of Central Missouri has increasingly documented its impact on the university and its students. A library statistics dashboard tool was developed internally to assist with increased assessment activities. The Information Technology Librarian and the Library Assessment Team collaborated to create the dashboard tool. This case study discusses the impetus for developing the tool and provides a detailed explanation of the creation and testing of the dashboard. The chapter also describes the outcomes of using the dashboard tool in the library's assessment activities, along with recommendations for how other libraries may develop similar tools and skills within their organizations.

DOI: 10.4018/978-1-5225-2676-6.ch009

INTRODUCTION

Cultures of assessment have been growing within American universities and academic libraries over the last 20 years. Interest in assessment has expanded since the Great Recession of 2008, due to limited state and university budgets. Many states began implementing specific performance indicators required for universities to obtain funding, shifting the focus from the number of students enrolled to student-focused goals, such as graduation rates and employment rates after graduation (National Conference of State Legislatures, 2015). As university budgets become more constrained, academic libraries must demonstrate their value to their larger organizations, using a variety of methods that include expressing measurable impact on student and faculty success in both quantitative and qualitative terms (Hernon, Dugan & Matthews, 2015; Oakleaf, 2010).

The James C. Kirkpatrick Library (JCKL) at the University of Central Missouri (UCM) faced the same increased levels of accountability that many academic libraries across the United States must satisfy. To demonstrate library impact, JCKL created a Library Statistics Dashboard that collected and visualized various library data, and allowed entering and visualizing data in one place. JCKL also used Application Program Interfaces (APIs) to pull data from different resources into the Library Statistics Dashboard. This dashboard enabled JCKL to maintain its assessment data and show administrators that the library had direct and positive value for college students.

Many academic librarians have felt that they lack the skills or resources necessary to build such a tool internally. However, building a tool such as a library statistics dashboard within a library organization is both doable and worth doing. This case study will show how a team at JCKL internally created a data dashboard. The authors will describe the impetus for developing a statistics dashboard, technological details of how it was built, the outcomes of using the dashboard, and recommendations for how a library organization can support an environment for developing internal tools.

BACKGROUND

The University of Central Missouri (UCM) is a master's-level public university situated in Warrensburg, Missouri, 50 miles east of Kansas City. Like many universities across the United States, UCM has had to increasingly demonstrate its value to students, parents, and the state. In 2015, UCM implemented a new performance-based funding model, known as the Strategic Resource Allocation Model (SRAM), which emphasized outcomes-based budgeting (University of Central Missouri, n. d.). The university appointed a cross section of university administrators, faculty, and staff to determine a more robust budgeting process. The Assistant Dean of Library Services, charged with library assessment, participated in the university's SRAM project. This newly developed funding model acknowledged three major trends: tightened state funding, tuition-increase caps, and demonstration of improved university performance.

Meeting Campus Expectations

The SRAM plan focused the university budget on meeting 16 key performance indicators (KPIs) (University of Central Missouri, n. d.). Five of these KPIs included performance indicators the state of Missouri required for institutions to receive additional funding (Missouri Department of Higher Education, 2012; University of Central Missouri, n. d.). UCM required all academic units to support appropriate KPIs, and develop goals to ensure that the university met these indicators within a three-year period. As a campus support unit, the library was allowed to select which KPIs it would directly impact. The Assistant Dean of Library Services coordinated the selection process. These duties included communication with library employees on the changing budget structure, and pulling together library statistics, benchmarking data, and usability studies to aid in choosing applicable KPIs.

Meeting Library Administration Expectations

During the implementation of the SRAM process, the university hired a new Dean of Library Services. The new dean instilled throughout the library organization an emphasis on evidence-based decision-making. This meant using some sort of data to justify decisions regarding library services, building hours, staffing, and collections. Upon the new dean's arrival, the Assistant Dean of Library Services and the Library Assessment Assistant (hereafter known as the Assessment Team) routinely met with her to present assessment data. This enabled the new dean to quickly learn the daily operations of JCKL, and to determine first priorities for short-term and long-term planning.

The library dean's need for and expectation of timely data drastically increased the amount of data created and analyzed within the library. The Assessment Team regularly produced statistics and reports for library administration. However, the new dean's increased requests for data challenged the team's ability to develop analysis and reports in a timely fashion. The team quickly realized their current method of using Excel spreadsheets to store library data and produce reports was not sustainable. They sought advice from the Information Technology Librarian, regarding data tools and more complex ways of structuring data to produce timely, accurate, and meaningful analysis for library administration. The Information

Technology Librarian recommended the creation of a library statistics dashboard to streamline the workflow. Built within the library organization, the dashboard would handle data entry and visualization to meet internal operational needs and demonstrate library impact on applicable KPIs.

LITERATURE REVIEW

Academic Library Assessment

Assessment of academic libraries increases as the need to provide evidence of impact grows. Library assessment is the study and evaluation of library space, services, collections and instruction as it relates to supporting users' needs. It covers an extremely broad range of activities including measuring the size and utility of physical and electronic materials, measuring library processes for efficiency, capturing usage patterns of library services and spaces, determining the library's impact on student success (learning outcomes, retention, graduation) and impact on research output and faculty success (Matthews, 2011; Matthews, 2015).

Assessment within a library rarely covers all potential aspects of library assessment previously noted; rather, libraries tend to focus on categories that reflect the values of the university. Matthews (2011) argues that the lack of agreed upon library objectives also contributes to the wide range of assessment activities. Library assessment approaches are also varied due to the evolution in how libraries have documented their import. Town (2011) categorized theses phases into three categories of value – library as storehouse, library as service and library as education. Heath (2011) provided a brief history of library assessment. He noted libraries initially focused on the size and contents of collections in the 1920s. In the 1930s, libraries began counting information on expenditures, staffing, and other quantifiable data points, many still captured today in the annual ACRL survey. Additional development happened in the 1990s, when librarians collected more qualitative data to understand how users saw the value of their academic libraries. This included local surveys and using the ARL LibQual survey that allowed libraries to compare the perceptions of their local users against a national average of research library users.

In the 2000s, assessment shifted again to include how libraries impact the research and educational endeavors of their universities. Tenopir (2010) researched how academic libraries provide return on investment (ROI) in faculty productivity. A number of studies have measured library impact on college students including student learning outcomes, student retention and graduation rates with mixed results (Mezick, 2007; Emmons & Wilkinson, 2011; Cooke & Rosenthal, 2011; Oakleaf, 2011; Schwieder & Hinchcliffe, 2012). During the same time period, there were several major ethnographic studies of how students use libraries and do research, done at the University of Rochester and participating libraries in the Ethnographic Research in Illinois Academic Libraries (ERIAL) Project (Foster & Gibbons, 2007; Asher, Miller & Green, 2012). These studies have helped develop student-centered library space and services to support student success.

As mentioned previously, libraries tend to focus their assessment to match the values of their parent institutions. UCM has a student-centered philosophy that emphasizes deep engagement in learning and strong interaction between students and faculty. Therefore, JCKL centered much of the library assessment activities around library impact on students. Even with a specialized assessment focus, there were still a large number of student-oriented assessment data points for JCKL to collect. A data dashboard tool enabled the Assessment Team to manage the hefty amount of data it needed to share with library and campus administrators.

Data Dashboards

Data dashboards gained popularity in the 1980s and 1990s, as businesses needed more data, and tools began to handle larger data sets (Few, 2006). Historically, the primary users of data dashboards were administrators; interestingly, this trend has continued (Few, 2006; Hernon et al., 2015; Matthews, 2011). Therefore, whether intentionally or not, dashboards acquired an administrator audience, and were often only available to senior management in an organization (Matthews, 2011). Few (2006) stated that first and foremost, dashboards are meant to be forms of communication. He defined a dashboard as a "visual display of the most important information needed to achieve one or more objectives; consolidated and arranged on a single screen so the information can be monitored at a glance" (p. 34). Few's definition of a dashboard reinforced the power of such a display to meet the purpose of graphical information. Tufte (1983) discussed the need for graphics to present a large amount of information in a small space. Tufte's point dovetailed with Few's requirement for arranging dashboard graphics in a consolidated manner. Morton-Owens and Hanson (2012) pointed out that a dashboard should also be simple and intuitive in its visualization. The user of a dashboard should readily understand what it conveys, without "reading too much text" or spending too much time figuring out what a graphic embodies (p.38). Morton-Owens and Hanson reminded tool builders that dashboards support analysis as well as communication. They stated that a dashboard enabled "closer scrutiny of trends in library use, ideally resulting in a more agile response to problems and opportunities" (p. 36). While dashboards were communication tools, they were also meant to aid decision-making.

BUILDING AN INTERNAL LIBRARY STATISTICS DASHBOARD

Once it was clear that a statistics dashboard tool was well suited to JCKL's assessment needs, the Assessment Team and the Information Technology Librarian (hereafter the Dashboard Team) worked to build a meaningful tool. They first determined the scope of the dashboard, considering a number of data sets for inclusion. The team decided to make the dashboard support the student-centered culture of the UCM campus. Therefore, they curated the tool to focus on statistics that demonstrated how students used the library, how the library impacted students, and how JCKL met selected campus KPIs.

The Dashboard Team compared locally gathered data and the literature on college-student library behaviors to determine what statistics went into the dashboard. College students considered library space the most important feature for them, as it aided studying and work (Applegate, 2009; de Jager, 2015; Gardner & Eng, 2005; Mizrachi, 2010). Analysis done by Schwieder and Hinchliffe (2012) demonstrated that the number of hours a library is open affected both student retention and graduation rates. Therefore, the Dashboard Team included the JCKL hourly headcount data and study-room usage data, to capture the time students spent in the building. The literature also showed that students made heavy use of library computers (de Jager, 2015; Mizrachi, 2010). This pattern also occurred at JCKL, so the team added data on computer usage.

Brief Background on Local In-House Development

Having determined the scope and initial content of the dashboard, developing a tool to analyze these data sets was a large undertaking. The Information Technology Librarian drew on previous programming knowledge to begin the dashboard design process. A change in position responsibilities occurred, due to migrating all of the library's in-house systems (such as EZproxy, ILLiad, DSpace, and the web server) to the campus IT department. This afforded the Information Technology Librarian the time and workload to undertake additional programming projects.

The first major project was a library website redesign. During this project, the Information Technology Librarian decided to base the website on some sort of dynamic web platform that would allow for complex, database-driven features. The librarian chose the Ruby on Rails framework for its flexibility, robust community, and excellent documentation, anticipating that Ruby on Rails could also work for other web-based projects in the future. About two years after implementing the new Rails-based library website, the need for a library-data dashboard arose. This was one of the projects the Information Technology Librarian initially imagined Rails handling.

Exploring Commercial Dashboard Solutions

Building a dashboard was a large project, and it was deemed prudent to explore third-party solutions before committing to in-house development. The third-party options were divided into all-in-one solutions and hybrid solutions.

All-in-one solutions were those that a vendor managed entirely, in terms of both data storage and reporting. Many all-in-one dashboard solutions, such as JasperSoft, were sold under the label of business intelligence tools, targeting enterprise markets. Academic libraries could not afford most of these products. The exception was Springshare's reasonably priced LibInsight platform. However, running a trial of LibInsight demonstrated that the platform was still too much in its infancy to meet JCKL's needs.

Hybrid solutions were considered next, because of much lower pricing and a high degree of flexibility. These tools are typically cloud-based web applications that contain a fully-featured front-end dashboard for analyzing data, but do not store the underlying data. In order to connect the hybrid solution to the data, the Information Technology Librarian would have to develop an internal database, data-entry methods, and a set of APIs. The amount of work required to use a hybrid solution was the same as building the tool in-house with Rails, but Rails had more flexibility. Rails also had the benefit of keeping the dashboard and the underlying data in a single application, resulting in a simpler structure. Therefore, Rails was chosen for building a custom in-house dashboard solution that handled all data-related functionality: data entry, data storage, and data analysis.

Setting Up the Rails Application

Since the dashboard would be built on top of the library's existing Ruby on Rails application, much of the initial groundwork was already complete when the dashboard project began. A brief account of the setup of the web server and Rails application precedes discussing the development of the dashboard.

Setting Up the Server

JCKL had retired all its in-house servers several years prior; the best option for a new server was to host the Rails application in the cloud—in this case, a Linux-based server, because Rails had difficulty in a Windows server environment. Creating and activating the server was fairly easy using the Linode cloud hosting platform. The complex part was configuring the server.

First, an Apache web server was installed using Ubuntu's software manager. Ruby was installed using RVM (Ruby Version Manager). Rails was installed using Gem,

Ruby's package management system. Phusion Passenger, an extension for Apache that allows Apache to run Rails applications, was installed. The MySQL server and database were installed to allow the Rails application to store data. Firewall rules were established to secure the server. Finally, a new Rails application was created using command line tools, and configured to connect to the MySQL database.

Developing the Rails Application

Initially, the Rails application consisted of a simple welcome page. Functionality within Rails required the creation of a development environment. This allowed the Information Technology Librarian to write and test code before publishing it to the server. The Information Technology Librarian created a development copy of the Rails application, which lived on a JCKL computer and used Atom text editor to write code.

There are three main components to a Rails application: models, controllers, and views. This is a common design pattern referred to as MVC (Figure 1). Models map application code to a database, with one model class per database table. The models provided a simplified way for the application to interact with the database without worrying about details like SQL queries and database connections. Controllers connect the models to views and handle URL routing. Controllers consist of actions

Figure 1. Ruby on Rails application diagram
(JCKL, 2016)

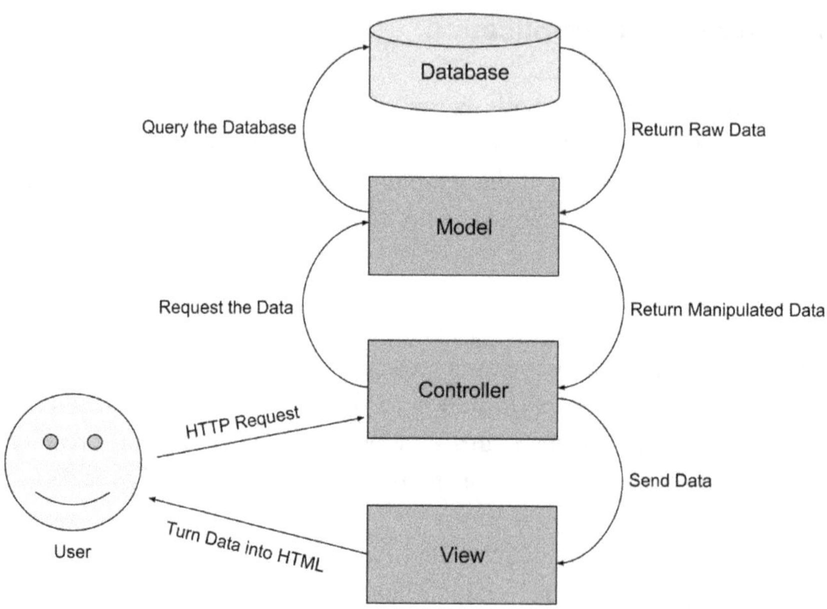

and an action typically initializes one or more models to hand off to a view. Views are the part of Rails that end users see, typically consisting of HTML code. Views typically do not contain complex code. Instead, they take data from models and controllers, and rearrange them into a user interface.

After learning the basics of Rails development, the Information Technology Librarian easily added new functionality to the library website. Features implemented early on included a database A-Z page, a library-hours display, a new-books feed, and a handful of complex forms. The new dashboard project was built using the same Rails architecture.

Developing a Dashboard In-House

With the Rails application already in place, the Dashboard Team needed to decide which data sets to include initially. Based on the most heavily used and most readily available data sets, the team identified three initial dashboard components: headcount data, study-room usage data, and computer usage data. These data sets were all very different and needed unique analysis. As a result, three separate components were added to the Rails application.

Headcount Data

Headcount data, deemed the most important data for initial inclusion based on its influence on decisions regarding building operations, provided a starting point for the dashboard project. The first task was to conceptualize the data and the dashboard, in terms of the MVC design pattern employed by Rails.

Historically, headcount data files were designed to make data entry easy. The form, designed in Excel, was not remotely machine-readable (Figure 2). Entering data was easy, but analyzing the data, especially over large time periods, was laborious. Even simple Excel functions like finding an average were time-consuming.

The data model required redesign from the ground up. In the new model, each headcount record had four basic components: a primary key, a building-location number, a time, and a headcount number (Figure 3). An SQL table with these four fields was created and mapped to a Rails model class. Structuring the headcount data this way enabled the use of SQL queries to automatically aggregate the data and perform mathematical operations.

The first challenge to the headcount dashboard was that the simple SQL structure was not conducive to ongoing data entry. The Dashboard Team solved this challenge by designing a human-readable data entry layer in the dashboard (Figure 4). A method added to the headcount model in Rails queried the database for all headcount data, across all locations for a single day. It sorted the data into a cross-tabular format,

Figure 2. JCKL's old headcount spreadsheets (JCKL, 2016)

3rd Floor Headcount Sheet — Monday 1-Oct

TIME	Center Carrels	North End	South End	West Side	Silent Room	Total
8:00	1			3		4
9:00	1	1		7		9
10:00	1	1	1	12		15
11:00		2	2	20		24
12:00		3	2	20		25
1:00	2	3	2	24		31
2:00	2	4	2	27		35
3:00	4	4	3	33		44
4:00	4	2	3	37		46
5:00	5	3	3	34		45
6:00	3	3	4	31		41
7:00	3	2	3	27		35
8:00	3	2	1	30		36
9:00	2	1	1	26		30
10:00	2	1	2	21		26
11:00	2	1	2	12		17
Total	35	33	31	364	0	463 463

3rd Floor Headcount Sheet — Monday 8-Oct

TIME	Center Carrels	North End	South End	West Side	Silent Room	Total
8:00	1			4		5
9:00	1			7		8
10:00	1			12		13
11:00	3		1	17		21
12:00	6		5	29		40
1:00	4	1	2	25		32
2:00	4	2	3	33		42
3:00	5	3	4	38		50
4:00	6	4	4	42		56
5:00	5	4	5	47		61
6:00	4	3	3	39		49
7:00	4	3	2	33		42
8:00	4	3	2	32		41
9:00	3	2	2	30		37
10:00	2	4	4	29		39
11:00	2	2	4	19		27
Total	55	31	41	436	0	563 563

3rd Floor Headcount Sheet — Monday 15-Oct

TIME	Center Carrels	North End	South End	West Side	Silent Room	Total
8:00	2	2		3		7
9:00	2	2		4		8
10:00	2	3	2	12		19
11:00	1	4	2	17		24
12:00	2	6	7	37	1	53
1:00	2	6	4	35	1	48
2:00	2	6		33		41
3:00	2	5		36		43
4:00	1	3	1	24		29
5:00	1	1	1	25		28
6:00	2	1	1	24		28
7:00	2	1	1	22		26
8:00	3	2	2	23		30
9:00	2	2	2	21		27
10:00	2	1	2	17		22
11:00	1	1	1	12		15
Total	29	46	26	345	2	448 448

3rd Floor Headcount Sheet — Tues 2-Oct

TIME	Center Carrels	North End	South End	West Side	Silent Room	Total
8:00				3		3
9:00	1	2	3	9		15
10:00	3	2	3	15		23
11:00	3	2	3	18		26
12:00	2	2	4	20		28
1:00	3	3	1	22		29
2:00	3	3	1	24		31

3rd Floor Headcount Sheet — Tues 9-Oct

TIME	Center Carrels	North End	South End	West Side	Silent Room	Total
8:00	1			2		3
9:00	3		1	4		8
10:00	2	1	1	9		13
11:00	2	2	6	20		30
12:00	2	2	7	24		35
1:00	3	1	6	26		36
2:00	3	1	6	26		36

3rd Floor Headcount Sheet — Tues 16-Oct

TIME	Center Carrels	North End	South End	West Side	Silent Room	Total
8:00				3		3
9:00	1	2		4		7
10:00	3	2	1	12		18
11:00	3	2	2	17		24
12:00	1	2	5	26		34
1:00		3	1	34		38
2:00	3	2	3	35		43

Figure 3. New headcount SQL table structure (JCKL)

id	location_id	headcount	count_time
14419	24	26	2014-09-17 17:00:00
14420	25	17	2014-09-17 17:00:00
14421	10	3	2014-09-17 17:00:00
14422	14	44	2014-09-17 17:00:00
14423	2	20	2014-09-17 17:00:00
14424	3	4	2014-09-17 18:00:00
14425	4	4	2014-09-17 18:00:00

showing headcount data for each location and each hour of the given day. The Rails view embedded the data into a table-based HTML form. Similar logic was added to transform the cross-tabular data back into the SQL data structure (Figure 5).

After handling data entry, the next task was to create the analytical layer using the tool Highcharts. Highcharts is a JavaScript library that automatically generates a graph from a data set and graph options. Similar to Excel, Highcharts requires series-based data. The x-axis values must be specified first, enabling any number of data sets containing y values to be specified separately, to correspond to each point on the x-axis. In terms of a line graph, each series is a line.

Figure 4. Headcount data entry form
(JCKL, 2016)

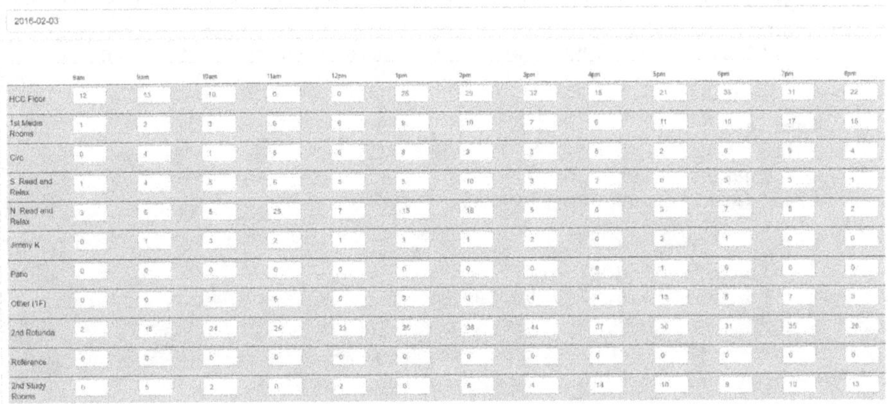

Figure 5. Headcount architecture diagram
(JCKL, 2016)

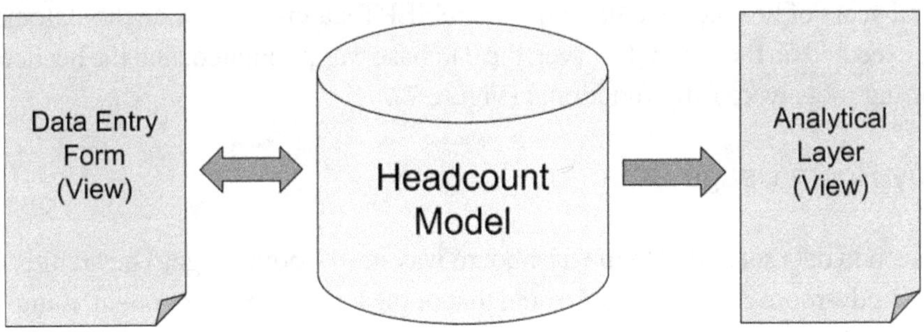

The SQL-based data required some tweaking to fit the Highcharts data structure. Another method added to the Rails headcount model accepted parameters like start date, end date, and means of grouping locations. The method generated an SQL query based on these parameters, read the data, and transformed it into a series-based data structure (Figure 6).

There was no straight path to pass the data from Rails (a server-side framework) to Highcharts (a client-side library). JavaScript Object Notation (JSON) was used as a crosswalk. JSON is a text-based data format that Rails can produce and Highcharts can read. The Rails headcount view rendered an HTML form into which the user entered a date range and other parameters. The form's submission triggered JavaScript code that requested the JSON data from the Rails application on server, and plugged it into Highcharts.

Figure 6. Series-based headcount data for Highcharts (JCKL, 2016)

```
"xAxis": {
  "categories": [
    "2016-09-01", "2016-09-02", "2016-09-03", "2016-09-04"
  ]
},
"series": [
  {
    "name": "1st Floor",
    "data": [267,300,290,235]
  },
  {
    "name": "2nd Floor",
    "data": [540,871,796,394]
  }
]
```

After building the data entry form and the analysis features, all that remained was to import the old Excel files. The Information Technology Librarian used a combination of Ruby scripts and manual data manipulation in Excel to convert several years of headcount data into SQL INSERT statements. Once the statements were executed on the MySQL server, the database was populated, and the headcount reporting tools were fully functional (Figure 7).

Study-Room Usage Data

The second data set added to the dashboard was study-room usage. The architecture of the study-room component mirrored that of the headcount component, minus the data entry form. Instead, study-room booking data was exported from Springshare's LibCal platform at regular intervals. A Ruby script was written to transform the exported LibCal data into a series of SQL INSERT statements. These statements

Figure 7. A headcount data report broken down by day and floor (JCKL, 2016)

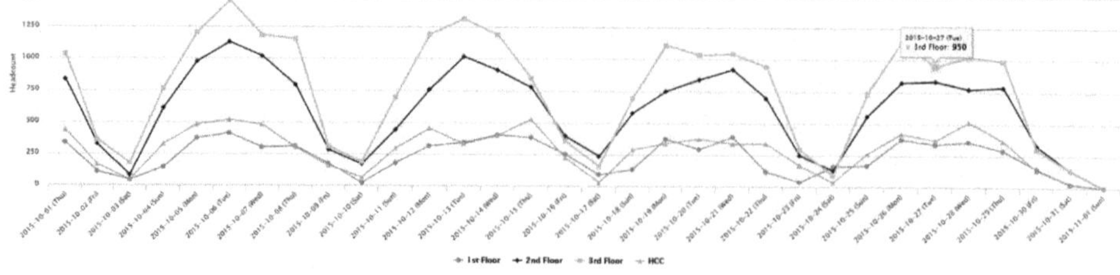

were executed on the MySQL server, in order to add them into a study-room booking table, the Rails application was used.

Library administration wanted to know the percentage of time that study rooms were booked. A new library hour database table was created, with a record for each day that included 24 fields for storing the number of minutes the library was open each hour. Another field was added for storing the total number of minutes the library was open over the course of a whole day. A scheduled script was created that queried LibCal for each date's library operating hours, and stored them in the database table. The script calculated and stored the number of minutes the library was open for each hour and for the whole day.

With the hour table in place, calculating a booking percentage was just a matter of division. The application queried all the study-room booking data during a time period, and summed the total number of minutes that rooms were booked. It then queried the database to find the total number of minutes the library was open during that same time period. The total number of minutes booked was divided by the total number of minutes open, and multiplied by 100 to calculate the booking percentage. The dashboard generated a graph showing the booking percentage used per day (Figure 8).

Computer Usage Data

Due to high student usage of library computers, the Dashboard Team designed a third component to visualize computer usage. This component differed from the previous two in both structure and visualization. The goal was to display the usage data as a heatmap. A map of the library and all its computers was color-coded to show how heavily the computers were used during a given time period.

The first step was to design a data structure. The basic data unit was a computer session, and the basic metric was the length of the session. Each session was tied to a particular computer, and each computer had a specific location on the heatmap.

Figure 8. A study room booking percentage report (JCKL, 2016)

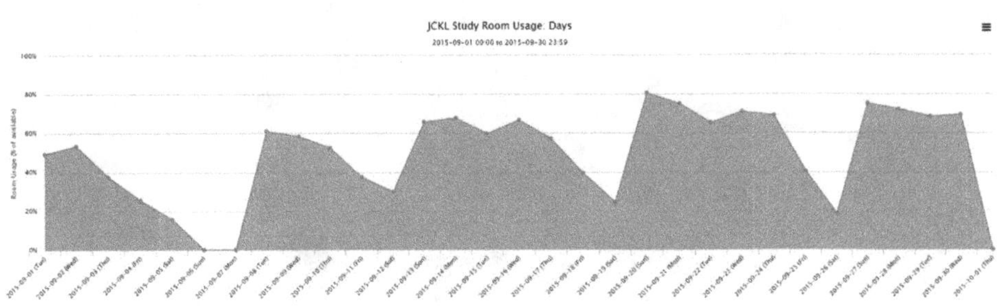

Two SQL tables were developed, one for computers and another for sessions. To collect the data, a startup script was added to all library computers. While a user was logged into a computer, the script pinged the Rails application once each minute, using an API. Rails collected the hostname and IP address of the computer, and created a session record. Each subsequent time the computer pinged the application updated a timestamp. The length of time between pings identified a new session. Subtracting the session start time from the session end time calculated the duration of the session.

Data visualization functionality consisted of a vector-based SVG map. The map showed the library floorplan, and each computer on the floor received a unique identifier corresponding to the computer table in the SQL database. Options at the top of the page allowed users to specify a time range and location parameters. The user's browser made a JavaScript request to the Rails server, which converted session data to a JSON format. Using the Chroma JavaScript library, the total use time for each computer was converted into a hexadecimal color value, scaled from black (lowest use) to red (highest use). The hexadecimal value was passed to the Snap SVG JavaScript library, which changed the color of the computer on the map (Figure 9).

The current architecture ties a computer's IP address to its physical location. If a computer is relocated in the library, the heatmap does not know anything about its previous locations. This is problematic because the main goal of the heatmap is to show how the computer's physical location affects its usage. The Information Technology Librarian is exploring ways to encode time ranges into the SVG map to make clearer which physical locations in the building receive the most computer usage.

Figure 9. A computer usage heatmap
(JCKL, 2016)

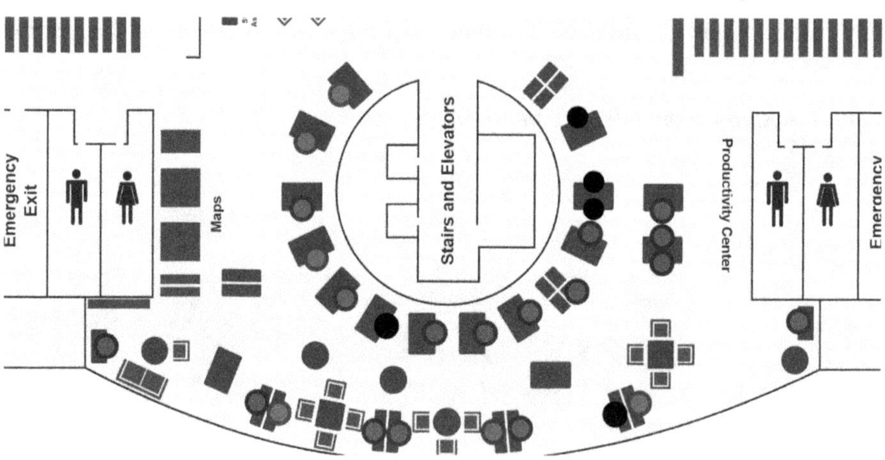

Putting It All Together

With the first three dashboard components constructed, the last step was to make them accessible to users. A dashboard landing page containing links to all the individual components contained smaller versions of the headcount and study room graphs (https://library.ucmo.edu/stats/dashboard). A time-range filter at the top of the page let users customize the time period for both graphs at once. Since the two components had such different filter parameters, all other filtering options were omitted. The graphs used default parameters and displayed data for the last 90 days (Figure 10).

The landing page was designed specifically for external stakeholders. Staff in the library had visualization preferences based on their relationships with the data, and needed advanced filtering options. Conversely, the landing page showed only the most important data sets, and used them to construct a brief visual story of recent happenings at the library. As more dashboard components are included in the future, those that tell the most powerful stories will be added to the landing page.

Squashing Bugs

After the initial three components and landing page were designed, the dashboard was published to the library's live production server. The Information Technology Librarian used simple FTP file transfer to move the Rails application files between the development and production servers. The limitations of FTP showed themselves quickly. The Rails application consisted of many modules that were often developed and modified in tandem. Many times, code in one module was finished, but another module was incomplete and buggy. It was difficult to remember which files were

Figure 10. JCKL statistics dashboard landing page (JCKL, 2016)

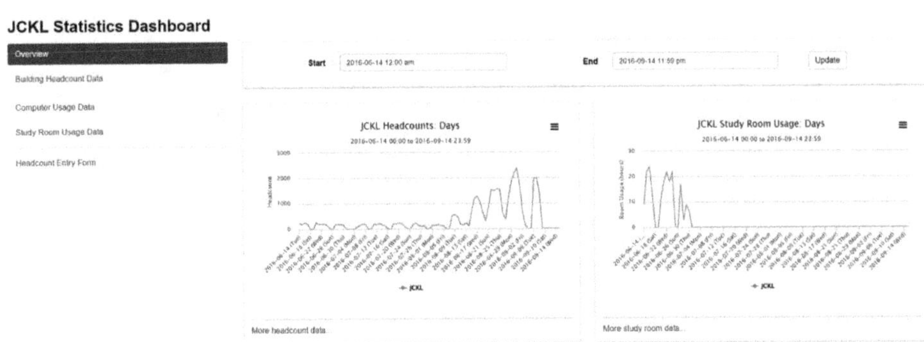

ready to publish and which were still in development, and bugs often appeared across the website.

To solve these problems, the Information Technology Librarian implemented Git, a software versioning system for tracking code changes. Git tracked and published code changes at a very granular level. Git used a branching system that isolated changes from one another and prevented publishing buggy code. The librarian created an online Git repository for the Rails application at BitBucket (https://bitbucket.org/ucm-jckl/jckl-website-public-version). Code was developed on a local PC and was pushed to the online repository using a graphical Git client called GitKraken. The production server used Git commands to publish specific updates. In the event that buggy code existed, Git commands rolled back the live application to an earlier working version. Git retained a complete history of all development in the repository and made it possible to see exactly where and when a bug appeared.

Git became an invaluable part of the development workflow. As development continued, a clear picture of the development workflow began to emerge. Figure 11 demonstrates a diagram of the entire development workflow and software tooling.

Figure 11. Development workflow and tools

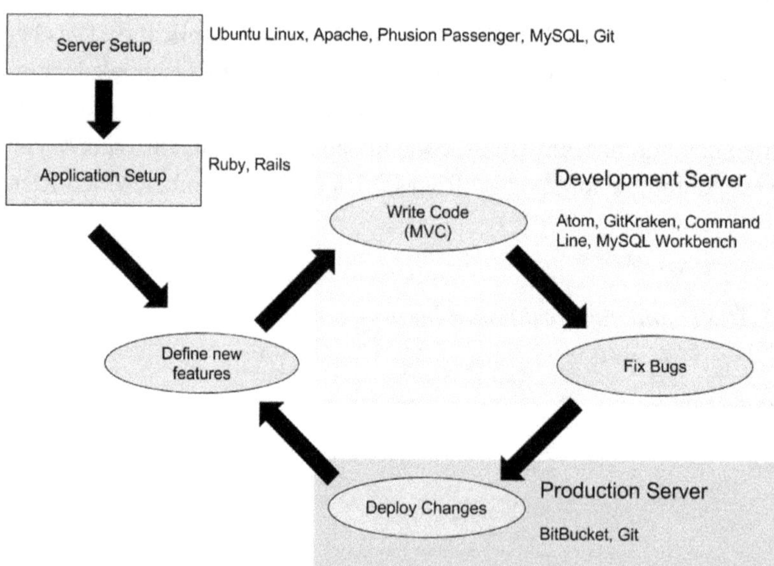

Future of the Dashboard

Libraries have no shortage of data, and there are several candidates for inclusion in the dashboard. Circulation, interlibrary loan, COUNTER e-resources, student printing, reference transactions, instruction, and research consultation data are all possibilities that the existing architecture could accommodate easily. Given the initial time investment in constructing a dashboard component, the Assessment Team must prioritize the most important data based on how frequently the data are used internally and how the data relate to JCKL's KPIs.

Internal audiences use circulation data heavily, mostly for collection development purposes. JCKL uses III's Sierra ILS, which has few built-in statistical tools for analyzing collection usage over time. Sierra's database stores circulation transactions (checkouts, checkins, renewals, and use counts) for only a few weeks. Sierra stores year-to-date and lifetime circulation data in individual item records. It is impossible to tell whether an item was used two years ago or twenty years ago. As a workaround, the Information Technology Librarian set up a MySQL database table for storing circulation transactions. A scheduled task in the Rails application runs each morning, connects to Sierra's PostgreSQL server, and queries all the previous day's circulation transactions. The transactions are saved to the MySQL database, where they can be kept permanently without fear of deletion. Since the data are already in the Rails application's database, all that remains is to design the analytical layer.

Another candidate for inclusion is printing data. Literature showed college students highly value the availability of computer services like printing (de Jager, 2015; Mizrachi, 2010). JCKL recently implemented WEPA, a cloud-based printing platform for students. The Assessment Team is interested in measuring how WEPA impacts student printing, and monitoring usage patterns to improve the student experience. Useful metrics include time of printing, number of pages printed, file-upload method, and whether color was used. An SQL table can easily accommodate these metrics.

Statistics on instruction, research consultations, and reference transactions are increasingly valuable. They are useful for both developing information literacy programs and demonstrating commitment to appropriate campus KPIs. Dashboard components are planned for traditional library metrics like reference transactions and instruction counts. Literature showed that information literacy instruction improved student work, and impacted student retention and graduation rates (Cooke & Rosenthal, 2011; Schwieder & Hinchliffe, 2012), making it an important indicator for demonstrating the library's value. The Dashboard Team also plans to explore data related to student learning by measuring the impact of instruction through pre-course and post-course surveys, to determine students' perceptions of their information-literacy skills after instruction.

OUTCOMES

Not surprisingly, JCKL's Assessment Team has been the heaviest dashboard user to date, both for data entry and data visualization. Additional intended audiences include library administration, other library employees, the university community, and external library stakeholders. The Dashboard Team took the data needs of each intended audience into consideration when creating the tool. As a result, filtering options allowed viewing a single data set in various ways to answer various data questions. The team anticipates that these intended audiences will become regular users of the dashboard as they come to know dynamic attributes of the dashboard better, get access to more data sets, and continue to emphasize data-driven decision-making.

The development and implementation of the dashboard provided solutions to JCKL's internal and external assessment needs. In particular, the Dashboard Team found a number of positive outcomes in developing this tool internally. The dashboard allowed for flexibility in data set availability and filtering. It also enabled the Assessment Team to spend more time on data analysis and reporting. The deeper analysis that this tool supported sustained the library focus on evidence-based decision-making. Also, the Library Statistics Dashboard demonstrated JCKL's ability to be accountable to the UCM community by providing transparent information on usage of library space and services.

The Dashboard Provided the Flexibility to Add Analysis and Reporting Features on Demand

Internal development of the dashboard provided the Dashboard Team with the ability to customize data output features at any time, including adding analysis features as needed, based upon current data needs. The Information Technology Librarian can make prompt changes or improvements when necessary, and delete features if they no longer serve the initial intended purpose of providing a richer understanding of the data set. This flexibility ensures that the Assessment Team stays relevant and timely in the data the dashboard provides. For example, library administration was particularly interested in viewing averages for headcount and study room data. (The averages provided a more accurate view of when and how long students used library space.) Therefore, average calculation features were added to the dashboard after its initial publication. The flexibility of the dashboard allows it to evolve to meet changing needs of the library for years to come.

The Dashboard Enabled the Assessment Team to Focus More on Data Analysis and Interpretation Than on Data Creation

The dashboard improved workflow for data entry and production of statistical reports. Previously, a single data set, such as headcount, called for utilizing multiple Excel spreadsheets. Using spreadsheets required painstakingly restructuring data to generate each requested report. Previous data collection and reporting methods also did not separate raw and analyzed data. The Assessment Team generated charts and graphs in the data-entry spreadsheet for some data sets. Creating new spreadsheets with copied data also became untenable, due to the sheer volume of spreadsheets produced using this process. Automating data entry into the dashboard eliminated the need to maintain multiple spreadsheets and manually juggle numerous formulas to compute sums and averages. Now the back-end of the dashboard handles computations, reducing the amount of time spent double-checking formulas. Likewise, statistical reports no longer required hours of labor-intensive work to restructure the data each time a user requested a report.

An additional benefit of the cloud-based system was that users could visualize the data in different ways, without changing the underlying data. This eliminated the risk of accidentally changing or deleting the raw data, and ensured the accuracy of generated reports. The new format created an analytical layer on top of the data by storing the underlying data in SQL tables. This allowed flexibility to add or change output features without changing the data. The dashboard enabled longitudinal comparison, regardless of changes to data collection categories. For example, as JCKL reallocated collection space to student-study space, the Assessment Team redefined the floor locations noted in the hourly headcount. The dashboard allowed the Assessment Team to redefine these locations without making data sets incompatible, by decoupling the raw data and the analysis.

By decoupling the data and the analysis, the dashboard opened the door for the Assessment Team to create deeper analysis than the manually completed process could. As the dashboard handled the majority of data storage, the Assessment Team shifted its focus from data maintenance to analysis for reports and recommendations. Requested reports were generated in less time because the dashboard provided immediate analysis for any included data set. Setting a few filters in the dashboard and generating the graph answered certain routine questions. As a result, the Assessment Team could meet the increasing demand for library data, produce a complete analysis, and submit well-reasoned recommendations for internal and external requestors.

The additional ability to download the raw data enhanced the analytical usefulness of the dashboard. The dashboard also allows users to download a comma-separated values (CSV) file of the filtered or complete data for further analysis. Library administrators could view both the numbers and the visualizations, to gain a deeper understanding of particularly complex library trends. This has proved helpful as library administration continues to request comparisons across data sets.

The Dashboard Supported an Increase in Data-Driven Decisions for Library Services and Operations

The dashboard allowed the Assessment Team to automate calculation of the data sets that would most impact data-driven decisions. Therefore, the Assessment Team produced a higher volume of statistical reports and analysis. The dashboard tool allowed the Assessment Team to focus on providing timely, meaningful reports and recommendations to library administration, using a variety of data, rather than simply calculating and answering factual questions. Library administration relied on the Assessment Team for deeper analysis that impacted decisions, because they used the dashboard themselves to respond to many of their immediate factual needs pertaining to library operations (for example, the number of students in the building at any given hour during a certain day of the week).

The Library Statistics Dashboard has become an especially useful tool in making decisions. Data from the dashboard supported revising library service staffing models, deploying updated technology, and informing space decisions to better benefit students. The dashboard provided evidence supporting adoption of a single service point model within the building, so research-help services and circulation services were combined into one desk in Fall 2016. The JCKL Technology Team used dashboard-generated data to identify the most heavily used library computers throughout the building, to target them for earlier upgrades than other computers, and thus better support student technology needs. The dashboard also provided headcount data that demonstrated where library administration needed to reallocate student study space in the library.

The Dashboard Provided Accountability to Library and Campus Administrators

Another positive outcome of the Library Statistics Dashboard was its support of JCKL's efforts to be more transparent. Historically, dashboards were rich in statistical insight, but severely limited because only administrators had access to them and the wealth of data they contained (Matthews, 2011). Because the dashboard was on the library's website without any authentication requirement, it was available to the world. Anyone with a vested interest in JCKL could view the data and library trends. This solved the traditional problem of demonstrating library value through dashboards. The public nature of the dashboard encouraged transparency by highlighting JCKL trends and activities. It also allowed JCKL to demonstrate its value and impact on student success to audiences beyond library administrators. Stakeholders could access library data on the dashboard, from any location at any time, without bottlenecks or passwords.

The dashboard has also increased a sense of accountability in JCKL. Emphasis on meeting key performance indicators required proof that JCKL met expectations set by library and campus administrators. The power of the dashboard allowed the Assessment Team and library administration to highlight those ways in which the library had a direct impact on their selected campus KPIs. Library administrators found the dashboard incredibly useful as they advocated for the library across campus. The creation of the Library Statistics Dashboard demonstrated JCKL's commitment to meeting appropriate campus KPIs, and exhibited solid stewardship of library resources.

The Dashboard Team created a tool that is both dynamic and powerful for many different stakeholders. Internally, the dashboard streamlined data collection for multiple data sets; externally, it expanded the library's ability to demonstrate value to the UCM community. By identifying the most heavily used data sets for initial inclusion, the Dashboard Team ensured that the dashboard would have immediate and lasting impact on internal and external stakeholders.

RECOMMENDATIONS

The Dashboard Team at JCKL learned a number of valuable lessons that ensured the success of the project. The knowledge gleaned from this experience led the authors to recognize several key recommendations to share with other academic library organizations. One takeaway was that successful internal tool development must have strong support from library administration, due to the time it takes to build such tools. Also, programming skills are essential to creating an internal digital tool. Therefore, the authors recommend that librarians, traditionally focused on library systems work, shift toward developing programming expertise. Also, a team-based approach is best for developing internal library tools, because a variety of expertise generates a more complete tool.

Strong Leadership Should Champion the Need for Internal Tool Development

Library administration's need for timely, inclusive, and customized data expedited the creation of JCKL's Library Statistics Dashboard. Library administration appreciated the availability of this dashboard as a tool to demonstrate library value to stakeholders across campus and in the community. As an initial beneficiary of the dashboard, the Dean of Library Services saw the immediate value of such a tool, and made the production of the dashboard a priority. The Dean shifted superfluous duties away from members of the Dashboard Team, to ensure the creation of the tool.

Therefore, the authors recommend presenting tool development proposals to library administrators, to encourage them to champion the project. Any potential tool-development proposal should have evident value in the eyes of library administrators to generate support from library leadership. Supportive library leadership should assist those who develop an internal tool in identifying priorities for tool development in relation to other responsibilities. Deeming a tool important enough to build internally requires library administration to provide the proper resources to assist in that work.

A Systems Librarian's Role Should Transition to a Programming Role to Meet the Unique Needs of Libraries

The Information Technology Librarian at JCKL had no formal training in programming or web development, having acquired programming skills over the course of just two years while working with library websites at a previous job. During that time, the librarian mostly worked with basic HTML, CSS, and JavaScript, but later added proficiency in MySQL and PHP applications like Wordpress and the Yii framework. The learning curve was gradual, and the only real impediment was a lack of time, since the position also included simultaneous liaison and electronic resource management responsibilities. The experience with PHP and Yii translated well to working with Ruby on Rails.

Libraries are outsourcing more and more application platforms to cloud-based vendors. Many institutions have already eliminated systems-librarian positions because they no longer find the work necessary. Rather than eliminating these positions, the authors recommend systems librarians shift their focus to spending more time developing in-house applications. There is a balance to strike between outsourcing functions common to all libraries, and insourcing custom applications unique to specific libraries. Systems librarians might require some additional training in technologies like Linux, SQL, Ruby, PHP, HTML, and JavaScript. They can learn many of these on the job while working on web-related projects.

Programming skills are best learned on the job. A good initial project is to automate small, mundane tasks, such as cleaning up spreadsheets. Ruby and Python are two powerful, beginner-friendly programming languages. Both have built-in tools for working with CSV files. They can save a large Excel file in CSV format; enable a Ruby or Python script to read through all the rows in the file; remove unwanted text using regular expressions; and split large cells to separate out different types of information.

As organizations around the world push for programming literacy, there has never been a better time to start learning. In the programming world, almost everyone learns by trial and error. Numerous free and low-cost tools, as well as Internet communities, provide modules and timely feedback for newcomers interested in developing coding skills. Codecademy and Treehouse both offer self-paced learning modules for Ruby and Python. While not quite as meaningful as a project to help with day-to-day library tasks, online programs are a cost-effective, accessible, and reliable way for librarians to begin developing their programming fluency.

A Successful Internal Tool-Development Team Should Include Experts With Different Roles and Knowledge, Who Actively Assist in the Project

Creating a team with experts in different roles was essential to the design and success of the Library Statistics Dashboard. The development of this sophisticated tool required a variety of knowledge and expertise. Individuals with knowledge of library assessment and external requirements of library operations and services, familiarity with end-user needs, and experience in programming were crucial. The Dashboard Team consisted of three members with varied expertise. The Assistant Dean's experience with library assessment and literature on library impact helped shape the scope of the dashboard. This helped the Dashboard Team identify which data sets should initially be on the dashboard to support expected library outcomes set by library and campus administrators. The Library Assessment Assistant provided valuable insight as the initial primary end-user of the dashboard. The Library Assessment Assistant worked closely with the Information Technology Librarian to develop a dashboard that could handle multiple data sets and data entry. This position was key to testing the dashboard before it went live. The Information Technology Librarian's experience in programming was vital in the creation of the dashboard. This librarian understood the Assessment Team's requirements and needs in making a successful tool. The Information Technology Librarian explored various programming frameworks and tools, enabling the creation of a Library Statistics Dashboard that robustly handled a variety of data sets .

The authors recommend including individuals with different strengths to foster a comprehensive approach to developing an internal digital tool. Successful tool development requires diverse expertise. Each member of a tool development team should be able to play a specific role that directly moves the project forward. Consider including the library end-user(s) of the tool on the development team, to ensure a meaningful tool. This will justify the resources it may take to build such a tool internally, because the end-user team member can continually advocate for the project. A team structure means that the group must work together regularly, not just see one another in meetings. Tool development happens between meetings; therefore, meetings should focus on decisions in the design of the digital tool, or testing the tool as a group. This approach ensures that team members share a common understanding of the purpose of the tool, and keep to a timeline that ensures real progress.

This project management team approach could be difficult in libraries that have extensive committee decision-making structures. The authors recommend developing a unique team specifically focused on the creation of a digital library tool, rather than attempting to include such a project in an existing committee structure. This will keep the development process focused and efficient, as each member has to provide unique, direct assistance on the development of a library-specific digital tool.

CONCLUSION

The James C. Kirkpatrick Library Dashboard Team found that building a statistics dashboard within the library organization was both doable and worth doing. Once the Assessment Team identified the need for a library statistics dashboard, the development process only took a few months, thanks to the previously established Rails framework and the support of library administration. Once published, the dashboard solved a number of internal and external issues related to library assessment activities. Internally, the dashboard was a time-saver in terms of both data entry and report creation. The ability to visualize data by setting a few parameters greatly increased the flexibility of data sharing with library administration and other internal and external stakeholders. Externally, the dashboard provided accountability for the library to meet campus KPI requirements. Building a dashboard internally in an academic library was a feasible task. Acquiring the programming skills seems daunting, but is achievable by anyone willing to put in the time. The tools that can be developed from this skill set are invaluable to libraries.

REFERENCES

Applegate, R. (2009). The library is for studying: Student preferences for study space. *Journal of Academic Librarianship*, *35*(4), 341–346. doi:10.1016/j.acalib.2009.04.004

Asher, A. D., Miller, S., & Green, D. (2012). Ethnographic research in Illinois academic libraries: The ERIAL Project. In L.M. Duke & A.D. Asher's (Eds.) College Libraries and Student Culture: What We Now Know (pp. 1-14). Chicago: American Library Association.

Cooke, R., & Rosenthal, D. (2011). Students use more books after library instruction: An analysis of undergraduate paper citations. *College & Research Libraries*, *90*(4), 332–343. doi:10.5860/crl-90

de Jager, K. (2015). Place matters: Undergraduate perceptions of the value of the library. *Performance Measurement and Metrics*, *16*(3), 289–302. doi:10.1108/PMM-08-2015-0021

Emmons, M., & Wilkinson, F. C. (2011). The academic library impact on student persistence. *College & Research Libraries*, *72*(2), 128–149. doi:10.5860/crl-74r1

Few, S. (2006). *Information dashboard design*. Cambridge, MA: O'Reilly.

Foster, N. F., & Gibbons, S. (2007). Introduction to the Undergraduate Research Project. In *N.F. Foster & S. Gibbons' Studying Students: The Undergraduate Research Project at the University of Rochester* (pp. v–vii). Chicago: Association of College & Research Libraries.

Gardner, S., & Eng, S. (2005). What students want: Generation Y and the changing function of the academic library. *portal. Libraries and the Academy*, *5*(3), 405–420. doi:10.1353/pla.2005.0034

Heath, F. (2011). Library assessment: The way we have grown. *The Library Quarterly*, *81*(1), 7–25. doi:10.1086/657448

Hernon, P., Dugan, R. E., & Matthews, J. R. (2015). *Managing with data: Using ACRLMetrics and PLAmetrics*. Chicago: American Library Association.

Matthews, J. R. (2011). Assessing organizational effectiveness: The role of performance measures. *The Library Quarterly*, *81*(1), 81–110. doi:10.1086/657447

Matthews, J. R. (2015). *Library assessment in higher education*. Santa Barbara, CA: Libraries Unlimited.

Mezick, E. M. (2007). Return on investment: Libraries and student retention. *Journal of Academic Librarianship*, *33*(5), 561–566. doi:10.1016/j.acalib.2007.05.002

Missouri Department of Higher Education, Performance Funding Task Force. (2012). *Performance funding model: Recommendations of the Performance Funding Task Force*. Retrieved from https://dhe.mo.gov/documents/PerformanceFundingReport.pdf

Mizrachi, D. (2010). Undergraduates academic information and library behaviors: Preliminary results. *RSR. Reference Services Review*, *38*(4), 571–580. doi:10.1108/00907321011090737

Morton-Owens, E. & Hanson, K. L. (2012, September). Trends at a glance: A management dashboard of library statistics. *Information Technology and Libraries.*

National Conference of State Legislatures. (2015). *Performance based funding for higher education*. Retrieved from http://www.ncsl.org/research/education/performance-funding.aspx

Oakleaf, M. (2010). *The value of academic libraries: A comprehensive research review and report.* Chicago: American Library Association.

Oakleaf, M. (2011). Are they learning? Are we? Learning outcomes and the academic library. *The Library Quarterly*, *81*(1), 61–82. doi:10.1086/657444

Schwieder, D., & Hinchliffe, L. J. (2012). NCES datasets and library value: An exploratory study of the 2008 data. In *Proceedings of the 2012 Library Assessment Conference* (pp. 657-667). Retrieved from http://libraryassessment.org/bm~doc/proceedings-lac-2012.pdf

Tenopir, C. (2010). Measuring the values of the academic library: Return on investment and other value measures. *The Serials Librarian*, *58*(1-4), 39–48. doi:10.1080/03615261003623005

Town, S. J. (2011). Value, impact, and the transcendent library: Progress and pressures in performance measurement and evaluation. *The Library Quarterly*, *81*(1), 111–125. doi:10.1086/657445

Tufte, E. R. (1983). *The visual display of quantitative information*. Cheshire, CT: Graphics.

University of Central Missouri. (n. d.). *Strategic Resource Allocation Model*. Retrieved from https://www.ucmo.edu/sram/

KEY TERMS AND DEFINITIONS

Highcharts: A JavaScript library for generating interactive graphs on HTML pages, free for noncommercial use.

HTML: Hypertext Markup Language. A programming language for building web pages viewed in a web browser.

JavaScript: A programming language run in a web browser interacting with HTML pages, allowing real-time, dynamic interaction and effects.

JSON: JavaScript Object Notation. A text-based data format easily read by JavaScript, therefore a common format for exchanging raw data between Internet applications.

KPI: Key Performance Indicator. A measure of a particular activity or outcome typically considered vital to the success of an organization.

Library Assessment: The study and evaluation of library space, services, collections, and/or instruction, as it relates to supporting the needs of library users.

Ruby on Rails: A framework providing an organized architecture for building database-driven web applications in Ruby, using models, views, and controllers.

SQL: Structured Query Language. An interface for obtaining data from relational databases, storing data as a series of tables consisting of records (rows) and fields (columns).

SRAM: (Strategic Resource Allocation Model). A process of aligning limited resources to meet specific goals, often using the key performance indicator process to identify said goals.

SVG: Scalable Vector Graphics. A format for designing images as a series of geometric shapes on a coordinate plane, rather than as a series of pixels, allowing graphics to be resized (scaled) infinitely without pixelation.

Section 3
Collections

Digital platforms offer new ways to showcase and disseminate library collections, as well as provide a means for preserving ephemeral works. The chapters in this section offer detailed accounts of building new apps and customizing existing platforms in order to create interactive digital experiences and communities of online users.

Chapter 10
Pulling Content out the Back Door:
Creating an Interactive Digital Collections Experience

Amy J Hunsaker
University of Nevada – Reno, USA

Natasha Majewski
University of Nevada – Reno, USA

Laura E. Rocke
University of Nevada – Reno, USA

ABSTRACT

The University of Nevada, Reno Libraries is building a project and assessment-based organization that utilizes applications to increase the discovery of digital collections, enhances the online user experience, supports a growing Digital Humanities measure on campus, and encourages faculty and students to create projects using digital curation and various existing tools. A GeoHumanities Digital Project Specialist and Digital Humanities Historian were added to the library organization to create interactive exhibits. ESRI software was employed to create place-based storytelling using digital content held by CONTENTdm, CatDV, and other library platforms. By reimagining how we use such tools at our disposal, we can create new ways of interacting with information to create innovative ways for our patrons to re-engage with our materials.

DOI: 10.4018/978-1-5225-2676-6.ch010

INTRODUCTION

Just as a brick and mortar library needs a solid foundation to support and build physical resources, a digital library needs to have a solid web framework and supportive organizational environment in place before developing tools to expand on standard systems. At the University of Nevada, Reno (UNR) Mathewson-IGT Knowledge Center, a small but goal-oriented staff is working toward building a project-based organization that focuses on utilizing or creating applications to increase the discovery of digital collections and enhance the online user experience. In addition, the Digital Initiatives team has expanded to support a growing Digital Humanities measure on campus and to encourage more faculty and students to create projects using digital curation and various existing tools. CONTENTdm is the technology tool we use to host and control content, but we have experimented with many ways of distributing the content so as to create a user-focused interactive environment. This chapter will discuss the organizational structure required to support the level of experimentation, development, and creative exploration that has been utilized by the UNR Library organization to make digital content more accessible and discoverable. In addition, specific software used by the Library to create interactive exhibits from digital content will be discussed in detail.

BACKGROUND

The UNR Libraries organization has gone through substantial shifts in the last few years. Although the Library does not have a large staff, personnel have been hired for new and existing positions, work groups have been created to tackle various tasks, and clusters handle projects that require various systems and skillsets. Part of the reorganization of the Libraries include the addition of an Assessment Librarian, Metadata Librarian, GIS Librarian, and Digital Initiatives Librarian. The Assessment Librarian has been instrumental in assisting with web and application development by designing and implementing methods to better understand how users experience digital content. Armed with a variety of assessment strategies, staff have used evidence to inform the design of web tools that are more intuitive, attractive, and consistent with users' work practices and preferences. Usability studies, which will be discussed later in this chapter, informed the most recent iteration of the Library website and Digital Collections interface. The Metadata Librarian provides support across departments by guiding the creation of non-MARC metadata in various systems so that content is easier to access in the web framework. Formatting and metadata standards within and across collections have been an important aspect of content interacting with the new website. In addition, the Metadata Librarian has been instrumental in organizing and making discoverable content held by the Digital Media Technology unit in the Libraries that supports campus photographers and videographers. UNR is deeply rooted in the physical sciences and hosts the prestigious Mackay School of Mines. A GIS Librarian was hired to meet the increasing demand for GIS support and instruction in the physical science departments and to also support the Delamare Science and Engineering Library Makerspace. The GIS Librarian has been instrumental in making geospatial tools and software available for students and faculty use while also offering technical support and training.

The Digital Initiatives Librarian provides guidance for various digital projects and digital preservation efforts and acts as a steward over content held in CONTENTdm. In addition, the Digital Initiatives team has expanded to meet the demands of campus faculty and students who wish to create digital projects. A Digital Humanities (DH) initiative has been embraced by the University and is manifested in the Nevada Center for Data and Design in the Digital Humanities (NDAD), an online DH center created in 2016 by a coalition of History, English, and Journalism professors on campus. The Digital Initiatives Librarian was invited to be an affiliate of the NDAD and has offered letters of support to several grant proposals created by campus faculty wishing to create interactive, online exhibits, further emphasizing that the Libraries are considered to be an important asset to the creation of digital projects and data visualization. It was increasingly clear to the Libraries that the Digital Initiatives team, consisting of one librarian and a few student workers, was not enough to meet the needs on campus and funds were made available to hire additional staff. However, rather than adding more librarians or library workers to the Digital Initiatives team, the Digital Initiatives Librarian hired a GeoHumanities Digital Projects Specialist in late 2015 and a Digital Humanities Historian in early 2016 to curate content and create exhibits. The addition of these professionals has enriched the Digital Initiatives team's ability to create interesting digital exhibits that reveal the Libraries' holdings in new and interesting ways, while providing examples of how the team can support digital project efforts on campus.

Although the collections are relatively small compared to those displayed by larger institutions, UNR Digital Collections has been known in library communities for its unique digital exhibits and holdings. UNR began creating digital exhibits in 2003 by curating digital objects that told a story when gathered together. These curated digital exhibits were given context through storytelling text presented on carefully designed CSS pages that invited users to explore the content. Often, these exhibits included special searches that were created using metadata assigned to the objects residing in CONTENTdm. The topics of the exhibits often coincided with physical exhibits put on by UNR Special Collections. For example, following a physical exhibit of photographs of Lake Tahoe created by Special Collections, a digital version, *Images of Lake Tahoe*, was created by scanning the photographs and building a digital exhibit. UNR Digital Collections also hosts a variety of "bucket-style" collections, a mass of digitized media with a common thread of resource origin and popularity. Three legacy UNR collections that fall into this category are the *UNR Special Collections Photographs* collection, the *Basque Library Photographs* collection, and *Campus Images*, a collection of photographs from the University Archives. These "bucket" collections each contain thousands of images and are created more as research tools for users seeking specific images rather than browsing experiences. The newest project, *Wolf Pack Athletics: A Visual History*, launched in October, 2016, consists of a collection of approximately 2,200 digital images curated from the UNR University Archives and Nevada Athletic Media Services and is accompanied by an interactive exhibit highlighting the materials. Many of the exhibits were sponsored through grants or donors who wished to have materials highlighted online. For example, *"The First Friend" of Ronald Reagan: Senator Paul Laxalt and Presidential Politics* is an online exhibit launched in early 2016 that was supported by the Laxalt family in an effort to highlight material included in the Paul Laxalt Papers donated to UNR Special Collections. The curation of the online exhibit *The Western Shoshone Defense Project* was supported by a grant from the National Historical Publications and Records Commission.

Almost all of the digitized materials that appear on the Library website were curated and published because of users' needs or demands. The *Wolf Pack Athletics* collection grew from the Athletic Department's desire to digitize their popular materials, in part to digitally preserve them, and also to make them more accessible to fans. Other collections were funded and supported by donors or through grants created by historians, faculty, or community members. Even UNR's generic "bucket" collections consist of items that are in high demand by users who are aware of the resources offered by the Libraries. However, as the Digital Initiatives team expanded in early 2016, strategies were created in an effort to reach users who are unaware of the holdings in Special Collections or of the Libraries' ability to create and support interactive online exhibits.

CREATING DISCOVERABLE AND INTERACTIVE DIGITAL EXHIBITS

Assessment of UNR Digital Collections

Google Analytics reports recorded activity on the UNR Digital Collections website reveals that most of our hits come from outside the Library website. In fact, Google is the largest driver of traffic, followed by direct links that lead to content held within the collections. Users do not seem to be entering the Library website with the idea to explore the clearly marked channels directing them to the Digital Collections pages (see Figure 1).

Google Analytics Report: Summary of All Traffic

With this in mind, UNR Digital Initiatives has been exploring different ways to create more interactive experiences that make digital content held by the Libraries more relevant to users and to expose digital collections to a larger audience. In addition to referring to the data provided by Google Analytics, assessment was used to gauge how the Libraries could proceed in creating more engaging and impactful projects.

The Library Web and Applications Team built a new web framework for the Libraries in 2016 and created a new interface for UNR Digital Collections. With the help of the Assessment Librarian, a usability study was created by the Digital Initiatives Librarian to not only test the operability and aesthetics of the new website,

Figure 1. Google Analytics report for UNR digital collections: September 13-October 6, 2016

Google Analytics Report: Summary of All Traffic		
Source/Medium	Sessions	Sessions
	3,591	3,591
	% of Total:	% of Total:
	100.00%	100.00%
	-3,591	-3,591
google / organic	1,112	30.97%
(direct) / (none)	1,032	28.74%
knowledgecenter.unr.edu / referral	175	4.87%
site-auditor.online / referral	163	4.54%
bing / organic	147	4.09%
guides.library.unr.edu / referral	146	4.07%
unr.edu / referral	105	2.92%
yahoo / organic	91	2.53%

but to address the basic question of how users interact with Digital Collections meant to provide guidance for future projects.

The presence of an Assessment Librarian has proven to be instrumental in the evaluation of web tools, the web interface, liaison activities, and other Library projects and exhibits. By allowing user feedback to guide library functions, a more functional and relevant experience will lead users to resources they need and provide a more positive outlook of the Library. Usability studies that influenced the design of this project include a study of Colorado State University's Digital Collections and the Western Waters Digital Library (Zimmerman & Pascal, 2009), emphasizing an iterative approach to effective website creation, and the Belgian-American Research Collection (Clark, 2004), which employed a task-oriented field test and exit questionnaire with a focus group. The Assessment Librarian worked closely with the Digital Initiatives Librarian to craft a set of questions and tasks that would allow testers to provide feedback while navigating through various digital collections and exhibits hosted on the new framework.

The usability studies took place during the last week of September, 2016. Five test subjects, all highly experienced library users, were recruited and given a $15.00 Amazon gift card for their participation. Four of the users were graduate students in History, Anthropology, Cultural Geography, and English, and one was an undergraduate who has worked at the Library Research desk for a year. Four of the test subjects were female and one was male. Two of the graduate students were studying at the doctoral level. The decision was made to test only experienced users whose research was primarily focused in the Humanities or Social Sciences. These users were likely to understand the importance of accessing primary resources like those offered within the Libraries' digital collections. While more experienced users were chosen for this first round of testing, subsequent testing will focus on less experienced users after changes have been implemented.

Each test took approximately 30 minutes to complete and was recorded using Camtasia video recording software. The testers were encouraged to verbalize their decisions while they navigated through assigned tasks. The tests took place over three afternoons in a quiet location in the Library. Two types of questions were asked to test the functionality and usefulness of digital collections and exhibits hosted on the website. The first set of questions was open-ended and gauged each user's basic knowledge and impressions of digital collections in general. The second set of questions was specific to tasks assigned to the users. The tests were verbally conducted by the Digital Initiatives Librarian and observed by the Assessment Librarian who noted observations and rated the difficulty of each of the task-based questions. The study also allowed the testers to ask questions and offer feedback after the experience. Although the study only worked with a small number of testers, the feedback offered a rich source of information about the strengths and weaknesses of the site design, and tester responses proved to be remarkably consistent across the board.

The first set of questions was created to gauge the testers' level of experience with the Library home page, knowledge of digital collections and exhibits held by the Library, and ability to easily navigate to the collections (see Figure 2). The first questions noted the testers' status, major, and how often they frequented the website. The testers were required to start at the Library home page and answer the question, "How do you get to Digital Collections from the Library home page?" A few testers wondered aloud what we meant by "digital collections," assuming that we equated digital collections with databases, e-reserves, or online journals. The Assessment Librarian noted the paths taken by the testers as they tried to find a link to the Digital Collections home page. After the testers reached the Digital Collections home page, they were asked the following question: "Looking at this page, what types of library resources do you think you might encounter?" One tester stated that she recognized these materials as being digital surrogates of items held in Special Collections. Another was surprised that these resources existed.

Once the subjects were allowed to explore the home page of Digital Collections, they were assigned a set of tasks that required them to find specific digital objects, exhibits, or collections (see Figure 3). The Assessment Librarian took notes and ranked each of the questions using the following scale, depending on the subject's ability to achieve the task (Teague-Rector, Ballard, & Pauley, 2011):

- **Easy:** First or second try; no problem
- **Medium:** First or second try; observed difficulty
- **Hard:** Second or third try; expressed difficulty
- **Fail:** Failed or gave up

The tasks were prepared with the idea of testing the functionality of the new web interface, but the study provided informal feedback about the subjects' perceptions of and interest in the actual digital collections and exhibits they explored. It also revealed that the subjects almost always preferred using the keyword search over

Figure 2. Usability Study Section A: General introduction

Look at the Digital Collections home page and click around for overall impressions.
How do you get to Digital Collections from the library homepage?
Looking at this page (the Digital Collections home page), what types of library resources do you think you might encounter?

the advanced search and that they preferred using the cross-collection search rather than explore specific collections or exhibits for content. For example, the Digital Collections site includes a collection of photographs of Lake Tahoe. The task given to the subjects was, "Try to find a collection of Lake Tahoe," then a follow up question, "Can you find an image of Emerald Bay?" Two of the subjects tried using keywords in the cross-collection search to find the collection of photographs, even though an icon leading directly to the collection existed under another icon labeled "Featured Collections." One subject looked in a couple of places first, and the other two were able to go directly to the collection.

The final portion of the usability study included the questions, "Now that you've had time to view and navigate different parts of the website, what observations, questions, or other feedback do you have about your experience? Is there anything that did not make sense or could be made clearer, or any task you'd like to be easier?" The feedback included many specific suggestions about the functionality of the website, compliments on the look of the collection pages, and statements about the nature of digital collections and exhibits in general. For the purposes of this chapter, a summary is provided that focuses only on feedback and observations pertaining

Figure 3. Usability Section B: Specific assignments

Begin each task on the Digital Collections home page
1. Find a photograph of a Basque dancer.
2. Try to find the Coffin and Keys Formation Petition in University Archives and Documents.
3. Can you find a photograph of a railroad depot?
3a. If you wanted to obtain a print of this photograph, how might you do so?
4. Try to find a collection that contains photographs of Lake Tahoe.
4a. Can you find an image of Emerald Bay?
5. How would you find an exhibit of photographs of Nevada barns?
6. Hypothetically you want to do some research on the history of UNR campus buildings. How would you go about finding an image of Getchell Library from the 1970s?
7. Find a map of wagon routes in Utah from the 1850s.
8. Hypothetically you are taking a seminar course on Women in Nevada and have been instructed to find primary resources. How many resources exist that deal with Women college students in Nevada?

to the subjects' perceptions of digital collections and exhibits, rather than including comments relating to search functionality or icon placement.

The UNR Digital Collections website separates access to digital content into eight categories: collections, exhibits, maps, Basque resources (UNR is home to the Basque Resource Center), documents & publications, oral histories, other resources, and music. Great thought was put into creating these groupings by librarians in Special Collections, the Digital Initiatives Librarian, and the Web and Applications team. However, only one tester utilized these categories. All others preferred to search across all collections using keywords rather than seeking out collections or exhibits that contained curated material. One tester who preferred to use the cross-collection search also said that she would prefer to have a listing of all curated collections that was easier to access. The meaning of the word "exhibits" was not clear and the name "Digital Collections" when referring to the general website was confusing to one because, as she stated, "They're all digital collections, aren't they?" Another tester stated that she would not know what was available in Digital Collections if she was not looking for it in this usability study. However, the testers all felt that the appealing new design made them want to explore more. They liked the addition of audio and video files. One stated, "You've taken advantage of the graphical aspect of the collection."

After completing each test, the Assessment and Digital Initiatives Librarians reviewed the test data and noted their observations. At the end, all testing was evaluated for general perspectives and patterns. For example, the librarians noticed that none of the testers located the "Digital Collections" icon on the Library home page and that one of them tried to find "digital collections" in the databases list and by using a keyword search in the discovery search bar. All of the users preferred to use the cross-collection search once they found the digital collections home page. Only two users seemed to understand the difference between digital exhibits and collections. All of the users were surprised when they discovered the quantity and variety of digital resources that are made available through the digital collections portal, and all of them appreciated the visual aspects of the website.

Although this was only the first of an iterative set of usability tests on the functionality of a new website, the Digital Initiatives Librarian concluded that the results could also inform other ways of providing access to library held digital content. These highly experienced users did not know much about digital collections and exhibits held by the Libraries. A highly-visible icon that would take the user directly to the Digital Collections home page was placed on the Library home page and none of the testers noticed it. Once they found the digital collections, they were surprised that they existed. The testers appreciated the look of the exhibits but were not enticed to explore or search for more digital content through the layers of the website. The testers were interested in tracking down a sought-after item. In short, the testers' search behavior implied that users will not go to a library website looking for exhibits. When they visit the Library website, they tend to look for specific items rather than exhibits to browse through. Librarians who designed the website did not have a problem understanding the nature of digital collections or exhibits or how to search through collections for specific objects. Perhaps the librarians could use a non-librarian point of view when creating ways to push digital content out to users. The next set of usability studies specifically focused on users' interaction with digital collections and exhibits are planned to take place in March or April 2017 and will offer more insight.

The Influence of Digital Humanities on Digital Exhibit Creation

For the last academic year, Digital Initiatives has been exploring ways to support the growing desire for DH projects on campus. The team has several collaborations under way, or is at least offering to provide a supporting role in different projects. The Libraries have been understaffed for many years due to budget cuts in the state. Now that the economy has rebounded, there is a wish list of faculty and staff positions that the Libraries hopes to fill. A Digital Humanities Librarian would be nice but is a lower priority than more desperately needed positions. The Libraries hired non-librarians to work with library collections who provided a unique perspective on how to best use and expose digital content in a way that can support DH projects without having to hire a specialized librarian. Since the History Department and School of Journalism teamed together with the Library to create a DH center, the NDAD, there is already a space on campus in place for collaboration and creation. Rather than continuing to create new library platforms and tools for exhibit curation and creation, why not use the tools that are used by the people the Library is trying to support? A geographer is not going to use the library platform to create an exhibit or interactive map. Historians and writers are going to create digital projects using software and tools such as Omeka, Scalar, or WordPress. There are many existing non-library tools that librarians can familiarize themselves with so that they can support the programs happening on campus rather than continuing to look inward at only using and developing tools within the Library framework.

The Digital Public Library of America (DPLA) offers millions of digital items to the public on an open platform that allows developers and scholars to create interactive applications, exhibits, and learning tools with the content using a variety of software and tools. In fact, the DPLA (Digital Public Library of America [DPLA] 2015) includes among their goals "an emphasis on collective action and collaboration across many institutions and individuals," and includes "A platform that serves those materials not only through our own website but through innovative and creative apps and other sites" as an important segment of its three-part plan (p. 3). The College of

Wooster Special Collections unit teamed with the Wayne County Historical Society and the Wayne County Public Library to create the *Wooster Digital History Project*, an interactive online exhibit that includes app-based walking tours, an interactive map, exhibits including audio and video elements, images, and a bibliography. This project, created from 2013-15 combined the talents of librarians, historians, and local community members to create a project utilizing library and non-library resources (Wooster College, 2015). These models are among those that inspired the UNR Digital Initiatives team to explore different avenues for exhibit curation and development that would encourage creative use of library materials to happen outside the digital "walls" of the library. Other libraries are also examining ways to support DH initiatives on campus by becoming familiar with and assessing DH tools and platforms. Librarians at the University of Illinois at Urbana–Champaign recently assessed Scalar, a DH publishing platform, in part to suggest "how libraries might partner with campus humanities centers to foster interest in new platforms by using the platforms as an opportunity for the conversations scholars already want to have about digital scholarship" (Tracy, 2016, p. 183). Another recent case study reviewed Omeka.net, the hosted version of Omeka, as a viable platform librarians could use to encourage collaboration between DH centers and libraries. Omeka.net is described in the study "as a platform to encourage cross-sector collaboration for digital humanities projects" (Rath, 2016, i).

Several platforms exist to support DH projects, but beginning in May 2016 the Libraries experimented with using Esri software to create Story Maps from digital content held by CONTENTdm and other library platforms. Initially, in order to make an existing collection of UNR campus images more accessible, a geographer with a background in journalism, the GeoHumanities Digital Projects Specialist, was hired to weed the collection by curating relevant images, clean and enhance the metadata to improve discovery, and create a more interactive experience for users. Because of her geography background, the GeoHumanities Specialist had used ArcGIS to create digital data maps, but had never used a cloud based product to create a project on this level. Using an existing library license, she created several interactive exhibits with this science-oriented software. This Qualitative GIS allowed for more in-depth geovisualization, with its abilities to layer meaning-making data such as research artifacts and multimedia like audio, video, photography, and hand-drawn maps and sketches, allowing for diverse possibilities of representations. By reimagining how to use such tools at their disposal, the Digital Initiatives team sought to create new ways of interacting with information and to create innovative ways for patrons to re-engage with materials.

In addition to adding a geographer to the team, the Digital Initiatives Librarian also hired the Digital Humanities Historian who had experience with place-based storytelling. The Historian worked with the Director of Digital Media Technology to provide metadata and time stamping for a large and diverse collection of historic videos that were digitally converted from tape. The Historian proved to have the technical skills necessary for working with digital materials and the domain knowledge to provide context in the descriptive metadata. She also worked with the GeoHumanities Specialist to provide research-based content for various projects created in the Libraries. In September 2016 they created interactive exhibits, a walking tour, and life sketch for Senator Harry Reid's retirement. In addition, the GeoHumanities Specialist and Historian have worked with the rest of the Digital Initiatives team, the Library Web and Applications team, and Nevada Wolf Pack Athletic Media to create an innovative and interactive website highlighting the *Wolf Pack Athletics: A Visual History* digital collection held by the Libraries. The *Wolf Pack Athletics* site is built on the web framework created by the Library Web and Applications Team but utilizes ArcGIS software, ESRI Story Maps, YouTube, and SoundCloud platforms. The energetic nature of the content, in addition to feedback collected from analytics reports and usability studies, informed the decision to create highly interactive experiences within the exhibit using a variety of tools, software, and platforms. The *Wolf Pack Athletics* digital collection and accompanying exhibit were launched on Homecoming game day in October 2016. The Athletics department promoted the launch by offering a daily "Historic Wolf Pack" moment count down leading to the launch, passed out "commemorative" pins created by the Libraries using historic images from the collection, and provided a page on their website with a link to the collection and exhibit to offer easier access to their fans. Although at time of publication a formal assessment of user interaction with the project has not been conducted, Digital Initiatives and Athletic Media Services have received informal positive feedback in the form of appreciative emails and requests for more information or access to more materials.

The diverse background of the professional but non-librarian staff has expanded the focus of the Digital Initiatives team to seek more diverse content and has encouraged the utilization of existing platforms and resources to create unique, interactive digital projects. The Digital Initiatives Librarian, Historian, and GeoHumanities Specialist have directly or indirectly shared Digital Initiatives projects with local and campus communities in an effort to further market the resources offered by the Libraries. Because of exposure to these projects, various entities have shown an increased interest in creating their own interactive digital projects through collaboration with the Libraries. In April 2017, the Digital Initiatives team will launch a campus walking tree tour created in partnership with the University Arboretum. The Art Department would like to work with the Digital Initiatives team to create online exhibits of their students' physical exhibits starting in the 2017-2018 school year. Local public libraries have asked the UNR Digital Initiatives team for support in implementing scanning days, oral history collection events, and in creating their own projects. For example, the Sparks Public Library is creating an LSTA grant proposal to work with UNR Digital Initiatives to digitize their Rail City collection, host scanning day events, and create an online exhibit in 2018. Although the positive reaction by the community toward efforts made by the Digital Initiatives team can be difficult to quantify, the Digital Initiatives team considers the increased attention to be a good sign that they are on the right track.

Using CatDv to Make Digital Media Discoverable

The Digital Humanities Historian, in collaboration with the Director of the Digital Media Technology department in the Libraries, used CatDV to digitally preserve a number of historic footage collections pertaining to the University and the state of Nevada, some dating all the way back to the 1930's. As a result, the content in these collections has not only been digitally converted and preserved from videotapes that were otherwise collecting dust, but it has also been made widely discoverable, via the Dublin Core metadata schema prepared by the Metadata Librarian, and usable across a variety of other digital projects. CatDV, as the Director of Digital Media Technology describes it, "is a media asset management/database software package that can ingest, catalogue, annotate, organize, archive, search, retrieve and export all digital media file types and formats" (M. Gandolfo, personal communication, October 13, 2016). The Historian utilized this program to create metadata and timestamps (or event markers, as they are referred to in CatDV) for individual videos, as well as to create and export smaller clips from the videos to be used in various other digital exhibits.

The Historian's experience with CatDV began when she was hired by the Digital Initiatives Librarian, in conjunction with the Director of Digital Media Technology, to create metadata and later curate a digital exhibit for a television series produced in the late 1970's and early 1980's by the UNR Office of Communications and Broadcasting, *Nevada Weekly* (name later changed to *UNR Today*). The series episodes had been converted to a digital format from videotape and were now held in CatDV. The Historian worked exclusively in CatDV due to its ability to store and play media, collect and store metadata, and mark and annotate event markers—a powerful feature that distinguishes the program from CONTENTdm. As an administrator within the program, the Director of Digital Media Technology is able to shape CatDV's functions. As he explains, "the framework for user contributed logging data, such as metadata fields, schema, and vocabularies can be created and defined by administrators based on what is deemed meaningful and valuable for the project and institution" (Gandolfo, 2016). The Historian, Director of Digital Media Technology, and Metadata Librarian (who is able to crosswalk the metadata created in CatDV over to CONTENTdm) collectively created metadata fields that seemed most relevant to this particular collection. Once the metadata fields were decided upon and created in CatDV, the Historian watched each episode, creating metadata along the way, while also meticulously time stamping them. The time stamps distinguish and separate different segments within a given episode as well as different topics and talking points within those segments, providing a considerable degree of granularity to the archiving of the footage.

Since completing the *Nevada Weekly/UNR Today* collection, the Historian has performed the same process on other historic video footage that has been in the possession of and digitized by the Director of Digital Media Technology. These videos include the following: miscellaneous footage pertaining to the University, ranging from footage of construction projects around campus to footage of numerous buildings around campus to events on campus such as the University's Centennial Celebration; historical footage of Nevada and the University that dates back to the 1930's; footage from 1991 of the well-known Burning Man Festival; and footage that was shot during Margaret M. Wheat's work making an oral history of Wuzzie George, an elder Paiute Tribal member and Indian medicine woman of the Stillwater, Nevada region.

The value of this process is multifarious. These videos are, for all intents and purposes, primary sources. Thus, digitizing and archiving them salvages and preserves their content and value as such, while simultaneously making them and their content discoverable and usable. In an effort to push the videos out to the public, a pilot group of five videos with all of their metadata and assigned time stamps were transferred to the University's YouTube station in December 2016. Informal feedback has been positive, and the Digital Initiatives team received the following message from Erin K. Cummings, a local Historian and Instructor at the University of Nevada, Reno, Truckee Meadows Community College, and Davison Academy:

Video or digital sources such as these are incredibly valuable for researchers and educators. Just as personal correspondence, journals, etc. give us access to real people and their genuine perspectives within particular social contexts prior to the advent of certain technologies, video and other digital sources (like the Nevada Weekly productions) feature equally real people speaking candidly on the issues of their day while simultaneously highlighting the cultural contexts that inform their sentiments. In my estimation, digital sources like these are invaluable particularly for those of us who work in the humanities and social sciences and aim to understand how real, ordinary people felt about themselves and the worlds they lived in, as well as the social/cultural bases from which they operated. The accessibility of digital sources for researchers and educators, as such, seems like a real no-brainer (E. K. Cummings, personal communication, January 20, 2017).

The discoverability and usability factor is what guided and motivated the Historian in her metadata and timestamp creation. In an attempt to make the historical footage as widely discoverable and consumed as possible, immense effort and care was taken to cast a wide and thorough metadata net, as well as to create as rigorous and precise of timestamps as possible. Additionally, the motivation behind creating such meticulous timestamps was the hope that an individual coming across the footage would not pass it over as a result of not wanting to sit through the entire duration of the particular video. The timestamps thus provide a convenient way for a viewer to jump ahead to sections that may be relevant to him or her, without having to sit through those that might not be—a scenario that might otherwise cause a viewer to skip watching the video altogether.

Beyond the value of digitally preserving these historic footage collections and making them widely discoverable, the Historian has been able to utilize them for collaborative projects that she and the GeoHumanities Digital Projects Specialist have been commissioned to produce (as members of the Digital Initiatives team and by other entities across campus). The Historian has extensive familiarity with the historic footage collections housed in CatDV as a result of working so intimately with them. She is able to call upon specific footage from them that will coordinate with and compliment particular digital projects and exhibits.

Such was the case with an interactive website highlighting the *Wolf Pack Athletics* digital collection held by the Libraries. The GeoHumanities Specialist requested from the Historian any footage pertaining to the project's subject. Utilizing CatDV's functionality to export portions of files (clips) that have been defined by the user (Gandolfo, 2016), the Historian created several clips from a variety of footage in the collections that she had archived and exported them in MP4 format for the GeoHumanities Specialist to work with. The GeoHumanities Specialist then applied her skill set to the creation of a video for the project, comprised of both these clips and other media she had acquired. The clips that were cut by the Historian came from the *Nevada Weekly/UNR Today* collection, as well as from a collection of silent footage of the University dating back to the 1930's. This added both authentic historic integrity and a nostalgic vintage quality to the project.

A similar process was used for several other projects, such as when the Digital Initiatives Librarian asked the Historian for any footage pertaining to the University's Marching Band. The Historian cut MP4 clips of such footage from the *Nevada Weekly/UNR Today* videos and the collection of silent footage. The Digital Initiatives Librarian then shared these clips with the University's Music Department.

As can be seen, one individual, the Historian, has been able to provide a variety of relevant and engaging media to a number of diverse projects across campus from a few relatively small footage collections. Ultimately, the Historian has collaborated on projects with the Digital Initiatives Librarian and the GeoHumanities Specialist, wherein all three apply their diverse expertise and skillsets to the production of innovate, interactive, and uniquely individualized digital projects.

Using Story Maps to Create Interactive Library Exhibits

Geographers can explore how to "know worlds" without driving a hard line between the physical and the imagined (DeLyser, Herbert, Aitken, Crang & McDowell, 2010, pp. 13-14). In this in-between state, concepts of place become experienced through our personal connections to the material, memory, imagination, stories, and our perceptions (Cresswell, 2004). Harris, Bergeron & Rouse write, "If one of the defining characteristics of place is the notion of meaning through experience, then exploring methods that can somehow represent these qualitative elements without destroying the essence of that meaning would be a valuable component to historical and literary research" (Harris, Bergeron & Rouse, 2011, p. 230). In this desire to connect methodologies and meaning, interactive, digital storytelling becomes a vehicle for understanding these human experiences expressed through visual, audio, cartographical, and narrative stories in place (Campbell & Moyers, 1988; Wood & Fels, 1992; Clandinin & Rosiek, 2006).

In creating online DH projects vibrant with interactive storytelling, libraries, museums, universities, and other organizations bridge digital preservation efforts with narrative curation. Projects engage their audiences in the ability to choose their own multi-dimensional experience. Examples of such projects include the Library of Congress' *Churchill and the Great Republic,* the United States Holocaust Memorial Museum's *Some Were Neighbors*, the University of Nevada, Las Vegas' *Documenting the African American Experience in Las Vegas*, and the Montana State Library's *Montana Memory Project.*

Digital geohumanites and geovisualization take such narratives one step further, grounding humanities in place (Knowles, 2008). Libraries such as the British Library, New York Public Library, Boston Public Library, and the Newberry Library have embraced these spatial storytelling formats (Thompson, 2013). Within this field, tools traditionally used for quantitative data storage and analysis, such as Geographic Information Systems (Longley et al., 2011), become platforms for humanities GIS and historical GIS, inspiring such projects such as the *Electronic Cultural Atlas Initiative* and the *Virtual Center for Spatial Humanities* at Indiana University-Perdue University Indianapolis (Harris et al., 2011). These projects not only arch the temporal/spatial divide but use dynamic, interactive storytelling to engage sense of place for creative user experience.

The Digital Initiatives team seeks to enliven digital resources using interactive, multimedia storytelling stretching between collection promotion and active audience participation. The projects delve into new ways of online curation, creating mapping tours and immersive experience. The goal of the team, in part, has been to intersect geography, history, and play by using the latest technologies from different fields to engage students, faculty, and community patrons in digital landscapes. As they have developed new mediums of multiple layers of story and Geographic Information Systems (GIS), Library patrons can literally walk through digital collections, engage imagination through creative interface, or simply browse Library collections. Some of the GeoHumanities projects created by the Digital Initiatives team include *Women at the University of Nevada, Reno* (see figure 4), *Forgotten Landscapes: Military at UNR*, and *Harry Reid and Nevada: A Love Story*. The curated collections deeply map the University's landscape, whether it be the rich history of women's stories on campus, a walking tour of military epochs told through the voices and photos of events no longer seen, or a heart-felt timeline of one of Nevada's state senators. The goal is to use in-house technologies that might not otherwise be combined to create a grander sense of play with UNR Libraries resources and the broader community. In addition, the Digital Initiatives team wishes to engage in the greater discussion on innovative ways to continually push boundaries in this newly-developing narrative field.

By combining geovisualization mapping and experiential storytelling, the GeoHumanities Specialist used in-house Library resources for various project creation. ERSI ArcGIS, both desktop and online, were used in the creation of GIS shapefiles and maps. Adobe Photoshop, Adobe Audition, Adobe Final Cut Pro, and

Figure 4. Women at the University of Nevada, Reno

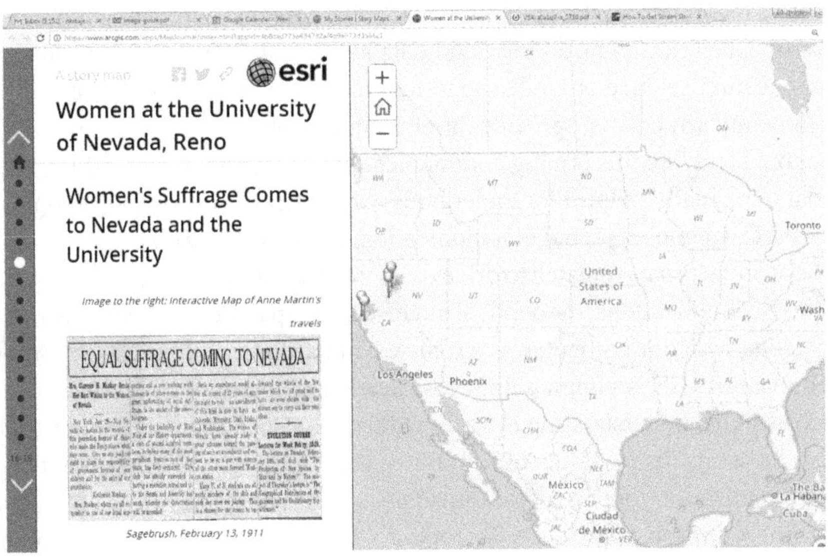

IMovie were used for audio and visual content creation. CONTENTdm was used for the creation of metadata and digital archiving of digital artifacts. The platform of ESRI Story Maps was then used as the template to create these interactive, place-based narratives, interweaving audio and visual stories, academic-cited research, writing, hyperlinks, and interactive GIS maps. Most content was driven through Library collections (the Nevada Oral History Archive, Digital Collections, Special Collections Archives, and content mined through CatDV) although first-account interviews and attributed outside media were additionally used to supplement curation.

These projects have required expertise in GIS software, multi-media production, engaging narrative creation, and an understanding of academic-level research. On one wilderness conservation mapping project, the team collaborated with an environmental non-profit GIS specialist in the community who had collected data and digitized it into shapefiles to create GIS maps. In using these already-created data layers, the GeoHumanities Specialist produced an interactive online map interlaced with storytelling to bring a stronger sense of narrative to the GIS layers themselves. This allowed users to click on individual spatial layers or inside of hyperlinked text to zoom to areas on the map with pop-up images and additional information told through photos, audio, video, historic documents, publications, speeches, and interactive GIS layers. This kind of cross-collaboration has allowed for multiple experts in their respective fields to imagine new possibilities while possessing the technical skills to create innovative products. Chrissy Klenke, the Maps Librarian at UNR, referring to the *Women at the University of Nevada, Reno* project, commented that "as a maps librarian, I am always looking for new and innovative ways to engage students and faculty with resources they have available to them. This project allows for people to creatively explore and navigate a variety of Library resources and with interactive mapping and storytelling" (C. Klenke, personal communication, January 20, 2016). Chelsea Canon, a PhD Candidate in Geography with a focus on GIS and communication science at UNR suggested that all the Story Maps created by the GeoHumanities Specialist "provides an entry into an otherwise overwhelming photo collection. I feel like this is a big communication asset and also something that will turn out to be really helpful for undergrads, especially if you keep developing it as a series" (C. Canon, personal communication, January 19, 2017).

These projects were created to drive users into Library resources, showcasing the breadth of our collections, the depth of our research capacities, and demonstrate what can be done with our computer programs when used in combined ways. Although GeoHumanites GIS is popping up across academic and public platforms, a divide still exists in the understanding of access to creating such projects and the tools the Library has at its disposal for such abilities. Highlighting cross-collaboration with unique organizations outside of the university setting has also allowed for innovation and public outreach across new sectors. As academic libraries desire to engage beyond their own campus boundaries, working with community organizations allows for a natural bridge into different levels of expertise, community engagement, and opportunities for marketing such projects.

Digital GeoHumanites and humanities GIS allows for more in-depth geovisualization, with abilities to layer meaning-making data such as audio, video, photography, artwork, artifacts, and maps, allowing for diverse possibilities of representations (Aitken & Kwan, 2010). As libraries contain great repositories of knowledge, we can also create new ways of interpreting and interacting with that knowledge, pulling from expertise found in colleagues with unique perspectives and backgrounds. By reimagining how we use such tools at our disposal and experts in our arena, we can create new ways to engage our patrons. As libraries strive to reinvent themselves in their own respective communities, by engaging in interactivity, innovation, creativity, and play, they can create new worlds of experiential knowledge and expand their impact across unusual divides.

SUMMARY

An expanding staff at the University of Nevada, Reno Libraries has allowed for creative support and collaboration among Library units. Assessment has played a vital role in web design and application development and was employed to test user's perceptions of the new Digital Collections website. Usability testing revealed that users may not use the Library website to access browseable exhibits but rather tend to seek directly for specific items held in digital collections.

The new web framework was supposed to create a more direct route for users to access digital collections, but since it is still part of the Library website, it does not seem to have done that. Users seem to be searching for specific items rather than for highly visual, interactive content on the Library website. In order to create interactive exhibits that will reach users outside of the Library website and support the growing Digital Humanities initiative on campus, a geographer with journalistic experience and a historian specializing in place-based storytelling were hired to curate content and create exhibits.

If the Library intends to support different units on campus, librarians should actively learn about their tools, software, platforms, etc. and implement these tools in collaborative projects. Working outside the Library with different units and a variety of experts increases our ability to create amazing new products. Hiring non-librarians who easily circulate among faculty and students in the humanities and social sciences to work on digital humanities projects provides a dynamic element to creating new user experience and redefine the library experience.

REFERENCES

Aitken, S. C., & Kwan, M. P. (2010). GIS as qualitative research: Knowledge, participatory politics and cartographies of affect. In D. DeLyser, S. Herbert, S. C. Aitken, M. Crang, & L. McDowell (Eds.), *The SAGE handbook of qualitative geography* (pp. 287–304). Los Angeles, CA: SAGE. doi:10.4135/9780857021090.n18

Campbell, J., & Moyers, B. (1988). *The power of myth*. New York: Doubleday.

Clandinin, D. J., & Rosiek, J. (2006). Mapping a landscape of narrative inquiry: Borderland spaces and tensions. In D. J. Clandinin (Ed.), *Handbook of narrative inquiry: Mapping a methodology* (pp. 35–76). Los Angeles, CA: SAGE.

Clark, J. (2004). A usability study of the Belgian-American Research Collection: Measuring the functionality of a digital library. OCLC Systems & Services. *International Digital Library Perspectives*, *20*(3), 115–127.

Cresswell, T. (2004). *Place: A short introduction*. Malden, MA: Blackwell Pub.

DeLyser, D., Herbert, S., Aitken, S. C., Crang, M., & McDowell, L. (2010). Introduction: Engaging qualitative geography. In D. DeLyser, S. Herbert, S. C. Aitken, M. Crang, & L. McDowell (Eds.), *The Sage handbook of qualitative geography* (pp. 1–18). Los Angeles, CA: SAGE. doi:10.4135/9780857021090.n1

Digital Public Library of America strategic plan 2015-2017. (2015). Retrieved from https://dp.la/info/about/strategic-plan/

Harris, T., Bergeron, S., & Rouse, L. J. (2011). Humanities GIS: place, spatial storytelling, and immersive visualization in the humanities. In M. Dear, J. Ketchum, S. Luria, & D. Richardson (Eds.), *GeoHumanities: Art, history, text at the edge of place* (pp. 226–240). London: Routledge.

Knowles, A. K. (2008). GIS and history. In A. K. Knowles & A. Hillier (Eds.), *Placing history: How maps, spatial data, and GIS are changing historical scholarship* (pp. 1–26). Redlands, CA: ESRI Press.

Longley, P. A., Goodchild, M. F., Maguire, D. J., & Rhind, D. W. (2011). *Geographic Information Systems & science* (3rd ed.). Hoboken, NJ: John Wiley & Sons, Inc.

Rath, L. (2016). Omeka.net as a librarian-led digital humanities meeting place. *New Library World*, *117*(3/4), 158–172. doi:10.1108/NLW-09-2015-0070

Sinton, D. S., & Lund, J. J. (2007). Critical and creative visual thinking. In D. S. Sinton & J. J. Lund (Eds.), *Understanding place: GIS and mapping across the curriculum* (pp. 1–18). Redlands, CA: ESRI Press.

Teague-Rector, S., Ballard, A., & Pauley, S. (2011). The North Carolina State University Libraries search experience: Usability testing tabbed search interfaces for academic libraries. *Journal of Web Librarianship*, *5*(2), 80–95. doi:10.1080/19322909.2011.568822

Thompson, L. (2013). Cartographic and literary intersections: Digital literary cartographies, digital humanities, and libraries and archives. Journal of Map and Geography Libraries, 9(3), 335-349.

Tracy, D.G. (2016, January). Assessing digital humanities tools: use of Scalar at a research university. *Libraries and the Academy, 16*(1), 163-189.

Wood, D., & Fels, J. (1992). *The power of maps*. New York: Guilford Press.

Wooster Digital History Project. (2015). Retrieved from http://woosterhistory.org/

Zimmerman, D., & Paschal, D. B. (2009, May). An exploratory usability evaluation of Colorado State University Libraries digital collections and the Western Waters Digital Library web sites. *Journal of Academic Librarianship*, *35*(3), 227–240. doi:10.1016/j.acalib.2009.03.011

APPENDIX: DIGITAL PROJECT EXAMPLES

College of Wooster, *Wooster Digital History Project* (http://woosterhistory.org/)
Electronic Cultural Atlas Initiative (http://www.ecai.org/)
Library of Congress, *Churchill and the Great Republic* (http://www.loc.gov/exhibits/churchill/interactive)
Montana State Library, *Montana Memory Project* (http://montanamemory.org)
United States Holocaust Memorial Museum, *Some Were Neighbors* (http://somewereneighbors.ushmm.org)
University of Nevada, Las Vegas, *Documenting the African American Experience in Las Vegas* (http://digital.library.unlv.edu/aae)
Virtual Center for Spatial Humanities at Indiana University-Purdue University Indianapolis (http://polis.iupui.edu/index.php/spatial-humanities/project-1/)
Recent University of Nevada, Reno Libraries Digital Initiatives projects:
Forgotten Landscapes: Military at UNR (http://arcg.is/24uZ4HI)
Harry Reid and Nevada: A Love Story (http://arcg.is/2bkSnyZ)
Wolf Pack Athletics: A Visual History (https://library.unr.edu/DigiColl/Exhibit/wolfpack)
Women at the University of Nevada, Reno (http://arcg.is/1XaFNG3)

Chapter 11
Drips Gallery:
A Community-Driven Graffiti Library and Archive

Alexandra Lederman
Drips Gallery, USA

Farah Jindani
Drips Gallery, USA

ABSTRACT

This paper explores the possibilities of using digital technologies in an archival setting. The hypothesis examined and investigated was: street art can be preserved and archived through archival websites and mobile applications. In order to explore this problem a community driven digital archive, Drips Gallery, was created. Drips Gallery is a new archive consisting of graffiti photograph collections and is available through a website and mobile app. The database, website, and mobile app was created, coded, and programmed specifically for the archival and community needs of Drips Gallery. Drips Gallery allows the community to drive the archive and changes the role of the archivist from record keeper to facilitator. By creating an archival mobile app and website, new and immediate ways of capturing and preserving culture as it is being created and consumed is now possible.

INTRODUCTION

Designedly displayed yet outlawed and elusive, graffiti is more complex than scrawled drawings and painted letters on city buildings and streets. It is a representation of a neighborhood; a voice of its inhabitants speaking to the public, to each other, and

DOI: 10.4018/978-1-5225-2676-6.ch011

to themselves. Graffiti is a worldwide subculture. It is political activism. It is art. Although the concept of graffiti dates back as far as Ancient Egypt, the art movement developed its roots and notoriety in 1970s New York City. Strategically glazed over subway cars were canvasses that travelled from the neighborhoods throughout the city. As city officials labored over the whitewashing of vandalism, advertisers adopted the style to sell clothes and music. The art form became popular and trendy. Since then, graffiti has evolved into a more accepted and often commissioned form of art. Walls around the city have been adopted for intricate murals, paintings are sold in galleries, books and documentaries on the subject are available, and all in homage to street sign scribbles. It's clear that from the birth of the movement to its current place in culture, graffiti has tremendous archival value. There are countless reasons why graffiti should be preserved including its role in art history and New York City, the socioeconomic connotations, the political stance, the effect on consumer culture, the controversy, and the acceptance. Of course, this is no easy task for archivists as graffiti is a transient street art. For the most part, graffiti is fleeting, constantly changing. Graffiti artists take risk with their art, exposing it to the world without knowing how many people will see it and how long it will survive. Thus, this radical type of art requires an unconventional, proactive archival approach. The best way for archivists to document graffiti would be to apply the technology that matches the mobile nature of this movement as well as rely on participation from the community.

Problem

Graffiti has tremendous archival value as an art form, a culture, and a political movement. However, there are many factors contributing to the reluctance in acquiring and maintaining these records. Similar to the internet; born digital material and social media, vital cultural material, are consumed as rapidly as it is being created occurring simultaneously across multiple platforms. With the rise of mobile technology, rapid creation and consumption becomes instantaneous creation and consumption; a stream of consciousness culture. A similar temperament is inherent within graffiti culture, except that it is also being destroyed at the same rate it is being created and consumed. The destruction of graffiti art stands against unpredictable forces including weather, property owners, and government sanitation. There is also the considerable issue of illegality; while graffiti art has become widely popular it is still often seen as vandalism. Artists, the primary sources, are hesitant to document their work and risk exposing their identities, which is paradoxical to their displays of activism which are meant for the public; a picture-taking, status-posting, auto-archiving, constantly mobile public.

The current state of the graffiti archive is a large gap of missed moments due to its original stigma of vagrant misdemeanors dirtying city streets, as well as its elusiveness and transient nature. Today, graffiti is being embraced by the art world, by communities proud to see displays of their roots on public walls, and by those who identify with the movements' politics. The archival gap is will be more apparent as the lack of documentation becomes more obvious. As previously stated, there are several challenges that face archivists in acquiring and preserving graffiti art. The greatest of which is its swift and simultaneous rate of creation, consumption, and destruction. Due to these challenges, a proactive approach will be necessary in the capture and documentation of this art form. The similarities between the nature of graffiti and the instantaneous use of mobile technology in today's culture suggest that a merger of the two could successfully result in a digital archive of graffiti guided by the community for which it is intended.

The purposes of this project were as follows:

- Capture and preserve graffiti by creating a digital archive, Drips Gallery, accessible via website and mobile application formats
- Encourage community contribution and usage by allowing users (creators and consumers) to create, edit, and share collections within the archive
- Introduce a radical archive fitting to its generation and subject matter – easily accessible, searchable, and instantly updated
- Evolve the role of creators, consumers, and record-keepers by using emerging technology and supporting proactivity

The main purpose of this venture (a MLIS capstone project) is to capture and preserve graffiti art through a community driven digital archive, Drips Gallery, created by the researchers. In order to create this community driven digital archive, a relational database of photographs and metadata will be built, a website and mobile application (app) prototype will be designed and programmed, and the users/contributors will derive from the researchers' personal and professional friends and family.

Secondly, this project aims to involve the creators and consumers of graffiti in the archival process. Drips Gallery's purpose is to give the users and community the power to add, subtract, and edit the photograph to the newly established archive. By allowing users to contribute towards the archive, the researchers hope to see higher usage and activity within the archive. Mobile accessibility is another mechanism to promote user activity. Drips Gallery hopes to promote the ease of capturing graffiti art by allowing users to instantly upload a digital photograph to the archive via mobile accessibility. The Drips Gallery mobile app will allow creators or consumers easy access, contribution power, and editing rights.

The third purpose of the Drips Gallery prototype is to create a radical archive while increasing searchability. Archives and reading rooms tend to have a reputation for being intimidating and geared towards academia or the intellectual elite. Drips Gallery will not look like other archives, nor will it work like the traditional archive. The archive will only exist in digital format, and the graffiti collections along with metadata will be created by the Drips Gallery community. The website itself will be easy to use, emulate the simplicity of a Google search, and will not require knowledge of Library of Congress Subject Headings or archival terminology. The vocabulary and terminology in Drips Gallery will derive from the graffiti community, artists, and photographers. Librarians, archivists, and educators can use this archive to introduce students and the general public to an archive.

As technology continues to evolve, so will the role of the archivist. The fourth, and final, purpose of Drips Gallery is to learn how to create a website and an app in order to further the role of the archivist. The archivist is no longer the record keeper; he/she will need to actively engage with the archive, its patrons, and other communities while relieving themselves of traditional archival duties. Allowing the community to control aspects of the archive shifts the role of the archivist. In this age of technology, the archivist will need to actively learn technical skills in order to create a relevant and heavily used archive.

LITERATURE REVIEW

Beginning with an examination of graffiti art, its background, cultural relevance and archival value, this section will display the reasons why a plan for archiving and preserving graffiti is necessary. Furthermore, this section will provide research relating to digital and contributor-based archives and mobile technologies, along with commentating on the use of digital technologies acting as a proper vehicle for building and maintaining a graffiti archive.

Graffiti: A Historical Background

The current art form of graffiti was established in New York City throughout the 1970's and 1980's. However, the concept of drawings or written text placed on various unconventional surfaces in order to convey a message dates back centuries. Articles on the subject provide varying time frames and locales for possibilities of origination such as the Pyramids of Ancient Egypt, IRA murals in Northern Ireland, and wall writings in Pompeii. In their paper, "A Gallery for the Outlaw: Archiving the Art of the Iconoclast", Cailtin M.J. Pollock and Andrea L. Battleground (2013) offer the story behind the World War II slogan "Kilroy was here," as a simple yet authentic representation of early graffiti and its relevance. James Kilroy was employed to mark machinery he had inspected, but soon the phrase began to appear on tanks before Kilroy had a chance to inspect. Then a man peering over a wall was being drawn above the slogan "Kilroy was here" and before the war's end, the slogan and image appeared on tanks, battleships, aircraft carriers, and cruisers. The evolution of the original message became a comforting message among soldiers who were far from home. Although the original purpose of Kilroy's designation was purely functional, it evolved into a repeated symbol implying a relatable identity or idea, similar to a graffiti artist's tag. A tag is the graffiti artist's signature, the primary and most common form of graffiti. They are "text-based and largely indecipherable by those outside the graffiti community. The intention behind the tag is the rebellious proliferation of the artist's signature, akin to brand name advertising" (DeNotto, 2014, p. 208). Whether the ideology behind the tag stems from the need to check something off, an egotistical mark of territory, or repetitive practice in lettering, it gave the history of graffiti a foundation in culture that matured into a movement of expression. As Tracey Bowen (2010) comments in her article concerning the visual literacy of graffiti, "the penchant to mark spaces we pass through and say 'I was here' to others known and unknown is gaining strength through the increasing complexity of urban street graffiti" (p. 85). The increasing complexity to which Bowen speaks only augments as the art becomes more intricate, the illegality a higher risk, as artists harness their talents, the power of expression is realized, and as the movement begins.

The New York City transit system acted as a catalyst for the graffiti movement, heightening every aspect from materials to audience. "Subway cars proved to be a strategic as well as convenient canvas for these new visual artists. Not only were various subway routes abandoned late at night...these cars traveled throughout the city. Therefore, the prospective audience... increased exponentially" (Pollock & Battleground, 2013, p. 242). The size of these canvases and the time available to tag overnight encouraged the evolution from markers to spray paint and from tags to throw-ups (grander, more artistic versions of tags). Rachel Masilamani (2008) explains this development:

When spray paint became the medium of choice, tags became more elaborate and more colorful. Several different lettering styles emerged, including Bubble Letters and Broadway Elegant, eventually culminating in highly abstract, often-illegible-to-outsiders, Wild Style writing. Writers referred to these pieces as "throw-ups," since they needed to create them quickly and move on to avoid being caught in the act. (p. 5)

The transit system not only enhanced the quality of art, but also the criminality of it. Many graffiti writers came from lower class neighborhoods in NYC's outer boroughs, including the Bronx and Brooklyn, where train yards were housed. The demand for larger quantities of better quality spray paint led to an increase in shoplifting crimes. "Some writers stole MTA uniforms to disguise themselves" and bypass security, "others acquired master key sets to trains and yards. Trespassing thus joined vandalism and shoplifting as crimes inherent in the art's production" (Masilamani, 2008, p. 5). The complexity of the production resulted in collaboration and graffiti crews, which resulted in graffiti wars. "Though there were rival crews, tension seemed to stem mainly from space issues, intellectual property disputes, and the politics of covering or touching each other's work" (Masilamani, 2008, p. 8). Regardless of these inevitable tensions, a subculture had been birthed and artists "shared and communicated across racial, ethnic, and neighborhood boundaries" (Masilamani, 2008, p. 8). Transit officials and law enforcement focused on cleaning up the transit system and putting a stop to the graffiti. Consequently, this pushed the movement further as every piece of graffiti became an act of resistance. "People in the transit system had spent the best part of the 1980s and hundreds of millions of dollars scrubbing and cleaning those markings, which ranged from the scribbled chaos of tags to glorious murals that spanned the length of two cars" (Dwyer, 2014, p. A20). Graffiti artists remained diligent in their protests, even as they watched their work being whitewashed away. That diligence has clearly paid off; the cultural, artistic, and archival value of the artwork from that time is tremendous and the current public opinion of graffiti art has mostly changed from negative to positive.

Graffiti: The Evolving Reputation and Cultural Relevance

Graffiti has evolved and influenced main stream art and popular culture. The research on this topic is consistent, citing the fame of well-known artists such as Jean-Michel Basquiat, Keith Haring, Shepard Fairey, and Banksy. The ability of these artists to work within the characteristics of the graffiti movement and obtain legitimate success and recognition from a wide range of communities is apparent. Although these artists have aided to ease graffiti's' negative stigma and motivate its celebration, the cultural relevance is deeply layered and has great potential as a source of study. It is important to acknowledge that graffiti, although more widely accepted and influential, is still illegal if unsanctioned and performed on private or city property. This is the reason why Banksy, perhaps the most successful street artist today, maintains his anonymity. Anonymity is simply part of the culture, part of the cause. Outlaw artists and art

...represent a larger marginalized artist community. With their work, they adopt guerilla tactics in their struggle to give voice to voiceless and often—but not necessarily—seek to be a catalyst for social justice and the elimination of racism, sexism, classism, ageism, homophobia, and/or transphobia. A marginalized or alienated art community often mirrors the similarly marginalized groups of society that have been divided by lines of gender, race, sexuality, class, or age... it becomes possible to identify outlaw art as a term used to describe artistic expressions that push societal norms, remove art from the gallery or museum, and place it in the everyday. (Pollock and Battleground, 2013, p. 240)

In the same sense that the art world will dissect color and lines to critique and place value on a piece of art, archivists can place cultural value on images of graffiti. The images of trains that have been acquired for the purpose of this project, speak not only to graffiti culture, but to the history of New York City, the transit system history, and the technological relics with which the images were captured. A graffiti archive will further the discovery and understanding of the movement. As DeNotto (2014) states, "Graffiti is now recognized as a legitimate source of academic study, and it is being studied as a reaction to injustice and disenfranchisement, a cry for revolution, a way to create awareness of socio-political issues, an expression of hope for the future, an effort to reclaim public spaces, or an attempt to beautify the urban environment" (p. 208).

Beyond the characteristics of graffiti that "confront us with questions about identity and the existence of others that live on the margins of the status quo," is the role it has played in pop culture. Graffiti has often been credited as one of the pillars of the Hip Hop movement along with rap music and break-dancing, as both were counter-culture movements emerging in the same locale at the same time. Artists' "renderings of cartoon characters such as Smurfs and Captain Crunch created instant connections with other young people through cultural reference" (Masilamani, 2008, p. 7). Essentially, their nods to popular culture caught the eye of the advertising world, which adopted the styles and branding methods invented by and intended for graffiti artists. In a New York Times article titled, "From Vandals to Artists: Time Rouses More Appreciation for Graffiti," Jim Dwyer (2014) reveals trains that were once canvasses to young graffiti mural artists, were scrubbed clean only to be sold for redecoration to advertisers at six-figure prices 25 years later (p. A20).

Archiving Graffiti: Challenges

There are several factors that inhibit the proper documentation of graffiti art. The most obvious are the legal issues involved. In reference to the previously described, "outlaw art," Pollock and Battleground (2013) explain:

There are often ethical and political implications to providing a forum for unsanctioned art objects. Implications that many in the art preservation establishment maybe more interested in eschewing than confronting on behalf of their institutions. It is often much more difficult to discover the creator of an art object if that art object is illegal. The artist has more than likely taken steps to keep his or her identity anonymous. For street art, the object itself is often a photograph of a mural or image as it appears on a wall or other outdoor surface. It is helpful that an archivist's host institution may claim creatorship of the photograph of said object, but even diligent research and interviews on the part of the librarian may yield no information on the authorship of the original product. (p. 243)

The ideal way to avoid this situation would be to acquire primary source material from the artists themselves, but again, because of the legality issues artists that are active may be hesitant sharing their personal collections. However, according to Masilamani (2008), "While documentary approaches enable graffiti task forces to anticipate future developments or increase officer presence in prime areas, the images are not overly useful for prosecution, since writers must be caught in the act or with graffiti-producing materials in hand for a conviction to adhere" (p.8). She also informs that these documentations are no longer useful in prosecution after the passing of a few years.

The other colossal challenge in attempting to archive graffiti is the ephemeral nature of the art form. "The consistent characteristic of ephemeral items is their short-lived existence and currency. Ephemeral art's brief life exists because it is consumed quickly by its audience who are very often transient; the hurried, harried, urban dweller" (Pollock & Battleground, 2013, p. 243). Graffiti is vulnerable to forces of nature such as precipitation and wind, as well as the laws of the city and its sanitation crews. Rarely created to have permanence, graffiti "is meant to exist for a brief episode of the viewer's life and affect - in that short exchange between the artist and the consumer - how the urban landscape is considered and experienced" (Pollock & Battleground, 2013, p. 243). Findlay argues that it is not only the fact that this type of art is ephemeral "in the sense that these traces are often fleeting and unavailable for future review" that hinders the existence of a proper archive, but just the classification of it (2012, p. 178). She states that graffiti art has "traditionally been regarded by archivists, librarians, and museum curators as 'ephemeral' and therefore of a lesser value to more formalised and structured methods of recordkeeping as is found in official files and volumes of government and corporations" (Findlay, 2012, p. 178). Essentially, traditional archival approaches are doomed here. Something radical is required, an approach that depends upon the same urgency as the culture.

Archiving Graffiti: Methods

In light of the research, the challenges acknowledged in these articles and suggestions offered thereafter, the two archival approaches presented in the hypothesis of this project have been proven necessary for the future of the graffiti archive. The first is to employ an active, ongoing collaboration with the community, users and contributors. Masilamani (2008) argues, "the ineffectiveness of...officially created and maintained records...especially for underrepresented and non-traditional groups, is an ongoing problem for archives" (p. 10). It is only natural to involve the community in a collaborative art that is representative of the voice of the community. It would be ideal to acquire materials through graffiti artists and photographers, but also through people who interact with the art- who stop and take notice of it in its short lifespan. Because the art is created specifically for public consumption, the public, alongside other artists and archivists, can determine its value. The second method Drips Gallery will use is the application of digital technologies and platforms to capture graffiti. Bowen (2010) comments on the nature of the graffiti movement and the nature of the digital world as follows:

The graffiti movement has embraced the digital world and exploited the opportunities to cover much more terrain on the virtual frontier with a plethora of statements about our human condition and existence. If graffiti includes the desire to make oneself known across a range of geographical areas, the Internet then, has multiplied this opportunity to include places and spaces beyond an accessible, physical locale. (p. 86)

Archiving graffiti through digital technology allows the culture a sense of permanence and legitimacy that the street cannot offer. Although this can be seen as a contradiction to the nature of the movement, synchronizing the user element with digital technology will help preserve the collaborative and communal voice. When speaking in regards to graffiti as a digital archive, Findlay explains that a shift takes place on the way that library professionals perceive graffiti. She states, "These new forms of archives are no longer relegated to the category of ephemera in institutional libraries and archives, or are dismissed as only 'fragments,' but rather are contextualised, shared, open and dynamic - and available in a time and (online) space that maximises their power to effect change" (Findlay, 2012, p. 181).

The Activist Archivist

The archive is the entryway to historical knowledge and the archivist acts as the gatekeeper. Documents contained in an archive are "often viewed as truthful and factual representations of individuals and significant events throughout history"

(Dalmer, 2012, p. 26). This thought may be misleading, many archival items are representations of the views and prejudices from the era in which the items were created. The archival items are not the only reason to be wary of the truthfulness of the archive. Archivists and their institutions are "influenced by political or cultural values, hampering the ability to incorporate or properly capture and describe records in the archive" (Dalmer, 2012, p. 26). Today, archivists and institutions are aware of the importance of documenting underrepresented communities while maintaining unbiased views.

Archivists and archives today are striving for unbiased inclusion while evolving with new technologies. The historical records of today and in the future, will rely increasingly on born-digital media and the archivist will need to capture, preserve, and maintain access. Cultural institutions collecting material of social and historical importance will need to ingest material from a variety of different sources, metadata, and file formats (Besser, 2014). The documentation of everyday activity is a vital product with enduring value (Besser, 2013). One way to document, capture, and curate vital products is by collaborating with the community, the individual, and those closest to where the events are occurring.

The archivist's role is beginning to blur in the digital age. This multifaceted role is made up of scholarly, editorial, publisher, stewardess, and collaborator functions (Clement, 2013). The activist archivist is collecting material from the creator while the material and the creator are still living. The activist archivist is a facilitator role; empowering communities to connect, create, share, learn, and teach. Remixing the traditional services of an archive and of the archivist not only portrays relevancy, but unbiased documentation and preservation.

Digital and Mobile Technology

Digital technologies and social media are evolving every day and creating new content rapidly. The content created on mobile phones, tablets, computers, and social media is important and relevant to libraries and archives. However, libraries and archives are rarely depositing the relevant content into their collections due to the quickly changing digital environment. "Archives and libraries need to be innovative and proactive about seeking" out digital content from numerous participants in real time (Besser, 2014, p. 2). Archives and libraries can access active users and communities by adopting into open-source projects committed to innovation and sustainability. A digital archive may act as a medium with different restrictions and different possibilities than the print environment (Clement, 2013).

Mobile technologies and devices providing portable access to the Internet have increased the past few years. Smart phones "have become the most prevalent tool for media consumption and communication worldwide, with 4.6 billion mobile phone subscriptions", compared to the "1.2 billion personal computers in use" (Hu, 2011, p. 18). Pew Research found adults aged 18-29 are more concerned with access to information on the go compared to staying in touch with others (Hu, 2011). That being said, many mobile Internet users become frustrated because the experience is different than using the Internet on a computer (Hu, 2011). Users "likened desktop Internet use to scuba diving, where search can be 'immersive' and 'invites exploration and discovery'" (Hu, 2011, p. 18). While "mobile Internet use is closer to snorkeling, where 'shallow dipping in and dipping out of content for quick checking of key content is desired'" (Hu, 2011, p. 18). Hu (2011) reports that "despite the disinclination to do heavy research on mobile devices, there does seem to be some interest in having the option to access library databases, catalogs and resources from mobile devices" (p. 21).

In order to attract and maintain users, the interactive and interaction designs of the mobile application or technology will be a determining factor. Interaction design is complex and various factors must be considered. Some factors to keep in mind are: "who is going to use the products, how these products will be used, where they will be used, and how emotions work during the interaction with a system" (Ardito, 2009, p. 85). Mobile technology has invited additional challenges in the interactive design development. The "pervasive and ubiquitous nature, the small size and the interaction modalities (e.g. touch-screens, stylus, fingers and combinations)," create a new range of interaction paradigms in mobile interactive design (Ardito, 2009, p. 80). While obstacles of mobile interaction/interactive design exist, the products can change the way information is accessed. Mobile learning "is the combination of e-learning and mobile computing...and provides opportunities to interact with learning materials in different ways while exploring a physical environment both outdoors...and indoors" (Ardito, 2009, p. 80). Different educational opportunities are being discovered through mobile learning technologies.

The growing educational opportunities made available through mobile technology are continuously being discovered. Geo-technologies, like GPS or digital mapping services are available through mobile technology and used frequently. Receiving directions through GPS is not the only benefit of Geo-technologies. GeoHistory, or history pinning, "uses geographic information systems to produce creative historical iterations of space and time" (Cocciolo, 2011, p. 100). Historypin.com (2014) utilizes GeoHistory and collaborates with individuals, museums, libraries, and archives to provide glimpses of the past and to build the story of human history. The augmented history available through mobile technology allows for users to emotionally connect with a geographical place. Philadelphia Department of Records launched PhillyHistory.org Mobile in 2007, allowing users the option to view historic images while walking near the original locations. Boyer (2011) reported "people could truly connect the past to the present and relate to the images from the Philadelphia City Archives in an entirely new and exciting way" (p. 50).

Mobile technologies have many potential benefits and obstacles for special collections, libraries, and cultural institutions. The ubiquity of various mobile devices creating numerous amounts of content is a major obstacle. Cultural institutions, libraries, and archives will need to creatively rethink the ingestion process in order to meet the demands of mobile content. While creative rethinking and brainstorming will need to take place, mobile technologies offer many benefits to libraries and archives. Many archival and special collections can reach new audiences, preserve photographs, "create additional learning and access opportunities, and redraw the geographic boundaries of a library collection" (Boyer, 2011, p. 52). The obstacle may be large, but the benefits of using mobile technology to provide access and to build collections are tremendous.

Drips Gallery used the case studies listed above as a guide while deciding and creating the type of archive most conducive to capturing and preserving graffiti. It was decided to focus on a mobile app because graffiti and "deep diving" research in regards to graffiti is more visual and less textual. Images of graffiti will be searchable through geolocation on a map visual, this allows users to walk in the present and view historical items. The most important aspect of using mobile technologies for Drips Gallery is to create accessibility to information. There will be no reading room or research requests, any user with a smart tablet and Internet will be able to research graffiti through Drips Gallery.

SUMMARY

Writing or drawing on unconventional surfaces to disseminate a message dates back centuries. The art form called graffiti established itself throughout the 1970's and 1980's in New York City. Graffiti was labeled and recognized as vandalism due to its invasive nature and use of MTA Transit trains as the medium. Law enforcement and transit officials focused on cleaning up the MTA, with a specific goal to end graffiti. This instigated an act of resistance within the graffiti community. This act of resistance and persistence has led to a more widely accepted view of graffiti, while maintaining its illegal status if on private property or unsanctioned. Graffiti provides a historical insight to injustice, the reclaiming of public spaces, socio-political issues, and urban beautification attempts. Graffiti has also been credited as one of the catalysts of the Hip Hop movement. The value in preserving graffiti is intrinsic.

Capturing, preserving and maintaining access to graffiti art is a mammoth obstacle. The first major challenge in archiving graffiti is the legalities. While documenting the art may increase law enforcement presence in particular areas, images of graffiti cannot be used against the artist. The artist can only be convicted if caught with graffiti producing materials. The second challenge in archiving graffiti is the ephemeral nature of the art form. Graffiti has a short lifespan and is consumed quickly. Traditional archival methods will be of no use when archiving graffiti, a radical method will need to be applied and enforced.

Redefining the role of the archivist is the first step in radically changing archival methods. An activist archivist collects living material while empowering communities to engage, connect, create, share, learn and teach. The archivist can transform into the activist archivist with the use of new technologies allowing archives to evolve in their methods and role. Mobile technologies have been increasing in usage and tend to be used for information access, the interaction/interactive design of mobile technology is complex, but attainable and worthwhile. Mobile technologies create new opportunities for learning and educational experiences, allowing libraries and archives to redraw the geographic boundaries of their collections. This allows individuals can emotionally connect with archival and special collections from the past and in the present beyond the walls of the institution.

Archiving graffiti with the use of mobile technology managed by a community of users is one radical method. Mobile technology will provide a method to capture ephemeral art, allow the graffiti community access to preserved photographs, provide control over collections, increase community activity, and evolve the archivist into a facilitator role.

Methodology

The completion of this prototype depended on four key elements: acquiring and curating preliminary collections, creating a relational database for those collections, designing and programming a website which interacted with that database, and separately designing and programming a mobile application to interact with the database.

Image Collections

Drips Gallery consists of images donated by Dennis Stumpo and Ray Mock. Dennis Stumpo a.k.a. RARE is a graffiti artist based in the Bronx, New York. He has been producing and documenting graffiti art since its emergence in the mid-1970s. His collection extends over 4,000 images, most of which he has personally digitized. Although he allowed Drips Gallery access to his entire collection, three collections were curated, shared and viewed via USB drives, DVDs, and Facebook, totaling fifty-three images. The collections contributed by Stumpo include Trains (photographs of New York City subway cars from the 1970s and 1980s), Subway Maps (images of tagged or stenciled transit maps), and Graffiti Universe. Graffiti Universe is the name given to a wall in the Bronx where Stumpo invites graffiti artists to come and display their work on private property owned by his uncle. The wall is buffed and the artwork is replaced with new pieces consistently on a weekly and bi-weekly basis. Dennis Stumpo has been documenting every piece of art displayed at Graffiti Universe since early 2011.

The other two collections in Drips Gallery, Brazil World Cup 2014 and Lisbon were contributed by Ray Mock a.k.a. Carnage. Based in Brooklyn, New York, Mock is a writer, photographer, and independent publisher who has been documenting street art around the world for the past 15 years. The Brazil World Cup and Lisbon collections are two of the locales where he has documented the street art culture through his photography. The photos for the two collections, totaling 34 images, were shared and curated via Flickr.

Prior to proceeding with the project, multiple in-person meetings occurred with both contributors to explain the Drips Gallery mission and how they would be credited. At the request of Dennis Stumpo, the photos that he contributed were watermarked with either "Stumpo" or "Graffiti Universe" logos using Adobe Photoshop. All the necessary metadata for the database such as image titles, dates, locations, etc. were acquired from the contributors in these meetings. The images were given file names, organized into collection folders, and stored on two external hard drives and one USB flash drive.

Database

The first step the creators of Drips Gallery took to create a community-driven digital archive involved designing the backend of the website and mobile app. The first decision was to determine the type of database in which the data would be contained. There were two ways to go about creating the database for Drips Gallery. The first option involved building a relational database from scratch and the second option comprised using a Content Management System (CMS). Systems reviewed include: Collective Access, Omeka, and Archivists' Toolkit. The types of data affiliated with Drips Gallery were taken into consideration when making this decision. Another aspect necessary to consider during the decision process was database accessibility. The connection and accessibility between the database and the mobile app is essential to Drips Gallery's web and mobile connection. Due to the type of data, the photographs, metadata, and mobile app accessibility Drips Gallery involved, the decision was made to create an original relational database with MySQL.

Before setting up the MySQL database, the creators began collecting all of the data and metadata for each image. Google Spreadsheets were used to organize the data because of cloud accessibility, multiple users, and CSV export features. The data was divided into tables based on metadata, keywords, collections, and browse capabilities in order to create a relational database. The tables created include: artist, collection, image origin, graffiti style, medium, Library of Congress Graphic Material Thesaurus, general location, exact location, file name, title, date taken, date uploaded, longitude, latitude, height, width, and pixels.

Once the tables on Google Drive were complete, the server location of the MySQL relational database needed to be determined. One option taken into consideration was Amazon Web Services (AWS). AWS is a cloud-based server available free of charge for the first twelve months followed by a monthly fee. This option would involve an entire server setup and software (PHP, SSH, Apache, MySQL) installation. The second option was donated Bluehost server space through DHALab.org. DHALab.org, Digital Humanities in Archives Lab, is a non-profit organization assisting archival students and archivists collaborating and experimenting with digital humanities. The DHA Lab server is located in the Bluehost Cloud and comes equipped with PHP, SSH, Apache, and MySQL.

Ultimately, Drips Gallery chose the Bluehost server because of its cost-effectiveness, capability of working with mobile apps, and the like-minded mission of DHA Lab. An additional benefit of collaborating with DHA Lab, and the archives housed within it, is increased visibility.

Now that the server had been determined, the tables needed to be transformed into a database. The tables located on Google Drive were converted into CSV files in order to upload the data to MySQL on the server. As the upload was taking place, a few flaws in the tables were noticed. By nature, tables are constructed of "one to one" relationships. A relational database allows for "one to many" or "many to many" relationships. In order to achieve that structure, it is necessary to create additional tables that cross-reference each other. At this point, only the simple tables had been constructed resulting in redundancies and duplications. For example, if one image has four artists, a conventional table would repeat an image four times with a different artist. In order to fix the problem, three additional relational tables were created: relational artists (artist x image), relational image origin (origin x image), and relational style (style x image).

Once the tables were complete, they were uploaded to MySQL. Next, it was necessary to upload the images to the Bluehost server. Prior to doing so, the image file names were adjusted in a manner that could be easily recognized by the program and constructed automatically from the metadata for organization and future growth. An open-source File Transfer Protocol (FTP), FileZilla, was used to transfer the computer files (images) from one host to another host over a TCP-based network (aka Internet). This allowed the image folder to be transferred with its given structure rather than consequently reorganizing single files within the server. The image FTP upload was completed smoothly and all of the data related properly to the images without any hiccups.

Website

The first step taken in creating the website was deciding whether to use a website builder or create the code via a developer tool. The creators decided the best way to tackle this decision was by investigating website builders. The conducted research included website builders such as Weebly, Squarespace, and LayoutIt! Ultimately, the creators decided on using LayoutIt!. The decision was based on financial terms, customization options, and ease of use. LayoutIt! uses Bootstrap, a front-end framework tool that specializes in developing websites that auto-adjust and transform for optimal viewing on mobile devices. Although Drips Gallery will offer a website and mobile application, it is beneficial that the website will be user-friendly on any mobile environment. Any additional level of access is considered a plus.

Before beginning to work on the website through LayoutIt!, the layout of the pages were sketched by hand. It was decided to place a menu bar at the top of each page with the Drips Gallery logo. The menu bar would include links to the following pages within Drips Gallery: Discover Drips, About Us, a search bar, Log In, and Register. In the future, Drips plans to include a Map Page with pins of all the locations of the graffiti. While this feature is not a priority for the website, it is an integral aspect of the mobile application. The original LayoutIt! design of the home page comprised one main image placed in the center of the page with two rows of smaller images below.

All of the images on the home page would be programmed to change whenever the site was refreshed. As the project actualized, the creators adjusted the home page to simply include one large centerpiece that cycled through each of the images on the database every few seconds. A loading speed issue presented itself with this change. As a result, all of the images were compressed and uploaded to the server in a low-resolution image folder from which the website was specifically programmed to pull the home page images. In the future, images that will be uploaded by users will automatically adjust to a size that works well for this purpose.

The pages created next included the Log In and Register pages. These pages are fairly standard, containing a username/email and password entry for the Log In Page and a form consisting of first name, last name, email address, username, password, and confirm password for the Register page. This was the least difficult part of the website building process because Bootsnipp.com, a resource for Bootstrap frameworks, provided the form builder code, equipped with text boxes and a submit button. It simply had to be customized and copy/pasted into the Drips HTML files.

The following page created was the Administrator page. The purpose of the Admin page is to allow the Drips Gallery creators and administrators to control and manage the database. Eventually, the database will no longer be accessed through MySQL, but rather through the Administrator page. This page will also allow the administrators to manage users and their contributions. In order to maintain the accessibility and accuracy of the archive, the images uploaded by users will be subject to a process of quality control. Although the Admin page has been created and uploaded to the server, it will not be programmed immediately. Because this preliminary process requires continuous interaction with the back-end, the utilization of the Admin page is not in the scope of this prototype project.

The most complex page, the Discover Page, is home to various search utilities. Drips decided that the easiest way for users to search is through drop-down search filters. The drop-down search filters are located at the top of the page and consist of: Collections, Artists, Medium, Location, Style, Photographer, Date Taken, User, Library of Congress Terms, and Image Origin (digital or analog). When the page is initially opened, the filters will not be set and all images can be viewed. The page will consist of four rows of one to four images, depending on size, with the remaining images separated by pagination. Each image will link to a landing page, which will include the singular image alongside its metadata. Clicking the image again via its landing page will link to the original photo at its highest resolution. After considering the inevitability of expansion, the creators decided to vary the style of the search functions. For example, more specific search criteria such as photographer or date taken have been separated out into an "Advanced Search" option as to not overwhelm the user. Some criteria such as Artist and Location are available as text boxes rather than drop-downs because those have the potential to grow tremendously and would not display well via a drop-down menu. The Discover Page will require the most ongoing maintenance and analysis as it is essentially the actualized form of the database and the surrounding pages are its bookends (see Figure 1: Drips Gallery Discover page).

The final page created was the About Us Page, which includes the Drips Gallery mission statement and team description. The mission statement appears at the top of the page followed by the team member bios and headshots. Originally, the researchers, Farah Jindani and Alexandra Lederman, were the only team members to be displayed online. However, they decided to include Allan Pichardo, the Drips mobile app consultant. Also, during this process, the creators decided it would be necessary to include a copyright statement to protect the archive and its contributors. The copyright disclaimer states: "Drips Gallery C. 2014. The material on this site may not be reproduced, distributed, transmitted, cached or otherwise used, unless used under the Fair Use Act." This statement appears as a static footer on the bottom of every page.

Figure 1. Drips gallery discover page (finished product)

As previously stated, the frameworks of the pages were built in Layoutit! They were downloaded as zip files, which included the HTML files and the Bootstrap CSS. The files were then opened in Adobe Dreamweaver to be stylistically manipulated. This is when the specific design aspects were determined. Since the archive consists of colorful photographs of graffiti and street art, toned down backgrounds were used. This ensures that the graffiti can speak for itself and boldly. Space, or padding, surrounds each image and everything is centered. The font type is Helvetica because of its natural easy to read on a screen characteristic. Following the initial alterations, the pages and corresponding CSS files were uploaded through Filezilla, thus making the website live. The PHP and Javascript code was programmed through Netbeans while accessing the live site via remote server, and synchronized repeatedly after testing each update.

Mobile Application

The Drips Gallery creators made a decision to produce an original relational database at the beginning of the process, resulting in a smoother experience in creating the mobile app. Before delving into the details, it is important to understand the basic mechanics of a mobile application and its relation to a website or a mobile website.

A mobile application functions on a Model-View-Controller architectural pattern. The model is the database, where the information is located, the view is the user interface, and the controller layer is the link between the other two layers. The controller extracts information from the model at the request of the view or user interaction and interprets that information so it can be displayed by the view. Although a mobile website essentially works the same way, an application is significantly more straightforward as it is a singular platform downloaded to live on a user's device and its sole purpose is to transmit and interpret requests between the three layers. A mobile website is simply a smaller version of an existing website that needs to be accessed via a web browser on a server and involves complex layers through which requests have to pass in order to achieve responses.

Drips Gallery's decision to create a mobile application alongside the website was because of the simplicity of working with images via mobile apps. The idea of capturing the images within the same platform as the archive is conceptual as much as it is convenient. This concept was a significant factor when determining the user interface of the app. The interface was first sketched on paper, similar to the origin of the website. The home page consists of several rows of multiple images that will continue as the user scrolls down the page. Each page is bordered with static header and footer navigation bars. The footer includes four icons: a home icon, a camera, a map icon, and personal profile. The header includes a list icon that opens on the left when clicked to show the available search criteria such as collections and artists. After these initial designs were completed, they were actualized through Eclipse with Android Developer Tools software. This software has the ability to drag and drop style elements to complete a design, then program those elements in the same developer environment (see Figure 11: Drips App Menu on Eclipse).

The coding was done in Java, the programming language for Android, and capable of interacting with the PHP scripts already written in the MySQL database for the website. As with the Discover Drips page of the website, the search criteria on the app filters the images available on the home page.

Each image leads to the larger resolution image with a list of metadata. The profile icon is not currently functional, but will be in the near future. The map icon leads to a map of the user's current location through the device's built-in GPS technology. As the archive grows and contributions are uploaded, the map will automatically generate pins of the various image locations. The camera icon offers the option of selecting an image from DropBox, the device's photo gallery, or taking a new image via the device's camera utility. Currently, these options can be seen are visible although the functionality is still in progress (see Figure 2: Drips Gallery Mobile App Home Page).

Figure 2. Drips gallery mobile app home page (finished product)

Findings

The purpose of the Drips Gallery project, to create a digital archive on a website and mobile app that support user contribution, was proven successful. However, several limitations and necessities for further development were also identified. They are as follows:

- Drips Gallery will require constant maintenance which equals more time, finance, manpower
- Expanding the archive will require technical expansion i.e. servers, bandwidth, storage, file migration
- Archival expansion will raise aesthetic arrangement questions and possible reprogramming
- Analytical studies need to be conducted in order to determine user efficiency and contribution rates

- Develop mobile app availability across operating systems i.e. Apple iOS, Microsoft
- Determine preservation best practices and longevity of born digital content

CONCLUSION

This project aimed to capture and preserve graffiti art through a community- driven archive with the use of a website and mobile app. The paper discusses the current state of graffiti art, the archivist's role, and the use of digital technologies in the archive. Graffiti art is currently becoming a more widely accepted art form and the archivist's role is evolving from record keeper to facilitator. Digital technologies can be and need to be used in archives, libraries, and cultural institutions in order to stay relevant in this digital age. Research questions were asked in order to guide the investigation and analysis. The questions explored the value of archiving graffiti art, whether or not copyright is an issue, the existence of a digital archive in a website and mobile app, and if a mobile app can increase user engagement in an archive. The hypothesis specifically examined whether or not street art can be captured and preserved through a website and mobile app. The research questions and the findings helped define the design of the Drips Gallery website and mobile app. Drips Gallery was designed to empower and engage a community within a digital setting by capturing and preserving graffiti art through a website or mobile app. The end result of this prototype project culminated in a community- driven archive capturing and preserving graffiti art through a website and mobile app. Drips Gallery was designed to engage the graffiti community with archives, evolve the Archivists' role, and increase accessibility while preserving graffiti art.

Recommendations

The purpose of this project was to build a prototype of a graffiti archive that lives and grows on a mobile app. Although Drips Gallery serves sufficiently as a prototype, it does not include a study analyzing overall usability, user accessibility and contribution, intuitiveness of interface, or testing for glitches that can occur with these types of technologies. This is a preliminary design created from donated images in order to inspire a larger scale of content through user participation. Another limitation in this project was limited app building knowledge, resulting in only an Android app. Mobile devices are computers with different operating systems; therefore, they are coded with different languages. The two most prevalent mobile devices on the market today are Apple and Android, and as of right now, Drips Gallery is only accessible via Android devices. The website, however, is accessible through any web browser.

With more time, financial means, and manpower, the necessary aspects can really be analyzed and adjustments and enhancements can be made.

Ideally, in the future, the current limitations of this project would be addressed and remedied. A study would be conducted to analyze the efficiency and usability of the archive so improvements could be made. As use increases over time and the archive grows, it will be necessary to expand the options or change the design. For example, it would be beneficial to have a map as a search function on the website tagging the different cities around the world that are represented within the archive. Drips Gallery would like to encourage user involvement by letting people have more control over what they contribute by being able to delete or edit their images. Challenges including digital preservation factors, server space, backup copies, and file migration are inherent in this as an ongoing project. Issues like being prepared to adapt to future technologies in order to maintain and preserve the archive itself as well as its content and concept are challenges that Drips Gallery, a born digital prototype, will engage as it flourishes.

REFERENCES

Ardito, C., Buono, P., Costabile, M., Lanzilotti, R., & Piccinno, A. (2009). Enabling interactive exploration of cultural heritage: An experience of designing systems for mobile devices. *Knowledge, Technology & Policy*, *22*(1), 79–86. doi:10.1007/s12130-009-9079-7

Besser, H. (2013). Archiving aggregates of individually created digital content: Lessons from archiving the Occupy Movement. *Digital Technology and Culture*, *42*(1), 31–38.

Besser, H., Farb, S. E., Grappone, T., & Jamshidi, A. (2014, August 16-22). Ethics, Technology and the Challenges of Documenting History in Real Time. In *IFLA WLIC 2014*, Lyon, France.

Bowen, T. (2010). Reading gestures and reading codes: The visual literacy of graffiti as both physical/performative act and digital information text. *Mapping Minds, 85*.

Boyer, D. (2011). From Internet to iPhone: Providing mobile geographic access to Philadelphia's historic photographs and other special collections. *The Reference Librarian*, *52*(1/2), 47–56. doi:10.1080/02763877.2011.521880

Clement, T., Hagenmaier, W., & Knies, J. L. (2013). Archive of the future. *Library Quarterly: Information, Community, Policy*, *83*(2), 112–130.

Cocciolo, A., & Rabina, D. (2011). Does place affect user engagement and understanding? Mobile learner perceptions on the streets of New York. *The Journal of Documentation*, *69*(1), 98–120. doi:10.1108/00220411311295342

Dalmer, N. (2012). Women in archives: Present contexts and future implications. *Feliciter*, *58*(4), 26–28.

DeNotto, M. (2014). Street art and graffiti resources for online study. *College & Research Libraries News*, *75*(4), 208–211.

Dunne, S., & Lerkenfeld, M. (2010). Digital graffiti: Urban subculture in digital environments. *Paper presented at the Young Investigator's Forum on Culture Technology, Korean Advanced Institute of Science & Technology*. Retrieved from http://itu.dk/people/mlsm/report/YCT2009 _Digital_Graffiti.pdf

Dwyer, J. (2014). From vandals to artists: Time rouses more appreciation for graffiti. *New York Times, 163*(56501), A20-A20.

Findlay, C. (2012). Witness and trace: January 25 graffiti and public art as archive. *Interface*, *4*(1), 178–182.

Hamilton, M., Sanidas, O., & Sweeney, C. (2012). Digital media labs: Thinking beyond the joystick. *Colorado Association of Libraries*. Retrieved from: http://coloradolibrariesjournal.org/articles/calcon-2012-digital-media-labs-thinking-beyond-joystick

Hu, R., & Meier, A. (2011). Planning for a mobile future: A user research case study from the California Digital Library. *Serials*, *24*(3), S17–S25. doi:10.1629/24S17

Masilamani, R. (2008). Documenting illegal art: Collaborative software, online environments and New York City's 1970s and 1980s graffiti art movement. *Art Documentation: Journal of the Art Libraries Society of North America*, *27*(2), 4–14.

Pollock, C. M., & Battleground, A. L. (2013). A gallery for the outlaw: Archiving the art of the iconoclast. Paper presented at the Association of College & Research Libraries (ACRL) Conference, Indianapolis, IN. Retrieved from http://www.ala.org/acrl/sites/ala.org.acrl/files/content/conferences/confsandpreconfs/2013/papers/PollockBattleground_Gallery.pdf

Compilation of References

9. to5 Staff. (2011, October). Jobs' original vision for the iPhone: no third-party native apps. *9to5Mac.* Retrieved from https://9to5mac.com/2011/10/21/jobs-original-vision-for-the-iphone-no-third-party-native-apps/

Aitken, S. C., & Kwan, M. P. (2010). GIS as qualitative research: Knowledge, participatory politics and cartographies of affect. In D. DeLyser, S. Herbert, S. C. Aitken, M. Crang, & L. McDowell (Eds.), *The SAGE handbook of qualitative geography* (pp. 287–304). Los Angeles, CA: SAGE. doi:10.4135/9780857021090.n18

Andrews, M. (2007). Changing Markets, changing relationships. *Library Hi Tech*, *25*(4), 562–578.

Angell, K. (2013). Open source assessment of academic library patron satisfaction. *RSR. Reference Services Review*, *41*(4), 593–604. doi:10.1108/RSR-05-2013-0026

Antoncic, B., & Hisrich, R. (2003). Clarifying the intrapreneurship concept. *Journal of Small Business and Enterprise Development*, *10*(1), 7–24. doi:10.1108/14626000310461187

Apple Inc. (2007, June). *Innovative new way to create applications for iPhone.* Retrieved from http://www.apple.com/pr/library/2007/06/11iPhone-to-Support-Third-Party-Web-2-0-Applications.html

Apple Inc. (n. d.). *iPod + iTunes Timeline.* Retrieved from https://www.apple.com/pr/products/ipodhistory/

Apple. (2016). *Common App Rejections.* Retrieved 10 16, 2016, from https://developer.apple.com/app-store/review/rejections/

Applegate, R. (2009). The library is for studying: Student preferences for study space. *Journal of Academic Librarianship*, *35*(4), 341–346. doi:10.1016/j.acalib.2009.04.004

Ardito, C., Buono, P., Costabile, M., Lanzilotti, R., & Piccinno, A. (2009). Enabling interactive exploration of cultural heritage: An experience of designing systems for mobile devices. *Knowledge, Technology & Policy*, *22*(1), 79–86. doi:10.1007/s12130-009-9079-7

Arthur, W. H., Robert, L. S., & Bradley, D. F. (2010). OpenRoom: Making Room Reservation Easy for Students and Faculty. *Code4Lib Journal,* (10). Retrieved from http://proxy.library.stonybrook.edu/login?url=http://search.ebscohost.com/login.aspx?direct=true&db=edsdoj&AN=edsdoj.f03e86ee6ca54827a209798ccb3ba7e4&site=eds-live&scope=site

Asher, A. D., Miller, S., & Green, D. (2012). Ethnographic research in Illinois academic libraries: The ERIAL Project. In L.M. Duke & A.D. Asher's (Eds.) College Libraries and Student Culture: What We Now Know (pp. 1-14). Chicago: American Library Association.

AVG Technologies, (2015, February). *A history of mobile apps* [Prezi Slideshow]. Retrieved from Prezi website: https://prezi.com/rwc6qmvqkrt-/a-history-of-mobile-apps/#share_email

Bainton, T. (2001). *Information Literacy and Academic Libraries: The SCONUL Approach (UK/Ireland).*

Beck, K., Beedle, M., van Bennekum, A., Cockburn, A., Cunningham, W., Fowler, M., . . . Thomas, D. (2001a). *Manifesto for agile software development.* Retrieved October 25, 2016 from http://agilemanifesto.org

Beck, K., Beedle, M., van Bennekum, A., Cockburn, A., Cunningham, W., Fowler, M., . . . Thomas, D. (2001b). *Principles behind the agile manifesto.* Retrieved October 25, 2016 from http://agilemanifesto.org/principles.html

Bell, S. (2015). Life, Library, and the Pursuit of Happiness. *Library Journal.*

Bell, S. J. (2014). Staying true to the core: Designing the future academic library experience. *portal. Libraries and the Academy, 14*(3), 369–382. doi:10.1353/pla.2014.0021

Bennett, C. (2001, November). A brief history of WAP. *InformIT.* Retrieved from http://www.informit.com/articles/article.aspx?p=23999

Besser, H., Farb, S. E., Grappone, T., & Jamshidi, A. (2014, August 16-22). Ethics, Technology and the Challenges of Documenting History in Real Time. In *IFLA WLIC 2014*, Lyon, France.

Besser, H. (2013). Archiving aggregates of individually created digital content: Lessons from archiving the Occupy Movement. *Digital Technology and Culture, 42*(1), 31–38.

Beyer, H., Holtzblatt, K., & Baker, L. (2004). An agile customer-centered method: Rapid contextual design. In C. Zannier, H. Erdogmus, & L. Lindstrom (Eds.), Extreme Programming and Agile Methods – XP/Agile Universe 2004, LNCS (Vol. 3134, pp. 50–59). Berlin, Heidelberg: Springer; doi:10.1007/978-3-540-27777-4_6

Bieraugel, M. (2015). Managing library innovation using the lean startup method. *Library Management, 36*(4/5), 351–361. doi:10.1108/LM-10-2014-0131

BlackBerry. (2009, April). *RIM launches BlackBerry App World.* Retrieved from http://press.blackberry.com/en/press/2009/pressrelease-2223.html

BnLViewer. (n. d.). Screenshots. Retrieved 23 Sept 2016, from http://sourceforge.net/p/bnlviewer/home/screenshots/

Bolin, M. (2005). The Library and the Computer Center: Organizational Patterns at Land Grant Universities. *Journal of Academic Librarianship, 31*(1), 3–11. doi:10.1016/j.acalib.2004.09.004

Bowen, T. (2010). Reading gestures and reading codes: The visual literacy of graffiti as both physical/performative act and digital information text. *Mapping Minds, 85*.

Boyer, D. (2011). From Internet to iPhone: Providing mobile geographic access to Philadelphia's historic photographs and other special collections. *The Reference Librarian, 52*(1/2), 47–56. doi:10.1080/02763877.2011.521880

Breeding, M. (2006). Reshuffling the deck. *Library Journal, 131*(6), 40–50.

Brown, M. (2012, October). The Lost Steve Jobs Speech from 1983; Foreshadowing Wireless Networking, the iPad, and the App Store. *Life, Liberty, and Technology*. Retrieved from http://lifelibertytech.com/2012/10/02/the-lost-steve-jobs-speech-from-1983-foreshadowing-wireless-networking-the-ipad-and-the-app-store/#

Bryan, S., & Holly, M. (2015). *Building a Culture of Innovation in Higher Education: Design & Practice for Leaders. EDUCAUSE*. EDUCAUSE.

Buckland, M.K. (1975). *Book availability and the library user*.

Cagan, M. (2008, July 6). Moving from an IT to a Product Organization. Retrieved from http://www.svpg.com/moving-from-an-it-to-a-product-organization

Campbell, J., & Moyers, B. (1988). *The power of myth*. New York: Doubleday.

Cervone, H. F. (2011). Managing digital libraries: The view from 30,000 feet: Understanding agile project management methods using Scrum. *OCLC Systems & Services: International Digital Library Perspectives, 27*(1), 18–22. doi:10.1108/10650751111106528

Chang, M. (2010). An agile approach to library IT innovations. *Library Hi Tech, 28*(4), 672–689. doi:10.1108/07378831011096303

Cheng, A. S., Fleischmann, K. R., Wang, P., Ishita, E., & Oard, D. W. (2010). Values of stakeholders in the Net neutrality debate: Applying content analysis to telecommunications policy. In *Proceedings of the 2010 43rd Hawaii International Conference on System Sciences (HICSS)*.

Churchill, N. C. (1992). Research issues in entrepreneurship. In *Sexton, Kasarda) The State of the Art of Entrepreneurship*. Boston: PWS-Kent.

Clandinin, D. J., & Rosiek, J. (2006). Mapping a landscape of narrative inquiry: Borderland spaces and tensions. In D. J. Clandinin (Ed.), *Handbook of narrative inquiry: Mapping a methodology* (pp. 35–76). Los Angeles, CA: SAGE.

Clark, J. (2004). A usability study of the Belgian-American Research Collection: Measuring the functionality of a digital library. OCLC Systems & Services. *International Digital Library Perspectives, 20*(3), 115–127.

Clement, T., Hagenmaier, W., & Knies, J. L. (2013). Archive of the future. *Library Quarterly: Information, Community, Policy, 83*(2), 112–130.

Cocciolo, A., & Rabina, D. (2011). Does place affect user engagement and understanding? Mobile learner perceptions on the streets of New York. *The Journal of Documentation*, *69*(1), 98–120. doi:10.1108/00220411311295342

Coffin, A., & Morril, S. (2015). Promoting Innovation: The WiLs Model. *Collaborative Librarianship*, *7*(1), 22–29.

Cohn, M. (2004, October 8). *Advantages of user stories for requirements* [Web log post]. Retrieved October 25, 2016, from https://www.mountaingoatsoftware.com/articles/advantages-of-user-stories-for-requirements

comScore. (2016). *comScore 2016 U.S. Mobile App Report* [SlideShare Slides]. Retrieved from http://www.slideshare.net/comScoremarcom/comscore-2016-us-mobile-app-report

Content Conversion Specialists. (n. d.). METS / ALTO introduction. Retrieved 23 Sept 2016, from http://content-conversion.com/wp-content/uploads/2014/09/CCS-METS-ALTO-Info_basic_20140909.pdf

Cook, C.C. (2001). *A Mixed-methods Approach to the Identification and Measurement of Academic Library Service Quality Constructs: LibQUAL.*

Cooke, R., & Rosenthal, D. (2011). Students use more books after library instruction: An analysis of undergraduate paper citations. *College & Research Libraries*, *90*(4), 332–343. doi:10.5860/crl-90

Corporation for Digital Scholarship. (2015). *Plans*. Retrieved November 3, 2016, from https://www.omeka.net/signup

Cresswell, T. (2004). *Place: A short introduction*. Malden, MA: Blackwell Pub.

Cullen, R. J., & Calvert, P. J. (1993). Further dimensions of public library effectivenes: Report on a parallel New Zealand study. *Library & Information Science Research*, *15*(2), 143–164.

Dalmer, N. (2012). Women in archives: Present contexts and future implications. *Feliciter*, *58*(4), 26–28.

Davis, M. H. (1983). Measuring individual differences in empathy: Evidence for a multidimensional approach. *Journal of Personality and Social Psychology*, *44*(1), 113–126. doi:10.1037/0022-3514.44.1.113

de Jager, K. (2015). Place matters: Undergraduate perceptions of the value of the library. *Performance Measurement and Metrics*, *16*(3), 289–302. doi:10.1108/PMM-08-2015-0021

DeLyser, D., Herbert, S., Aitken, S. C., Crang, M., & McDowell, L. (2010). Introduction: Engaging qualitative geography. In D. DeLyser, S. Herbert, S. C. Aitken, M. Crang, & L. McDowell (Eds.), *The Sage handbook of qualitative geography* (pp. 1–18). Los Angeles, CA: SAGE. doi:10.4135/9780857021090.n1

DeNotto, M. (2014). Street art and graffiti resources for online study. *College & Research Libraries News*, *75*(4), 208–211.

Desmet, P., & Hassenzahl, M. (2012). Towards happiness: Possibility-driven design. In Human-computer interaction: The agency perspective (pp. 3-27). Springer. doi:10.1007/978-3-642-25691-2_1

Digital Public Library of America strategic plan 2015-2017. (2015). Retrieved from https://dp.la/info/about/strategic-plan/

Doherty, M. T., & White, E. R. (2012). Room reservations at VCU Libraries How we coped with rapid growth and overwhelming demand for student study space. *College & Research Libraries News*, *73*(3), 142–146. Retrieved from http://proxy.library.stonybrook.edu/login?url=http://search.ebscohost.com/login.aspx?direct=true&db=edselc&AN=edselc.2-52.0-84859732064&site=eds-live&scope=site

Donald, N. (1988). *The design of everyday things*. Doubled Currency.

Drake, M. A. (1979). Managing innovation in academic libraries. *College & Research Libraries*, *40*(6), 503–510. doi:10.5860/crl_40_06_503

Draper, H. L., Oswald, T. A., & Renfro, M. (2007). Student Workers: Cross Training in the Academic Environment. *Journal of Access Services*, *5*(1/2), 133–137.

Duffy, J. A. M., & Ketchand, A. A. (1998). Examining the role of service quality in overall service satisfaction. *Journal of Managerial Issues*, *10*(2), 240-255.

Dunne, S., & Lerkenfeld, M. (2010). Digital graffiti: Urban subculture in digital environments. *Paper presented at the Young Investigator's Forum on Culture Technology, Korean Advanced Institute of Science & Technology*. Retrieved from http://itu.dk/people/mlsm/report/YCT2009_Digital_Graffiti.pdf

Dunphy, C. (2011, March). Palm: the rise and fall of a legend. *Maximum PC*. Retrieved from http://www.technobuffalo.com/2011/03/31/palm-the-rise-and-fall-of-a-legend/

Dwyer, J. (2014). From vandals to artists: Time rouses more appreciation for graffiti. *New York Times, 163*(56501), A20-A20.

Emmons, M., & Wilkinson, F. C. (2011). The academic library impact on student persistence. *College & Research Libraries*, *72*(2), 128–149. doi:10.5860/crl-74r1

Estimote. (2014). *Beacon Tech Overview*. Retrieved 10 2016, 17, from http://developer.estimote.com/

Fagan, J. C., Mandernach, M. A., Nelson, C. S., Paulo, J. R., & Saunders, G. (2012). Usability test results for a discovery tool in an academic library.

Fetterman, D. M. (2010). *Ethnography: Step-by-step* (Vol. 17). Sage.

Few, S. (2006). *Information dashboard design*. Cambridge, MA: O'Reilly.

Findlay, C. (2012). Witness and trace: January 25 graffiti and public art as archive. *Interface*, *4*(1), 178–182.

Fisher, E. (2007). Ethnographic invention: Probing the capacity of laboratory decisions. *NanoEthics*, *1*(2), 155–165. doi:10.1007/s11569-007-0016-5

Fleischmann, K. R., Oard, D. W., Cheng, A. S., Wang, P., & Ishita, E. (2009). Automatic classification of human values: Applying computational thinking to information ethics. *Proceedings of the American Society for Information Science and Technology* 46 (1):1-4. doi:10.1002/meet.2009.1450460345

Fleischmann, K. R., & Wallace, W. A. (2005). A covenant with transparency: Opening the black box of models. *Communications of the ACM*, *48*(5), 93–97. doi:10.1145/1060710.1060715

Forrest, C. (2009). Academic libraries as learning spaces: Library effectiveness and the user experience. *Georgia Library Quarterly*, *46*(3), 4.

Foster, N. F., & Gibbons, S. (2007). Introduction to the Undergraduate Research Project. In *N.F. Foster & S. Gibbons' Studying Students: The Undergraduate Research Project at the University of Rochester* (pp. v–vii). Chicago: Association of College & Research Libraries.

Fuld, H. (2012, March). After 16 months Windows phone has 70k apps how long did it take iOS and Android. *Inneractive.* Retrieved from http://inner-active.com/2012/03/25/after-16-months-windows-phone-has-70k-apps-how-long-did-it-take-ios-and-android/

Galinsky, A. D., Maddux, W. W., Gilin, D., & White, J. B. (2008). Why it pays to get inside the head of your opponent the differential effects of perspective taking and empathy in negotiations. *Psychological Science*, *19*(4), 378–384. doi:10.1111/j.1467-9280.2008.02096.x PMID:18399891

Gardner, S., & Eng, S. (2005). What students want: Generation Y and the changing function of the academic library. *portal. Libraries and the Academy*, *5*(3), 405–420. doi:10.1353/pla.2005.0034

GitHub. (n. d.). Retrieved from https://github.com/inuitcss

Gordon, R. S. (Ed.). (2007). *Information tomorrow: reflections on technology and the future of public and academic libraries*. Information Today, Inc.

Grönroos, C. (1984). A service quality model and its marketing implications. *European Journal of Marketing*, *18*(4), 36–44. doi:10.1108/EUM0000000004784

Gurgov, V. (2016, December). (Personal communication).

Hadro, J. (2008). OCLC Aquires EZProxy. *Library Journal*, *33*(3), 23.

Hamilton, M., Sanidas, O., & Sweeney, C. (2012). Digital media labs: Thinking beyond the joystick. *Colorado Association of Libraries.* Retrieved from: http://coloradolibrariesjournal.org/articles/calcon-2012-digital-media-labs-thinking-beyond-joystick

Hanington, B., & Martin, B. (2012). *Universal methods of design: 100 ways to research complex problems, develop innovative ideas, and design effective solutions*. Rockport Publishers.

Harris, T., Bergeron, S., & Rouse, L. J. (2011). Humanities GIS: place, spatial storytelling, and immersive visualization in the humanities. In M. Dear, J. Ketchum, S. Luria, & D. Richardson (Eds.), *GeoHumanities: Art, history, text at the edge of place* (pp. 226–240). London: Routledge.

Hassenzahl, M. (2008). User experience (UX): towards an experiential perspective on product quality. *Proceedings of the 20th Conference on l'Interaction Homme-Machine*. doi:10.1145/1512714.1512717

Hassenzahl, M., Eckoldt, K., Diefenbach, S., Laschke, M., Len, E., & Kim, J. (2013). Designing moments of meaning and pleasure. Experience design and happiness. *International Journal of Design*, *7*(3).

Heath, F. (2011). Library assessment: The way we have grown. *The Library Quarterly*, *81*(1), 7–25. doi:10.1086/657448

Heath, F. (2011). Library assessment: The way we have grown. *The Library*, *81*(1).

Hernon, P., Dugan, R. E., & Matthews, J. R. (2015). *Managing with data: Using ACRLMetrics and PLAmetrics*. Chicago: American Library Association.

Higginbotham, B. (1997, December) Marriage, Brooklyn Style: How the Library, the Faculty and Administrative Computing Deliver Brooklyn College's Academic Computing Program. *Paper presented at the CAUSE annual conference*, Orlando, FL.

Highsmith, J. (2009). Agile project management: Creating innovative products (2nd ed., Kindle version). Amazon.

Hinchliffe, L. J., & Askey, D. From Invasive to Integrated: Information Technology and Library Leadership, Structure, and Culture.

Hisrich, R. D., & Peters, M. P. (1998). *Entrepreneurship: Starting, Developing and Managing a New Enterprise*. Chicago: Irwin.

Hossain, M. J. (2016). Determining the Key Dimensions for Evaluating Service Quality and Satisfaction in Academic Libraries. *The International Information & Library Review, 48(3), 176-189.*

Hu, R., & Meier, A. (2011). Planning for a mobile future: A user research case study from the California Digital Library. *Serials*, *24*(3), S17–S25. doi:10.1629/24S17

Ingraham, I. (2013, October). Apple announces 1 million apps in the App Store, more than 1 billion songs played on iTunes radio. *The Verge*. Retrieved from http://www.theverge.com/2013/10/22/4866302/apple-announces-1-million-apps-in-the-app-store

Inman, R. A., Sale, R. S., Green, K. W., & Whitten, D. (2011). Agile manufacturing: Relation to JIT, operational performance and firm performance. *Journal of Operations Management*, *29*(4), 343–355.

Järs, J. (2014). IT-based solutions for users and library staff: case study of the Tallinn University of Technology Library. In *Proceedings of the IATUL Annual Conference* (Vol. 35, pp. 1-5). Retrieved from http://proxy.library.stonybrook.edu/login?url=http://search.ebscohost.com/login.aspx?direct=true&db=lih&AN=97787043&site=eds-live&scope=site

Joy, P. A. (2014). Law Schools and The Legal Profession: A Way Forward. *Akron Law Review, 47*(1).

Kantar Worldpanel. (2016). *Smartphone OS sales market share*. Retrieved 10 2016, 17, from http://www.kantarworldpanel.com/global/smartphone-os-market-share/

Kautz, J. (n. d.) Small Business Notes - History of Intrapreneurship. Retrieved from http://www.smallbusinessnotes.com/choosing/intrapreneurship/inthistory.html

Kim, B. (2013). The Present and Future of the Library Mobile Experience. *Library Technology Reports*, *49*(6), 15. Retrieved from http://proxy.library.stonybrook.edu/login?url=http://search.ebscohost.com/login.aspx?direct=true&db=f5h&AN=90405355&site=eds-live&scope=site

Kinner, L., & Rigda, C. (2009). The integrated library system: From daring to dinosaur? *Journal of Library Administration*, *49*(4), 401–417. doi:10.1080/01930820902832546

Knowles, A. K. (2008). GIS and history. In A. K. Knowles & A. Hillier (Eds.), *Placing history: How maps, spatial data, and GIS are changing historical scholarship* (pp. 1–26). Redlands, CA: ESRI Press.

Koepfler, J. A., & Fleischmann, K. R. (2012). Studying the values of hard-to-reach populations: content analysis of tweets by the 21st century homeless. In *Proceedings of the 2012 iConference*, Toronto, Ontario, Canada. doi:10.1145/2132176.2132183

Kong, V. (2015). *The 2015 U.S. Mobile App Report by ComScore* [SlideShare Slides]. Retrieved from http://www.slideshare.net/VictorKongCisneros/the-2015-us-mobile-app-report-by-comscore

Krug, S. (2009). *Don 't make me think: A common sense approach to Web usability: How we really use the Web.*

Krug, S. (2014). *Don't make me think, revisited: A common sense approach to Web usability. (n.p.).* New Riders.

Kucsma, J., Reiss, K., & Sidman, A. (2010). Using Omeka to build digital collections: The METRO case study. *D-Lib Magazine*, *16*(3/4). doi:10.1045/march2010-kucsma

Kuniavsky, M. (2003). *Observing the user experience: a practitioner's guide to user research.* Morgan kaufmann.

Kuniavsky, M. (2010). *Smart things: ubiquitous computing user experience design*. Elsevier.

Lallemand, C., Gronier, G., & Koenig, V. (2015). User experience: A concept without consensus? Exploring practitioners perspectives through an international survey. *Computers in Human Behavior*, *43*, 35–48. doi:10.1016/j.chb.2014.10.048

Lancaster, F. W. (1978). Guidelines for the evaluation of information systems and services. In *Guidelines for the evaluation of information systems and services*. Unesco.

Langer, A. M. (2016). Build Versus Buy. In Guide to Software Development (pp. 37-48). Springer London.

Lascarides, M. (2009). Infomaki: An open source, lightweight usability testing tool. *Code4lib 8*.

Latour, B., & Woolgar, S. (1979). *Laboratory life: The social construction of scientific facts*. Beverly Hills: Sage.

Law, E. L. C., Roto, V., Hassenzahl, M., Vermeeren, A. P., & Kort, J. (2009). Understanding, scoping and defining user experience: a survey approach. In *Proceedings of the SIGCHI Conference on Human Factors in Computing Systems*.

Ledeen, K. S. (2014). Build v. buy: a decision paradigm for information technology applications.

Leiter, R. A. (2003). Reflections on Ranganathan's five laws of library science. *Law Library Journal*, *95*, 411.

Library of Congress USA. (n. d.). ALTO: Technical Metadata for Optical Character Recognition. Retrieved 23 Sept 2016, from http://www.loc.gov/standards/alto/

Library of Congress USA. (n. d.). Metadata Encoding and Transmission Standard (METS) Official Web Site, Retrieved 23 Sept 2016, from http://www.loc.gov/standards/mets/

Longley, P. A., Goodchild, M. F., Maguire, D. J., & Rhind, D. W. (2011). *Geographic Information Systems & science* (3rd ed.). Hoboken, NJ: John Wiley & Sons, Inc.

Madsen, D. L., & Oleen, J. K. (2013). Staffing and workflow of a maturing institutional repository. *Journal of Librarianship and Scholarly Communication*, *1*(3), 1–12. doi:10.7710/2162-3309.1063

Mamoli, S. (n.d.). On acceptance criteria for user stories [blog post]. Retrieved November 3, 2016, from http://nomad8.com/acceptance_criteria/

Marsh, A. C. (2013). Omeka in the classroom: The challenges of teaching material culture in a digital world. *Literary and Linguistic Computing*, *28*(2), 279–282. doi:10.1093/llc/fqs068

Masilamani, R. (2008). Documenting illegal art: Collaborative software, online environments and New York City's 1970s and 1980s graffiti art movement. *Art Documentation: Journal of the Art Libraries Society of North America*, *27*(2), 4–14.

Mathews, B. (2012). *Think Like A Startup: a white paper to inspire library entrepreneurialism.* Virginia Tech.

Matthews, J. R. (2011). Assessing organizational effectiveness: The role of performance measures. *The Library Quarterly*, *81*(1), 81–110. doi:10.1086/657447

Matthews, J. R. (2015). *Library assessment in higher education*. Santa Barbara, CA: Libraries Unlimited.

Maurer, Y. (2013). *Presentation on BNL viewer*. Amsterdam.

McAfee, A. (2009). *Enterprise 2.0: New Collaborative Tools for Your Organization's Toughest Challenges* (Kindle ed.). Harvard Business School Press.

McCulley, L. (2010). Sustaining Feedback: Assessment in the Liberal Arts College Library. In *Proceedings of the 2010 library assessment conference*.

Memorandum from Provost Christopher Kimmich and VP for Administration and Finance Patricia Hassett to Brooklyn College Faculty and Staff. (1994, November 14).

Mezick, E. M. (2007). Return on investment: Libraries and student retention. *Journal of Academic Librarianship*, *33*(5), 561–566. doi:10.1016/j.acalib.2007.05.002

Missouri Department of Higher Education, Performance Funding Task Force. (2012). *Performance funding model: Recommendations of the Performance Funding Task Force*. Retrieved from https://dhe.mo.gov/documents/PerformanceFundingReport.pdf

Mizrachi, D. (2010). Undergraduates academic information and library behaviors: Preliminary results. *RSR. Reference Services Review*, *38*(4), 571–580. doi:10.1108/00907321011090737

Moreno, A. M., & Yagüe, A. (2012). Agile user stories enriched with usability. *Lecture Notes in Business Information Processing*, *111*, 168–176. doi:10.1007/978-3-642-30350-0_12

Morton-Owens, E. & Hanson, K. L. (2012, September). Trends at a glance: A management dashboard of library statistics. *Information Technology and Libraries*.

N.Y.U. Libraries. (n. d.). User Experience (UX). Retrieved from https://library.nyu.edu/departments/user-experience/

National Conference of State Legislatures. (2015). *Performance based funding for higher education*. Retrieved from http://www.ncsl.org/research/education/performance-funding.aspx

National Library of Luxembourg. (n. d.). BNLViewer. Retrieved 23 Sept 2016, from http://www.eluxemburgensia.lu

New Media Consortium & Balboa Park Online Collaborative. (2015). *NMC horizon report*. Retrieved from http://cdn.nmc.org/media/2015-nmc-horizon-report-museum-EN.pdf

Nicomsoft. (n. d.) Optical Character Recognition (OCR) – How it works. Retrieved 23 Sept 2016, from http://www.nicomsoft.com/optical-character-recognition-ocr-how-it-works/

Nie, G. P. (2009). Customer Satisfaction Management with Counting Opinion Surveys. *Public Library Quarterly*, *28*(3), 204–211. doi:10.1080/01616840903106980

Nielsen, J. (2001). First rule of usability? Don't listen to users. *The Alertbox: Current Issues in Web Usability*. Retrieved from http://www.useit.com/alertbox/20010805.html

Nielsen, J. (2012). How many test users in a usability study. *Nielsen Norman Group*.

Nielsen. (2014, July). *Smartphones: so many apps, so much time.* Retrieved from http://www.nielsen.com/us/en/insights/news/2014/smartphones-so-many-apps--so-much-time.html

Nilsen, K., & Ross, C. S. (2006). Evaluating virtual reference from the users perspective. *The Reference Librarian, 46*(95-96), 53–79. doi:10.1300/J120v46n95_05

Nokia Corporation. (2005, June). *Snake creator receives special recognition from mobile entertainment forum.* Retrieved from http://company.nokia.com/en/news/press-releases/2005/06/16/snake-creator-receives-special-recognition-from-mobile-entertainment-forum

Nowviskie, B. (2013). Skunks in the Library: A path to production for scholarly R&D. *Journal of Library Administration, 53*(1), 53–66. doi:10.1080/01930826.2013.756698

Oakleaf, M. (2010). *The value of academic libraries: A comprehensive research review and report.* Assoc. of College & Research Lib.

Oakleaf, M. (2010). *The value of academic libraries: A comprehensive research review and report.* Chicago: American Library Association.

Oakleaf, M. (2011). Are they learning? Are we? Learning outcomes and the academic library. *The Library Quarterly, 81*(1), 61–82. doi:10.1086/657444

Olsen, L., Baillargeon, T., & Maringanti, H. (2012). Developing an open access croplands research database through global collaboration. *Journal of Agricultural & Food Information, 13*(1), 35–44. doi:10.1080/10496505.2012.639272

Owens, T. (2012.) Crowdsourcing cultural heritage: The objectives are upside down [blog post]. *User Centered Digital History.* Retrieved November 1, 2016, from http://www.trevorowens.org/2012/03/crowdsourcing-cultural-heritage-the-objectives-are-upside-down/

Parasuraman, A., Zeithaml, V. A., & Berry, L. L. (1985). A conceptual model of service quality and its implications for future research. *Journal of Marketing, 49*(4), 41-50.

Payne, P., & Conyers, A. (2005). Measuring the impact of higher education libraries: the LIRG/SCONUL impact implementation initiative. *Library and information research,* 29(91).

Pendell, K. D., & Bowman, M. S. (2012). Usability study of a librarys mobile website: An example from Portland State University. *Information Technology and Libraries (Online), 31*(2), 45. doi:10.6017/ital.v31i2.1913

Perenson, M. (2008, October). Google launches Android market. *PCWorld.* Retrieved from http://www.pcworld.com/article/152613/google_android_ships.html

Perniciaro, K. (2017). *Mobile/Digital Now Vision Aims to Transform the Stony Brook University Experience.* Retrieved from https://it.stonybrook.edu/news/articles/mobiledigital-now-vision-aims-to-transform-the-stony-brook-university-experience

Pew Research Center. (2017). [Charts illustrating mobile phone ownership and device ownership from 2004-2016] Mobile Fact Sheet. Retrieved from http://www.pewinternet.org/fact-sheet/mobile/

Pinchot, G. (1985). *Intrapreneuring: Why You Don't Have to Leave the Corporation to Become an Entrepreneur*. New York, NY: Harper & Row.

Pitt, L. F., Watson, R. T., & Kavan, C. B. (1995). Service quality: A measure of information systems effectiveness. *Management Information Systems Quarterly*, *19*(2), 173–187. doi:10.2307/249687

Pollock, C. M., & Battleground, A. L. (2013). A gallery for the outlaw: Archiving the art of the iconoclast. Paper presented at the Association of College & Research Libraries (ACRL) Conference, Indianapolis, IN. Retrieved from http://www.ala.org/acrl/sites/ala.org.acrl/files/content/conferences/confsandpreconfs/2013/papers/PollockBattleground_Gallery.pdf

Primack, D. (2012, April). Breaking: Facebook buying Instagram for $1 billion. *Fortune*. Retrieved from http://fortune.com/2012/04/09/breaking-facebook-buying-instagram-for-1-billion/

Quesenbery, W., & Brooks, K. (2010). *Storytelling for user experience: Crafting stories for better design*. Rosenfeld Media.

Quinlan, C., & McHarg, H. (2012). The Emerging Library: Structure, Culture, and Lessons Learned from the Dissolution of a Combined Libraries-IT Organization. *Journal of Library Administration*, *52*(2), 147–161. doi:10.1080/01930826.2012.656483

Rath, L. (2016). Omeka.net as a librarian-led digital humanities meeting place. *New Library World*, *117*(3/4), 158–172. doi:10.1108/NLW-09-2015-0070

Renfro, P., & Neal, J. (2012). The Integration of Libraries and Academic Computing at Columbia: New Opportunities for Internal and External Collaboration. *Journal of Library Administration*, *52*(1).

Roy Rosenzweig Center for History and New Media, George Mason University. (2016). *Preparing to install*. Retrieved October 27, 2016, from http://omeka.org/codex/Preparing_to_Install

Rubin, J., Chisnell, D., & Spool, J. M. (2008). *Handbook of usability testing: How to plan, design, and conduct effective tests*. Indianapolis, IN: Wiley.

Ryan, J., & Boyer, J. (2011). GroupFinder: A Hyper-Local Group Study Coordination System. *Code4Lib Journal*, (13). Retrieved from http://proxy.library.stonybrook.edu/login?url=http://search.ebscohost.com/login.aspx?direct=true&db=edsdoj&AN=edsdoj.55dd1303be374518a28b212d8abd952e&site=eds-live&scope=site

Schonfeld, R. C. (2016). Organizing the work of the Research Library.

Schwieder, D., & Hinchliffe, L. J. (2012). NCES datasets and library value: An exploratory study of the 2008 data. In *Proceedings of the 2012 Library Assessment Conference* (pp. 657-667). Retrieved from http://libraryassessment.org/bm~doc/proceedings-lac-2012.pdf

Shannon, C. E. (2001). A mathematical theory of communication. *Mobile Computing and Communications Review*, *5*(1), 3–55. doi:10.1145/584091.584093

Sharma, P., & Chrisman, S. J. J. (2007). Toward a reconciliation of the definitional issues in the field of corporate entrepreneurship. In *Entrepreneurship* (pp. 83–103). Springer Berlin Heidelberg.

Sharon, T. (2013). A Collaborative Lean UX Research Tool. *Smashing Magazine*. Retrieved 10/14/2016 from https://http://www.smashingmagazine.com/2013/04/rainbow-spreadsheet-collaborative-ux-research-tool/

Sherwin, D. (2013). A 5-step process for conducting user research. *Smashing Magazine*. Retrieved from: http://uxdesign.smashingmagazine.com/2013/09/23/5-step-process-conducting-user-research/

Sinton, D. S., & Lund, J. J. (2007). Critical and creative visual thinking. In D. S. Sinton & J. J. Lund (Eds.), *Understanding place: GIS and mapping across the curriculum* (pp. 1–18). Redlands, CA: ESRI Press.

Smith, B. R. (2016). Book-a-Room Software.

Sofronijevic, A. (2011). New Paradigm of Library Collaboration. In S. Gradmann, F. Borri, C. Meghini (Eds.), *Research and Advanced Technology for Digital Libraries - International Conference on Theory and Practice of Digital Libraries, TPDL 2011*, Berlin, Germany, LNCS (Vol. 6966, pp. 519-522). Springer.

Sofronijevic, A., Milicevic, V., Ilic, B., & Seaman, S. (2011). Enhancing Library Business Performance by Implementation of Enterprise 2.0 via Intrapreneurship: The Case of a Serbian Library. *Journal of Academic Librarianship*, *37*(4), 358–362. doi:10.1016/j.acalib.2011.04.010

Solr Wiki. (n. d.). Analyzers, Tokenizers, and Token Filters Retrieved 23 Sept 2016, from https://wiki.apache.org/solr/AnalyzersTokenizersTokenFilters

Solr Wiki. (n. d.). Data Import Request Handler. Retrieved 23 Sept 2016, from https://wiki.apache.org/solr/DataImportHandler

Solr Wiki. (n. d.). SchemaXml. Retrieved 23 Sept 2016, from https://wiki.apache.org/solr/SchemaXml

Solr Wiki. (n. d.). Solr Query Syntax. Retrieved 23 Sept 2016, from https://wiki.apache.org/solr/SolrQuerySyntax

SpringShare. (n. d.). About. Retrieved from http://www.springshare.com/about.html

Stephan, E., Cheng, D. T., & Young, L. M. (2006). A usability survey at the University of Mississippi Libraries for the improvement of the library home page. *Journal of Academic Librarianship*, *32*(1), 35–51. doi:10.1016/j.acalib.2005.10.011

Stevenson, H. H., & Jarillo, J. C. (2007). A paradigm of entrepreneurship: Entrepreneurial management. In Entrepreneurship (pp. 155-170). Springer Berlin Heidelberg

Sula, C. A. (2013). Digital humanities and libraries: A conceptual model. *Journal of Library Administration*, *53*(1), 10–26. doi:10.1080/01930826.2013.756680

Szebeko, D., & Tan, L. (2010). Co-designing for Society. *Australasian Medical Journal, 3*(9), 580–590. doi:10.4066/AMJ.2010.378

Teague-Rector, S., Ballard, A., & Pauley, S. (2011). The North Carolina State University Libraries search experience: Usability testing tabbed search interfaces for academic libraries. *Journal of Web Librarianship, 5*(2), 80–95. doi:10.1080/19322909.2011.568822

Tempelman-Kluit, N., & Pearce, A. (2014). Invoking the User from Data to Design. *College & Research Libraries, 75*(5), 616–640. doi:10.5860/crl.75.5.616

Tennant, R. (2005, April 15). Digital Libraries: "Lipstick on a Pig." Retrieved from http://lj.libraryjournal.com/2005/04/ljarchives/digital-libraries-lipstick-on-a-pig/

Tenopir, C. (2010). Measuring the values of the academic library: Return on investment and other value measures. *The Serials Librarian, 58*(1-4), 39–48. doi:10.1080/03615261003623005

The Apache Software Foundation. (n. d.). Apache Lucene Query Parser Syntax. Retrieved 23 Sept 2016, from http://lucene.apache.org/core/3_6_0/queryparsersyntax.html

The Apache Software Foundation. (n. d.). Apache Solr. Retrieved 23 Sept 2016, from http://lucene.apache.org/solr/

The Apache Software Foundation. (n. d.). Package org.apache.lucene.codecs.lucene40. Retrieved 23 Sept 2016, from http://lucene.apache.org/core/4_0_0/core/org/apache/lucene/codecs/lucene40/package-summary.html#Limitations

The New Media Consortium (2016). NMC Horizon Report: 2016 Higher Education Edition.

The New Media Consortium. (2015). The NMC Horizon Report: 2015 Library Edition.

Theimer, K. (2010). *Web 2.0 tools and strategies for archives and local history collections*. New York, NY: Neal-Schuman Publishers.

Thompson, B., Cook, C., & Kyrillidou, M. (2006). Stability of library service quality benchmarking norms across time and cohorts.

Thompson, L. (2013). Cartographic and literary intersections: Digital literary cartographies, digital humanities, and libraries and archives. Journal of Map and Geography Libraries, 9(3), 335-349.

Torres-Pérez, P., Méndez-Rodríguez, E., & Orduna-Malea, E. (2016). Mobile Web Adoption in Top Ranked University Libraries: A Preliminary Study. *Journal of Academic Librarianship, 42*(4), 329–339. doi:10.1016/j.acalib.2016.05.011

Town, S. J. (2011). Value, impact, and the transcendent library: Progress and pressures in performance measurement and evaluation. *The Library Quarterly, 81*(1), 111–125. doi:10.1086/657445

Tracy, D. G. (2016). Assessing digital humanities tools: Use of Scalar at a research university. *Portal: Libraries and the Academy, 16*(1), 163–189. doi:10.1353/pla.2016.0004

Tracy, D.G. (2016, January). Assessing digital humanities tools: use of Scalar at a research university. *Libraries and the Academy, 16*(1), 163-189.

Trubitt, L., & Muchane, M. (2008). In plain English, please: Effective IT communications. *EDUCAUSE Quarterly, 31*(2), 62.

Tufte, E. R. (1983). *The visual display of quantitative information*. Cheshire, CT: Graphics.

Tweney, D. (2011, March). Amazon launches its own Android app store. *Wired*. Retrieved from https://www.wired.com/2011/03/amazon-android-app-store-2/

U. Hub. (n. d.). Five second test. Retrieved from http://fivesecondtest.com/

UMKC School of Law. (2016). *Admissions Facts at a Glance*. Retrieved 09 2016, from http://law.umkc.edu/prospective-students/jd-program/admissions-facts-at-a-glance/

UMKC School of Law. (2016). *Employment Summary For 2015 Graduates*. Kansas City: UMKC School of Law.

University Library SvetozarMarkovic. (n. d.). Search Guide. Retrieved 23 Sept 2016, from http://www.unilib.rs/istorijske-novine/about#search-guide

University Library SvetozarMarkovic. (n. d.). Searchable Digitized Historical Newspapers. Retrieved 23 Sept 2016, from http://www.unilib.rs/istorijske-novine/advanced-search

University Library SvetozarMarkovic. (n. d.). Searchable Digitized Historical Newspapers. Retrieved 23 Sept 2016, from http://www.unilib.rs/istorijske-novine/browse

University Library SvetozarMarkovic. (n. d.). Searchable Digitized Historical Newspapers. Retrieved 23 Sept 2016, from http://www.unilib.rs/istorijske-novine/browse?newspaper=UB_00029

University of Central Missouri. (n. d.). *Strategic Resource Allocation Model*. Retrieved from https://www.ucmo.edu/sram/

Vesper, K. H. (1990). *New Venture Strategies*. Englewood Cliffs, USA: Prentice-Hall.

Walters, T., & Skinner, K. (2011). *New roles for new times: Digital curation for preservation*. Association of Research Libraries.

Watson, C. A., & Reeves, L. (2011). Technology Management Trends in Law Schools. *Digitalcommons*. Retrieved from http://digitalcommons.law.uga.edu/law_lib_artchop/21

Whitchurch, M. J. (2012). A quick response: QR code use at the Harold B. Lee Library. *The Reference Librarian, 53*(4), 392–402. doi:10.1080/02763877.2012.704573

Wikipedia. (2016, October 18). *iBeacon*. Retrieved 10 18, 2016, from https://en.wikipedia.org/wiki/IBeacon

Wikipedia. (n. d.). Intrapreneurship. Retrieved 23 Sept 2016, from https://en.wikipedia.org/wiki/Intrapreneurship

Wikipedia. (n. d.). Optical character recognition explained. Retrieved 23 Sept 2016, from https://en.wikipedia.org/w/index.php?title=Optical_character_recognition&oldid=686827150

Wikipedia. (n. d.). Stemming. Retrieved 23 Sept 2016, from https://en.wikipedia.org/w/index.php?title=Stemming&oldid=685786913

Wise, N. (2016, April 11). *Sonic Foundry Announces Finalists in the 12th Annual Enterprise Video Awards*. Retrieved from http://www.sonicfoundry.com/sonic-foundry-announces-finalists-12th-annual-enterprise-video-awards/

Wood, D., & Fels, J. (1992). *The power of maps*. New York: Guilford Press.

Wooster Digital History Project. (2015). Retrieved from http://woosterhistory.org/

Zagar, C. (2007). Unlocking Library Subscriptions. *Library Journal netConnect*.

Zimmerman, D., & Paschal, D. B. (2009, May). An exploratory usability evaluation of Colorado State University Libraries digital collections and the Western Waters Digital Library web sites. *Journal of Academic Librarianship*, *35*(3), 227–240. doi:10.1016/j.acalib.2009.03.011

About the Contributors

Laura Costello is the head of research and emerging technologies at Stony Brook University Libraries. She formerly served as the head of library materials and acquisitions at EdLab, a design and development unit of the Gottesman Libraries at Teachers College, Columbia University. She received her MLIS from the University of Wisconsin and BA in English literature from the University of Minnesota. Highlight projects include Roomer, a mobile room reservation system and Pocket Knowledge, a social and digital archive at Teachers College. She has also been deeply engaged in the library redesigns at both Teachers College and Stony Brook University. Her research interests include data and demand driven strategies for acquisitions and other library management decisions, emerging technologies in libraries, education technology, and designing digital and physical library learning spaces. Laura's professional goals include changing everything, not destroying the library, and maintaining the delicate balance between old skool librarianship and newfangled technology.

* * *

Ayyoub Ajmi is a Digital Communications and Learning Initiatives Librarian at the University of Missouri Kansas City, School of Law. He is building and managing an integrated digital communications platform which provides access to the Law School library and its digital resources, supports law faculty's effective use of technology to enhance student learning, and facilitates information and communication among various constituencies of the law school.

Jennifer L. Anderson is a UX Designer and Information Architect with nearly 20 years experience making web interfaces. She has an MLS from Pratt Institute, and was the Senior UX Designer for the New York Public Library for 8 years. She is currently at Hook & Loop, a creative agency focused on the UX of enterprise software design.

Prof. Colleen Bradley-Sanders (MA., M.L.I.S.) has over 15 years of experience in the archival field, and has experience utilizing technology to support the archival process and improve and expand access for researchers.

Alexandra Dolan-Mescal is a user experience designer and archivist focused on designing digital spaces of, by, and for marginalized communities. She has worked in the libraries of the University of California, Riverside and City University of New York, Queens College, two of the most diverse campuses in the United States, and works for Documenting the Now, a grant-funded project developing tools to build ethical social media archives.

Houda El Mimouni is a doctoral candidate at Drexel University's College of Computing and Informatics. She is doing research in the domain of Human Computer-Interaction and she is interested in UX in libraries and other educational spaces. Houda received her Bachelor degree from the Ecole des Science de l'Information in Morocco and her MLIS from Pratt Institute with support from Fulbright.

Shafeek Fazal is the Assistant Dean for Library Technology, Discovery and Digital Initiatives, University Libraries, Stony Brook University.

Dana Haugh is the Web Services Librarian at Stony Brook University Libraries where she leads the design and development of the library's web presences. Her research interests include web design & development, marketing & outreach in libraries, and information literacy.

Laura Horne-Popp is the Assistant Dean of Library Services and coordinates library assessment programming at the James C. Kirkpatrick Library at the University of Central Missouri. She received her MLIS from the University of Washington.

Amy J. Hunsaker is the Digital Initiatives Librarian at the University of Nevada, Reno where she provides leadership in the development and management of digital collections in collaboration with other Library and University departments.

Farah Jindani although a minimalist in most aspects of her life. Farah is interested in the collection, organization, and accessibility. Currently, she is helping nonprofits make the best use of technology as a Product Specialist at Jacobson Consulting Applications, Inc. Her hobbies include creative writing, podcasts, and television.

Milena Kostic is a librarian, English language teacher and translator. She earned her BA and MA degrees in the field of pragmatic analysis of the discourse of advertising at the Faculty of Philology of the University of Belgrade where she is currently a PhDc. Her dissertation is in the field of cognitive linguistics and education. She has worked at the University Library in Belgrade since 2013 where she has participated in various activities regarding professional training of librarians, international cooperation and adapting new library spaces and services. In 2015 she held a workshop series entitled Digital Marketing Culture, which had a sequel in 2016 as a workshop on Social Media and Digital Storytelling which is accredited by the National Library of Serbia and it includes digital marketing, storytelling, creative communication, trends, standards and rules, researching target groups, setting goals and evaluation. Milena was also involved in the project "Safeguarding the fragile collection of the private archive of the Lazic family" funded by the British National Library and coordinated by the University Library in Belgrade. She worked for 2 years as a project manager assistant on Reforming Foreign Language Studies Tempus Project where she maintained social media, worked in surroundings organized according to agile culture and gained experience in working with various target groups. Ms Kostic has published both scientific and research papers on agile management, online open knowledge resources, information literacy, linguistics, education and foreign language teaching. She regularly presents at conferences in Serbia and abroad.

Alexandra Lederman is a digital humanitarian, a staunch supporter of equal access to information, and is interested in capturing and preserving culture while it's being created and consumed. Foodways, blockchains, net neutrality, and social justice in the library and archive are her passions. After 5 years in the hospitality industry, Alexandra finally took the plunge to advocate for equal access to information. She is a MLS graduate from Queens College and was one of three Graduate Fellows collaborating with the Citi Center Culture x Queens Library. Previously, she was the Technology Materials Librarian at Teachers College, Columbia University. Alexandra is currently the Digital Archivist & Rare Books Librarian at the American Jewish Historical Society and co-founder of Drips Gallery, a community-driven, digital archive and library.

Natasha Majewski curates media-based library collections to create interactive, online stories at the University of Nevada, Reno Libraries. Her background blends multi-media storytelling, creative cartography, and project management and outreach. Her focus on place-based stories showcases library collections and resources through visual and audio media, interactive maps, and researched content to engage audiences ranging from academics to the general public. She holds a Master's of

Science in Cultural Geography with a Master's Minor in Business Administration from the University of Nevada, Reno with a research focus on interactively mapping stakeholder needs, place attachment, and stewardship in community development initiatives. She has also professionally managed prestigious local and international non-profit programs targeting youth leadership, diverse community engagement, multicultural education, democracy, and social media.

Harish Maringanti started my career in Libraries as a programmer at K-State Libraries managing various systems including digital repositories and subsequently managing a team responsible for desktop support, application development and system administration. In my current role as the Associate Dean for IT & Digital Library Services at J. Willard Marriott Library, I am responsible for advancing Library's technology initiatives including strategy, policies, compliance, business processes, and infrastructure. My educational background includes an M.S. in Computing and Information Sciences and a graduate certificate in organizational Leadership, both from K-State.

Susan Chesley Perry is the Head of Digital Initiatives at the University of California, Santa Cruz Library, responsible for the Library Digital Collections and the Grateful Dead Archive Online. These collections include born-digital and digitized materials from the Library's Special Collections and Archives. She works with archivists, metadata specialists, technologists, digital production staff, and preservation specialists as materials move through the digital production lifecycle. She's presented on Omeka at Code4Lib, the Digital Library Federation Forum, and Internet Librarian conferences.

Meredith Powers is a reference librarian at Brooklyn Public Library. She previously worked as part of a team of librarians at EdLab, a design and development unit at the Teachers College, Columbia University library, as well as part of the Web Archiving team for the New York Art Resources Consortium. She received her B.A. from the City College of New York and a Masters of Library & Information Science from Pratt Institute. Meredith's personal and professional goals have always been oriented toward providing equitable and sustainable access to information and knowledge—whether she's capturing websites for the Internet Archive or wireframing the world, Meredith is particularly interested in leveraging new technologies to make information accessible and usable for everyone.

Laura Rocke was born and raised in Reno, Nevada. She moved to Las Vegas, Nevada and attended the University of Nevada, Las Vegas, receiving a Bachelor of Arts in History in 2008. She then attended the University of Nevada, Reno (U.N.R.) and received a Master of Arts in History in 2015, focusing on the cultural study of: Early American History; Race and Ethnicity in the United States with an emphasis on Slavery in Colonial America; and Public History. Her professional experience during and since the pursuit of her MA includes: teaching Core Humanities at U.N.R. and Truckee Meadows Community College; Academic Advising for the College of Liberal Arts and the College of Engineering at U.N.R.; and serving as the Historian, Author, and Copy Editor for the Digital Initiatives Unit in the Matherwson-IGT Knowledge Center at U.N.R.

Alex Rudshteyn, Director of Library Technology, Entrepreneurship, Systems and Network Support at Brooklyn College has an M.S. in Mechanical Engineering, and M.A. in Computer and Information Science, and has worked at the Brooklyn College Library since 1998.

Nikola Smolenski (1979) is a programmer from Serbia, who worked on various cultural and digitalization-related projects, by education an engineer of electrotechnics. He worked as a freelance journalist and published short SF stories. He established Wikipedia in Serbian language and was a founding and board member of Wikimedia Serbia; he has been presenting at various Wikimedia-related conferences. He is working at the University Library in Belgrade since 2014, his most important project being Searchable Digitized Historical Newspapers.

Adam Sofronijevic (1973) holds a PhD in library and information science from University of Belgrade, a MSc in management and a MSc in library and information science and a BSc in information and communication technologies. Adam is certified with CISCO CCNA industrial certificate and over 40 Coursera, Udacity and MITx online certificates in fields of computing, management and humanities. He has eight years of managerial experience as a department head and a deputy director of University library Belgrade and rich experience as a board member of University library Belgrade, ''Milutin Bojic'' library in Belgrade and DART Europe. Adam was the driving force behind participation of University library Belgrade in two EU CIP ICT-PSP projects and is currently heading the participation of the library in Horizon 2020 READ project. He was also responsible for implementation of 5 projects granted by Serbian Ministry of culture and is a national MC in EU COST Action E-READ. Adam has published internationally over 60 peer reviewed articles and book chapters and has been presenting at more than 30 international scientific conferences in 12 European countries. He is a member of LIBER annual conference program committee since 2012.

Nadaleen F Tempelman-Kluit is the head of the User Experience Department at New York University Libraries. She focuses on creating and supporting user-centered design for Libraries interfaces, resources, and services.

Elisabeth Bliese Tessone is the Library Assessment Assistant at the James C. Kirkpatrick Library at the University of Central Missouri. She received her MLIS from the University of Wisconsin-Milwaukee.

Jessica Waggoner is a Digital Projects Librarian at the University of California, Santa Cruz. She is the project manager for the library's Omeka Curator Dashboard project.

Joshua Welker is the Information Technology Librarian at the James C. Kirkpatrick Library at the University of Central Missouri. He received his MLIS from the University of Missouri.

Index

I

J

K

L

M

O

P

R

S

T

U

www.ingramcontent.com/pod-product-compliance
Lightning Source LLC
LaVergne TN
LVHW081329300926
849161LV00008B/1919
* 9 7 8 1 5 2 2 5 2 6 7 6 6 *